CONSUMING OCEAN IS

CONSUMING OCEAN ISLAND

Stories of People and Phosphate from Banaba

Katerina Martina Teaiwa

Indiana University Press

Bloomington and Indianapolis

This book is a publication of

Indiana University Press
Office of Scholarly Publishing
Herman B Wells Library 350
1320 East 10th Street
Bloomington, Indiana 47405 USA

iupress.indiana.edu

Telephone   800-842-6796
Fax   812-855-7931

Manufactured in the United States of America

Library of Congress Cataloging-in-Publication Data

Teaiwa, Katerina Martina.
   Consuming Ocean Island : stories of people and phosphate from
Banaba / Katerina Martina Teaiwa.
      pages cm
      ISBN 978-0-253-01444-3 (cl) — ISBN 978-0-253-01452-8 (pb)
— ISBN 978-0-253-01460-3 (eb) 1. Banaba (Kiribati)—History—
20th century. 2. Phosphate mines and mining—Kiribati—
Banaba—History—20th century. 3. Banabans (I-Kiribati people)—
Relocation—History—20th century. I. Title.
   DU615.T45 2014
   996.81—dc23

                                                    2014009591

1 2 3 4 5 20 19 18 17 16 15

*For John Tabakitoa and Joan Kathryn Martin Teaiwa,
and with thanks to Nick, Tearia, Tere, Maria, and
our multisited kainga*

Naturally some think the native owners are right, yet it is inconceivable that less than 500 Ocean Island–born natives can be allowed to prevent the mining and export of a produc[t] of such immense value to all the rest of mankind.

—*Sydney Morning Herald,* April 13, 1912

Contents

Prelude

Three Global Stories

Heaven was a rock lying over the earth and rooted in the deep places of the sea.

All the lands of the ancestors were embedded in the rock and stood out like hills on the topside. Banaba was the *buto*, the navel, and all the multitudes of lands and ancestors in Te Bongiro, the darkness, lay around it. In the time of Te Bongiro, heaven began to move and the earth began to move; they rubbed together as two hands are rubbed together, and from this came Tabakea, the first of all. Tabakea, the turtle, lived on Banaba with Nakaa, his brother. With them lived Auriaria the giant, Tabuariki the shark and thunder, Tituabine the stingray and lightning, and Taburimai, Nawai, Aorao, and many others. Beneath the rock were *te baba ma bono*, the deaf mutes, and *te rang*, the slaves.

The inhabitants of the rock began to have children. A woman of Banaba, Tangan-nang, conceived and bore a child; it was the bird Te Kunei. The bird grew large and flew over the sea to catch fish, and often it would bring back food for its mother.

There came a time when the bird flew far to sea and caught a *rereba* fish, which it carried home to Banaba. Tangan-nang did not kill the fish; she kept it in a bowl of seawater. But the small rereba grew into a large *urua* fish, the full size of a man. They feared it and cast it into the sea, but the urua returned with many great and fierce fish. Tabakea had an idea about how to save them from the urua and his multitude—Tabakea took a little *beru*, or lizard, and cast it into a fire. He put the ashes into a clam shell filled with water, and after three moons Nareau, a tiny dark man, emerged from the shell. Tabakea repeated this process with Nareau several times until he was the size of a small man. He then claimed him as a son. Nareau destroyed the urua and scattered its bones around Banaba.

Auriaria became the lord of Te Bongiro, and he pierced heaven with his staff. The rock then fell into the sea, upside down with its roots in the air, burying Tabakea underneath. Auriaria traveled southward until his foot struck a reef-rock. There he stayed and made a great land, which he named Samoa. He met a razor clam, Katati, which he flung into the east and that was the sun. And again he took a shellfish, Nimatanin, and that was the moon. Then he took the body of Riki, the eel, and laid it across heaven. The white belly of Riki is seen across the sky today: it is the Milky Way. Then Auriaria planted a tree on Samoa, from which sprang a host of ancestors. He returned to Banaba and his children are there to this day.[1]

*   *   *

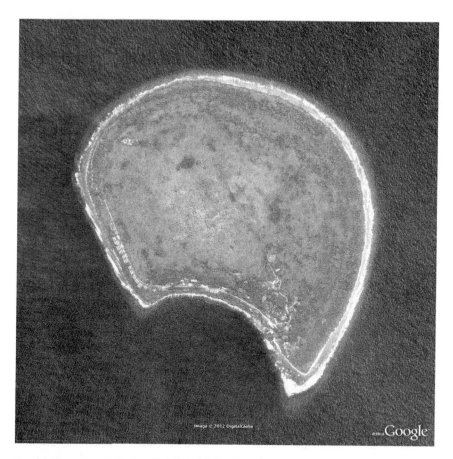

Banaba/Ocean Island. Digital Globe/Google Earth

March 15, 1997

I arrived on the island of Banaba in the western part of Kiribati on a government boat filled with all manner of cargo: women and children; male crew members; freely wandering chickens, ducks, and dogs; tinned corned beef and tinned fish of various sizes; sacks of rice; kilograms of pounded, paper-bagged *kava;* and my father, Tabakitoa.[2] With no visible moon or light of any kind, we somehow disembarked, clutching our bags, and ascended slippery invisible steps from the wharf landing. The total darkness was overwhelming to me, the sound of the ocean deafening. Yet everyone else seemed to be able to see perfectly and were less bothered by the din.

I was deposited on the back of a small, sturdy motorbike which then sped up a bumpy, dark road to a grand but dilapidated house. I later discovered that

Banaba pinnacles, April 2000. Photo by Katerina Martina Teaiwa

the driver was my father's younger brother Eritai, whom he had not seen for over thirty years. After a night mostly devoid of sleep but including several encounters with large, healthy-looking rats, I awoke to an extraordinary view.

Banaba was a desiccated field of rocks and jagged limestone pinnacles jutting out of a gray earth, laced with patches of dark green foliage. Roofless concrete buildings and corrugated iron warehouses littered the vista, which was punctuated here and there by startling red flame trees and coconut trunks weirdly devoid of fronds. An indigo ocean encircled the island, filling the horizon that seemed to curve outward from my window. Jagged rock and rusted iron in a vast blue sea: not an idyllic island scene, but an industrial oceanic wasteland.

*   *   *

April 10, 2002

My younger sister Maria and I traveled to Rabi in Fiji. After the plane trip from Suva to Savusavu and four hours in a truck along the bumpy coastal road of northern Vanua Levu, we arrived at Karoko Point across the bay from the village of Tabiang. My cousin Lala and uncle Teruamwi were waiting for us in a boat named *Manoa,* after my elder sister Teresia's son. I had never seen the sea so rough, and the twenty-minute crossing took almost an hour before we arrived at the *kainga,* the family hamlet, at Tabona, just outside Tabiang. The turbulent seas were just the beginning of three harrowing days to come. The rain arrived that night, turning into a deluge so deafening that by the second night we could barely hear each other speak inside my father's tin-roofed house.

The next morning there was over two feet of water across the kainga, and a large stretch of road had washed away. The brand-new trenches dug around each house to accommodate the much-anticipated electricity lines now overflowed with muddy water. A pipe had burst during the downpour and all the taps were dry. Our rainwater tank quickly became an invaluable source of clean drinking water for people in Tabona and Tabiang. Two of my cousins placed the one-ton ice chest, normally used for storing fish, just below the tank to catch the overflow, and this provided extra water for washing dishes and clothes and for bathing, though most of us ended up showering in the rain.

On the third day, when the storm finally broke, we attempted a short fishing trip. The sea was brown and filled with debris; it seemed impossible to catch anything in the murky water. After traveling for only two minutes, the engine on the boat died. One of the men, an experienced diver, jumped into the water and with the rope in one hand pulled us back to shore, where a mechanic just happened to be working on a second boat. He quickly fixed the problem and we set out again, this time accompanied by a wooden outrigger canoe. Lala caught a few fish from the canoe, but no one on the motorized vessel caught anything. On our return we learned that six people—two adults and four children—had tragically been killed in a landslide in Buakonikai village to the east of Tabiang. They had all been sleeping when the mountain behind them came crashing into their homes.

The reality of regular heavy rains and cyclones on Rabi contrasts rather starkly with the dryness of the original home island of Banaba in the central Pacific. Nevertheless, despite the rain, the flood, the road washing away, and the brown muddy sea, our kainga had an improvised *bootaki*, or celebration, to mark the rare family reunion. Someone managed to catch more fish; someone caught and cooked several chickens; taro and cassava from the gardens appeared for boiling; and despite all the mud, family members walked from at least two villages over an hour away to join us. We all sat crowded on the balcony of my father's house, now sheltered on two sides with a tarpaulin and a bed sheet, and ate, sang songs, and drank kava, that ubiquitous Fijian drink, till very late.

A couple of weeks later we cleaned the house, packed our bags, and said our goodbyes. After we'd boarded the boat, waved teary-eyed to our relatives, and traveled for exactly one minute while still furiously waving at those on-shore, the engine died, again. Two of my cousins hopped into the outrigger canoe and swiftly paddled out to tug us back to shore, where the same mechanic fixed our little twenty-five-horsepower engine. At this point the outrigger canoe was looking like a far better alternative to the outboard motor. But we made it to Savusavu and were back in Suva that evening.

Preface

On Other Ways of Tracking the Global

This is a Banaban story and a global story—one of assemblage, linking many stories that are much more than a collection of incidental sites, nodes, or points in a web or network.[1] Histories of the Banaban people and their home island require a reader to challenge the standard conventions of literacy and to contemplate the relations between the deep past and the present; the personal and the political; the organic and the inorganic relations between distant peoples, nation-states, and territories; and the multilayered connections that emerge from and between oral, visual, and textual forms of knowledge production.

In this book I ask what kind of scholarly knowledge is produced while we inhabit and move between the deep past and the present, the realms of the ancestors and the living, and between islands and cities, histories and cultures, texts, images, and film. What kind of global perspective emerges from the exploration of these seemingly contrasting spaces, and what are the stakes of globalization for those who are displaced by the values, demands, expectations, and extractive activities that go along with it? My work is concerned with the political, ethical, and epistemological assumptions inherent in our approaches to tracking and framing globalization, and with the question of whether we can truly dismantle the dominant frameworks, the presumed binaries such as local-global or national-international, and the ontological hegemonies that shape global processes and our representations of them. To challenge such dominant approaches, to ground our studies, and to find more truly inclusive ways to tell global stories without ignoring the very present effects of colonialism and imperialism, we have to put forth other ways of knowing, being, doing, and writing from other, non–Euro American spaces of power and agency.

This book explores these personal and scholarly concerns by presenting stories of mining, agricultural, political, and social history and culture in sites still very much at the edges of global studies—the nation-states of Kiribati, Australia, New Zealand, and Fiji—using a combination of archival research, autoethnography, visual and critical discourse analysis, and storytelling. I highlight the relevance of geological and spiritual processes in deep time to contemporary social, political, and environmental issues. This work is broadly engaged with the phosphate mining that occurred between 1900 and 1980 on the tiny Pacific island of Banaba, also known as Ocean Island, in Kiribati and its more recent sociopolitical effects.

The mining of Banaba was facilitated and conducted by various agents across the British Empire, and the Banaban people were moved to Rabi in the Fiji islands in 1945. Banaban land became part of a global commodity chain of superphosphate fertilizer and agricultural products, such as grain, lamb, beef, milk, and cheese. The multiscalar nature of the Banaba story, and particularly the manner in which it tacks between temporal and geographical contexts, resonates with a Banaban and Gilbertese (I-Kiribati) and, more generally, indigenous Pacific understanding of and approach to time and place.

Ultimately I am arguing for transdisciplinary research: research that both links and moves beyond disciplinary boundaries, that considers the very real differences and connections between the stories explored here, as well as the personal, political, material, epistemological, ontological, methodological, and pedagogical implications and stakes of multisited knowledge production. The multisited, multiscalar, or multivocal must refer not just to the theory or content of our research endeavors, but to the very form of scholarly production as well. The ethics and strategies I use in challenging and expanding the forms of scholarship are a result of my interdisciplinary Pacific islands studies training; my inspiration from feminist ethnography, indigenous studies, and dance studies; my collaborations with various Pacific artists over the years; and my skepticism toward the still-normative social science "eye of God" approach.[2]

While a linear or encyclopedic approach to Banaban history is possible and has been presented by a handful of travel writers and historians, it does not resonate with the partial and often fragmented manner in which Banaban land or people, or any of the other agents involved in mining, experienced the last one hundred years. *Te aba,* that fundamental and corporeally grounded ontological premise linking land and people and regularly invoked by Banabans and I-Kiribati, was devastated and dismantled at a rapid rate by mining. This can be seen as especially dire when compared with geological time and the natural rate at which islands and mineral deposits are formed. The name *Ba-n-aba* means "rock land" and, simultaneously, something both fixed and fluid, material and human. Banaba is the body of the land and the bodies of the people. To track Banaba is to track fragmented and dispersed stories, peoples, and landscapes, which throws up challenges to conventional history and literacy.

On balancing monocultural literacy with mixed cultural literacy, Ramona Fernandez states the task elegantly: "The encyclopedic impulse must be balanced by its counterpoint: the impulse to travel across local knowledges, making a map as you go, weaving a net of connections as you meander and discover. Reading practices are not about creating a canon of knowledge; they are about entering a rhizomatic web of meaning created through association. Reading practices cannot be fixed, texts are not static lumps yielding to invariant decoding."[3]

Simply put, phosphate rocks and islands are also not static lumps. To track this story, I ask the reader to read telescopically and imagine a piece of phosphate from its tiniest unit as a molecule—phosphorus with four oxygen atoms attached—to its much larger form as an entire island, and all the chemical processes, particles, pinnacles, rocks, dust, and fertilizer pellets in between. Each chapter in this book comprises a journey through some of the stories, events, hopes, losses, and gains that were made possible by Banaban phosphate.

Throughout this research journey, my own understandings of colonial history, place and power, and the potential of one tiny island to make a global difference were transformed. I am Banaban and I find much of what happened in the past deeply troubling. Justice and reparation for our people and the physical rehabilitation of our original homeland are still required. Moreover, if the islands of Kiribati sink below the sea, as predicted by climate change scientists, the mined landscape of Banaba may be the only one left above water.

Notes on Orthography and Geography

Kiribati Language

"Ti" in all words in the Kiribati language is pronounced "s." So Kiribati is pronounced "Kiribas."

"I" in I-Kiribati refers to "the people of" Kiribati.

There are three different spellings of certain words using the "a" vowel in the archival literature, Kiribati dictionaries, and online language sources when the pronunciation is "ah" as compared with the "a" in apple. A source might spell the word maneaba as either mʻaneaba or mwaneaba. Except in direction quotations, I have generally adopted the use of "w" to indicate the "ah" sound in words such as mwaneaba, unimwane, mwakuri, rabwa, bwangabwanga, and umwa, except when referring to the village of Uma. Uma is often referred to as "Ooma" in the British Phosphate Commissioners archives and Tabwewa as "Tapiwa."

"Kiribati" is the indigenous way of pronouncing "Gilbert." Kiribati, Gilbertese, and the Gilberts are used interchangeably. The Gilbert Islands was the name used by the British colonial government for the chain called Tungaru by the indigenous inhabitants. Since independence in 1979 those islands are just part of the main chain of islands in Kiribati. There are several other islands outside the Gilbert chain.

The Gilbert and Ellice Islands are now the separate independent nation-states of Kiribati and Tuvalu in the Pacific.

The Banabans spoke their own language, but many Gilbertese words were introduced through intermarriage. Banabans began to speak Gilbertese primarily after it was established as the language of Christian worship toward the end of the nineteenth century and as the official language of the Gilbert and Ellice Islands colony in the early twentieth century.

Fijian Language

"C" is pronounced "th"; "g" is pronounced "ng" (as in sing); "q" is pronounced "nga" (hard g); "d" is pronounced "nd"; and "m" is pronounced "mb." Rabi Island is thus pronounced "Rambi" and sometimes spelled Rambi, Rambe, Rambey, or Rabe in the literature.

"Ratu" is a title used to indicate Fijian males of chiefly rank. "Adi" indicates female chiefly rank. "Tui" indicates a paramount chief.

Other

The term "European" is used regularly throughout the book in accordance with how Pacific Islanders generally refer to white folk; this reflects the terminology used during the colonial period by whites themselves. "European" thus refers to Australian, New Zealand, and British Company officials, investors, and their families.

PART I
PHOSPHATE PASTS

There can be no civilization without population,
no population without food,
and no food without phosphate.

—Albert Ellis, *Phosphates: Why, How and Where?*

1   The Little Rock That Feeds

Let's-All-Be-Thankful Island

On September 20, 1919, Thomas J. McMahon, one of the most prolific journalists and photographers of the South Pacific of his time, published a story in an Australian magazine called the *Penny Pictorial.* It was replete with the usual Pacific imagery and language—paradise, romance, natives, South Seas, balmy breezes, and so forth—with one notable exception. The title of the piece proclaimed: "Let's-all-be-thankful Island. A Little Spot in the South Pacific That Multiplies the World's Food." McMahon had just visited Ocean Island, indeed one of the tiniest inhabited dots in the Pacific, and produced extraordinary images of productive, orderly, brown laborers and impeccably clad white folk—men, women, and children—against a backdrop of less than tropical rock pinnacles and mining fields. Less than a year later the governments of Australia, New Zealand, and the United Kingdom bought out the Pacific Phosphate Company and created the British Phosphate Commissioners (BPC), tasked with mining Nauru and Ocean Island in the Pacific and, later, Christmas Island in the Indian Ocean. Across the seas, the Cherifian Phosphates Board (Office Chérifian des Phosphate), today the world's major phosphate supplier, was established in Morocco that same year.

In 1900, two of the world's highest-grade sources of phosphate rock were identified on Nauru and the island of Banaba in what is now the Republic of Kiribati in the central Pacific. The history of Nauru has been told in a variety of forms, but that of the smallest of the phosphate islands is much less well known.[1] In this book I present a series of stories about Banaba from 1900 through the present, with a focus on the political and social impacts of phosphate mining and the displacement of both the land and the indigenous Banabans. While deeply concerned with the ethical and moral implications of unbridled resource extraction for indigenous peoples and global consumers, I also reflect on the process of tracking this multisited, multiscalar, and multivocal history and the varying ideological and ontological positions taken by what some might call the major and minor agents of change. Of central concern are the relations between people and the land, people's relations to each other, and the relations between the past and the present. The island of Banaba is an entry point and the key motif linking these stories; we spiral through time, experiencing the island's material development, decimation, and global consumption as well as the changing sociopolitical landscapes created across the mining enterprise. From the past we can see the future, and vice versa.

"Babes in the Pinnacles" by Thomas J. McMahon.
Courtesy of the National Archives of Australia

Banaba, mapped by Europeans in the early nineteenth century as "Ocean Island," is a two-and-a-half-square-mile (six-and-a-half-square kilometer) island in the central Pacific.[2] Now in a state of relative obscurity, the island was the intense focus of British imperial agricultural desires for most of the twentieth century. Phosphate rock is the essential ingredient in phosphate fertilizers, which are crucial for the maintenance and expansion of global agriculture and therefore key to global food security. Both of these island landscapes were essentially eaten away by mining, which devastated both the land and spirit of their respective peoples while supporting thousands of Company[3] employees and families and fueling agriculture in the British Antipodes for much of the twentieth century.

Nauru, once known as Pleasant Island and a former colony of Germany, eventually acquired international rights to self-determination and independence after World War II, initially as an Australian Trust Territory of the United Nations. These rights did not extend to Banaba, however, which was colonized by Britain. Nauru gained independence in 1968, and from 1970 the Nauruan government itself ran the mining industry, becoming temporarily one of the wealthiest countries in terms of income per capita. In the 1990s the Commission of Inquiry organized by the Nauruan government focused on the requirements for the environmental rehabilitation of worked-out phosphate lands. This resulted in the Nauru and Australian governments signing the Compact of Settlement, which provided for remining by Australian companies followed by rehabilitation of the mined-out lands.[4]

Since independence, however, a string of bad investments and dealings left Nauru in debt, reliant on Australian aid, and with a 90 percent unemployment rate and a range of challenging health issues.[5] It is currently the smallest republic in the world with a land mass of eight square miles (twenty-one square kilometers) and approximately 9,000 people. While their culture has been heavily influenced by mining and colonialism, and Nauru is now a major and controversial center for the processing of asylum seekers who want entry into Australia, Nauruans are active in revitalizing their culture through fishing, sport, music, and dance.

There is a population of approximately 400 Banabans and I-Kiribati on Banaba today, living there as caretakers while the majority of Banabans live on Rabi in Fiji. On Banaba, where fishing grounds, homes, villages, and ritual and burial sites once existed, there are now stark limestone pinnacles, decaying processing plants, rusted storage bins, algae-congested water tanks, and a massive maritime cantilever with its giant arm crippled and submerged. The island is administered by the Rabi Council of Leaders and the Kiribati government.

Two other Pacific islands, Angaur in the Caroline Islands and Makatea in French Polynesia, are much smaller but still have been critical sources of phosphate. They are both sparsely populated but still of significance to their indigenous peoples. The same Company that mined Banaba and Nauru partnered with a Tahitian-based syndicate to mine Makatea. While the Pacific phosphate deposits constituted only about 8 percent of the world's annual output at their peak, they were for decades essential regional sources for Australia, New Zealand, and Japan, which were without domestic supplies and would incur great freight costs to import phosphate from the United States, Morocco, or South Africa.[6]

During almost a century of mining, shipping, and manufacturing, the rock of both Nauru and Banaba was scattered across countless fields in and beyond the British Pacific. In this period the United Kingdom, France, the United States, Australia, and New Zealand all had colonies in the Pacific islands, some as a result of the post–World War I League of Nations Mandate, and others as a result of prewar imperial claims and divisions that initially included German and Japanese territories. The Pacific was yet another theater for the expression of British, American, European, Japanese, and later Indonesian martial power, as well as a strategic opportunity for securing natural resources and expanding metropolitan business interests. The development of mines and plantations was also a necessity on some islands for funding the administration of the colonies, and Banaba was no exception. Phosphate mining, even on an island as tiny as Banaba, made British, Australian, and New Zealand investors very wealthy; supplied farmers with cheap fertilizer while stimulating various chains of commodity production, distribution, and consumption; and funded the administration of the Gilbert and Ellice Islands colony through taxes.

While expanding populations were enjoying the agricultural benefits of intensive fertilizer application and the phosphate-hungry high-yielding crops of what USAID director William Gaud coined the "Green Revolution" in 1968, there was and continues to be little public education or awareness about humanity's reliance on phosphorus. What the Green Revolution failed to acknowledge was the reliance not just on land for agricultural development and the expansion of monocropping, but on resources that would fuel the entire chain of agricultural outputs, most significantly fertilizer. Knowledge of certain key ingredients, such as phosphate, was specialized and rarely successfully popularized, in spite of the attempts of various travel writers and journalists.

The epigraph for this part of the book was originally by Clemson University founder Thomas Clemson. His statement on the crucial link between food and phosphate was quoted in a speech by Pacific "phosphateer" Sir Albert Ellis to the Auckland Rotary Club in New Zealand in 1942: "Phosphates: Why, How and Where? . . . Why Needed? How Used? and Where Found?"[7] Media coverage of phosphorus and phosphate issues more than seventy years later still sustains this curious tone of excited discovery, as if telling the story for the first time to an unknowing audience. For his lay listeners, Ellis adjusted Clemson's original line, which contained the more accurate technical term "phosphoric acid," the industrial shorthand P_2O_5 for water-soluble phosphate, rather than "phosphate."

For the layperson, there is often confusion about the differences between guano and rock phosphate. Guano, from the Quechua word *wanu,* is the excrement of seabirds, bats, and seals. There were major guano sources across the Pacific and Caribbean with the largest deposit in Peru, in some cases mined by slave labor from the Pacific.[8] Rock phosphate is the result of millions of years of sedimentation while guano, which also provides nitrogen, is younger in formation. They both yield phosphoric acid with the latter an ostensibly more "natural" fertilizer. Organic farmers, for example, prefer to use guano, and journalists and travel writers thrive on the vivid metaphors and images conjured up by humans' obsession with bird and bat shit.[9]

Maslyn Williams, Barrie Macdonald, Christopher Weeramantry, and Nancy Viviani have all produced important scholarship on the history of mining on Banaba and Nauru.[10] Williams and Macdonald's celebratory account of the BPC is a careful distillation of a large collection of archival records organized into an evocative and entertaining narrative that gives a dense and temporally linear view of the economic and political stakes of this industry for the three stakeholder nations: Great Britain, New Zealand, and Australia. Much less attention is given to any Pacific Islander actors, indigenous or otherwise. Their voices and experiences are muted in these political histories.

Land: Sedimentation, Traveling Rocks, and Fragments

Throughout this book I bring indigenous Banaban concepts and experiences into dialogue with competing regimes of value and the industrial processes applied to Banaban land by powerful actors and agencies from across the former British Empire. I track the phosphate, stories of life on the island, the Banabans, and various events in which they were entangled over several landscapes. Each story is an interlocking piece of the puzzle, partially sedimented, layered, and overlapping, but ultimately fragmented and diffracted in parallel with the now-dispersed phosphate landscape.

In most Pacific languages there are central concepts linking the people and the land metonymically, ontologically, and spiritually: *vanua* in Fijian, *aina* in Hawaiian, and *whenua* in Māori, for example. *Te aba, kainga,* and *te rii* in Gilbertese (the Kiribati language) refer, respectively, to the land and the people, home or hamlet, and bones. All have linguistic, human, and material forms that can be interchangeable, substituted, or used to indicate linked parts of a whole, which is the land and people together. "Te aba" thus means both the land and the people simultaneously; there is a critical ontological unity. When speaking of land, one

"Postcards from Pleasant Island III: Te Aba n Rii," by Robin White.
Used with permission of the artist and courtesy of the National Gallery of Australia.

does not say *au aba,* "my land," but *abau,* "me-land." Te aba is thus an integrated epistemological and ontological complex linking people in deep corporeal and psychic ways to each other, to their ancestors, to their history, and to their physical environment. Sigrah and King speak of "te rii ni Banaba," the backbone of Banaba, as the spiritual wealth and well-being of a person involving three pieces of knowledge: knowledge of one's genealogy, knowledge of one's customary rights, and knowledge of one's land boundaries.[11] Relations to land are extremely serious. Though it might increasingly be used as such, land is not merely for exploitation or profit. Land is the very basis for relationality and for knowing and being.[12] These various facets of land and the manner in which they relate to the area's mining history are captured lucidly in New Zealand artist Robin White's *Postcard from Pleasant Island III.* She manages to evoke the land as body, blood, and rock, the mined landscape resembling a gravesite that has become te aba n rii, the land of bones.

Banaba was viewed as the buto, the navel or center of the world, by Banabans, much as other islands, including Nauru and Rapa Nui, were viewed by their indigenous inhabitants.[13] While Banaba was settled by at least three waves of migration beginning over two thousand years ago, emplaced identities were forged and consolidated over the centuries so that personhood was shaped within a network of both kinship-based and environmental relations and connections. Most significant, on Banaba, in contrast with most Pacific societies, including in the Gilbert Islands, land was not held communally.[14] Each individual, male and female, adult and child, had their own carefully demarcated plots that they could keep, exchange, or dispose of at will.[15] Land was thus the ground for individual agency and efficacy within a communal system of social organization. The subsequent transformation of the land by mining and colonial regulation disrupted and unraveled the whole complex of social and material relations.[16]

The Banaban and Gilbertese concept of kainga refers to the local extended family unit and their place of residence.[17] Kainga is "home." The people of a kainga eat and live together, sharing resources and responsibilities. But both te aba and kainga were completely transformed as mining consumed the original island, and the ideas of people, place, and home were reconstructed in new ways on a different island, Rabi, 1,600 miles (2,575 kilometers) away in Fiji.

My research began several years ago with a primary concern for the indigenous Banaban experience of betrayal, loss, displacement, and cultural revitalization. However, further engagement with archival Company records, films, and photographs exposed the materiality of the enterprise and the loss of the island itself. "The land," te aba to Banabans and te tano (or "soil") to the Gilbertese and Ellice Islander workers, was for the Australian prospectors and fertilizer manufacturers, layers of sedimented phosphate rock containing a significant ratio of calcium phosphate that, when subjected to sulfuric acid, unlocked a valuable source of phosphoric acid, the key ingredient of all phosphorus-bearing fertilizers. These fertilizers increased the capacity of plant roots to absorb minerals and water from the soil, added to its fertility, increased crop yields, and fostered the growth of grass fields for grazing. My contemplation of this shift in scale and perspective had the effect of both optical zooming and diffraction.[18] I stopped thinking of Banaba as a Pacific island located at 0° 52' S and 169° 35' E, and began to think of it as a place that was in motion, making and breaking both human and environmental connections while it was constantly in a state of chemical transformation.

Banaban history has been represented by others in a linear manner in both text and performance, but I contend that an island in a constant state of transformation and fragmentation requires a different mode of storytelling. Moreover I am concerned with what these various forms of Banaba in place and in transit meant to the ever-expanding population of indigenous, mining, and agricultural stakeholders and their families. The interchangeable use of the terms "Banaba" and "Ocean Island" signals the competing and complex indigenous and foreign values attributed to the island. The Banabans themselves often used the English

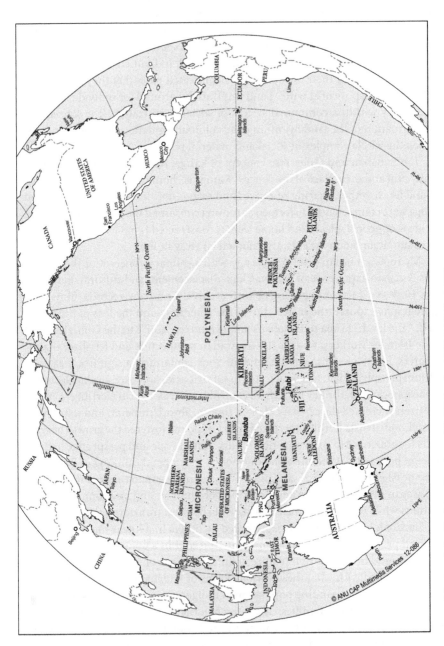

Map of the Pacific highlighting Banaba and Rabi Islands. ANU CAP CartoGIS

name to mark the past and the period of colonialism and mining, but it is not uncommon to hear the island referred to as Ocean Island in casual Banaban conversations or for former European residents to correct themselves and call it Banaba instead of Ocean Island.

Throughout this account, I juxtapose the stories and perspectives of several communities and individuals connected to the mining venture with a fragmented and transnational biography of the phosphate rock. This results in a multisited, multivocal, and temporally disparate narrative informed by the work of anthropologists, historians, scientists, and Pacific studies scholars. A variety of both major and minor characters and events are included. There are the indigenous Banabans who lost their cultural and physical land rights; Gilbertese laborers who signed up to work in the mines on the lands of their distant Banaban relatives; the resident commissioners and representatives of the British Empire; Australian and New Zealand Company employees and their families; fertilizer manufacturers and farmers; and the Rabi Islanders, the Banabans who now live in Fiji and perform a historical dance theater every year on December 15, the anniversary of their landing in 1945.

The experiences of these groups are combined in this book with an ethnographic reading of phosphate records from the rich textual and visual archives of the BPC held in the National Archives of Australia and in the State Library of Victoria; documentary films, newspapers, and journals from Britain, Australia, New Zealand, Kiribati, and Fiji between 1900 and 2010; and the H. E. and H. C. Maude Papers and the Arthur Grimble Papers in the Pacific Collection of the Barr-Smith Library at the University of Adelaide in South Australia. These sources are used to track both Banaba's fragmented history and the fragmented rocks across islands, cities, and archives. The goal is not to provide a neat synthesis of the phosphate enterprise, which has been done by other writers, but rather to offer what I see as an appropriately partial view, in the sense of expressing specific interests and in the sense of both an incomplete and a motivated reading of diverse Banaban sources and experiences.

The anthropologist James Clifford has written, "Thinking historically is a process of locating oneself in space and time. And a location . . . is an itinerary rather than a bounded site."[19] The histories of Banaba embody the spirit of this statement. Banaba is no longer a place, an island in the middle of an ocean, but rather a flow of rocks with multiple trajectories and itineraries. And if indigenous identities were or are rooted in specific landscapes and seascapes, then Banaban land and Banaban identities have now become coordinates between islands and continents. My account thus represents one form of the multisited research theorized by George Marcus in the 1990s.[20] I am following not just the stories, the people, and the ideas, but the land itself and its sequelae as commodities.

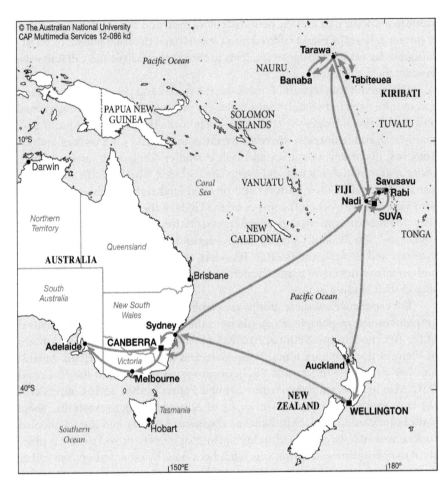

Katerina Teaiwa's research itinerary, 1997–present. ANU CAP CartoGIS

Land Before Mining

The premining social organization on Banaba was significantly different from that of many other Pacific societies. On most islands, land is communally held or administered in trust for the broader community by chiefs or aristocratic families (Tonga, Fiji, and Samoa), or by male leaders of clans and tribes (the Solomon Islands, Vanuatu, and many parts of Papua New Guinea). In contrast, on Banaba the land, usually bearing coconut, pandanus, breadfruit, noni, mango, and almond trees, was held by individuals and was a form of currency in the sense that it could be exchanged between people according to various rules of transaction.[21] The result was that everyone could have a connection to some other part of the island in addition to the district where they lived. This gave Banabans a range of options for accessing resources, acquiring new knowledge or counsel, and receiving support in times of need. Land also provided the basis for payment or compensation for serious crimes. Maude and Maude detail several recognized categories of landholding and transactions for transferring land:

> *Te katautau:* dividing land among children by walking with them along boundary lines, mother and father deciding which children should receive maternal or paternal lands
>
> *Te aba ni kara:* land for the aged, the land set aside for parents in their old age after te katautau
>
> *Te aba n nati:* land for adopted children
>
> *Te nenebo:* the blood payment, when a murderer's lands pass to the family of the victim in two portions: *kie na* (the "mat" for the victim) and *rabuna na* (the "shroud" of the victim); the murderer's canoe would also be passed along as *bao na* (the coffin)
>
> *Te aba n rau:* the land of peacemaking, passing from a man to the husband of a woman with whom he had committed adultery
>
> *Te aba ni kamaiu:* the land of life giving, land given to people with food or with skill in fishing who shared their stores and knowledge with others, especially in times of famine and drought
>
> *Te aba n iein:* the land of marriage, signaling the end of an engagement (if the girl ended the marriage no land would pass, but if the boy ended it he would give two plots if there had been no intercourse and four or five plots if there was)
>
> *Te aba ni butirake:* land of the asking, if land had gotten into the wrong hands and needed to be returned to the rightful person
>
> *Te aba n ira:* the land for theft (the thief passes land to the owner of stolen property)
>
> *Nenebo n te man:* blood payment for animals if another's tame frigate bird or other animal is killed
>
> *Te aba n tara:* the land for looking after, given in return for nursing during illness or old age
>
> *Te aba ni karaure:* the land of farewell, in exchange for great friendship outside the kindred group
>
> *Te aba n riring:* the land for bone setting, given by a patient to the bonesetter[22]

Maude and Maude write, "These conveyances were the chief means by which justice and peace were maintained on the island."[23]

These transactions would have helped sustain social stability and would have created avenues for the distribution of resources, though in times of drought, resources such as water, coconuts, and knowledge of fishing were held very tightly. But the introduction of Christianity in the 1880s, the arrival of the Pacific Islands

Company in 1900, the monetization of the land and the fixing of land tenure, the transformation of consumption norms, British colonial governance, and the eventual displacement of the population to Rabi brought an end to many of these indigenous cultural practices and to this system of peace and justice. Rather, the native magistrate, the police, and the *kaubure,* or village council, came into prominence. The council was usually populated by the *unimwane,* or elderly males, while male Protestant church ministers increasingly took on key political and economic roles. Women's political voices and agency were rapidly diminished in this period.

Before mining, Banaba was organized into districts with kainga, or hamlets, consisting of *utu,* or family households, with couples, their children (both natural and adopted), and one or both sets of parents, who might stay for a period with each of their children throughout the year. The kainga usually consisted of a family descended from a common ancestor, and either husband or wife would relocate upon marriage while maintaining links and rights to their original, ancestral kainga.

Each household consisted of a central house, a *mwenga* or *bata;* a kitchen; an *umwa n teinako,* or house for menstruating women; and a *bareaka,* or canoe shed. Young men who were ready for marriage spent most of their time in the *umwa n roronga,* or men's house, where they learned *te kauti,* or family magic, and the important skills of catching and taming frigate birds. Each kainga was headed by an unimwane, who was consulted on all affairs of the hamlet as a whole and served as the spokesperson for the group. Each kainga had its own sitting place, or *boti,* in the *mwaneaba,* or meetinghouse, of the district, which was demarcated by the *oka* (roof beams) or rows of pandanus thatch on the roof. A member of the kainga could sit there regardless of where they were living on the island, and each had well-guarded rights and privileges. Both men and women could speak in the mwaneaba. The *umwa n anti,* or house of spirits, was a ceremonial meetinghouse, a sacred version of the mwaneaba where feasts were held, offerings were made, and spiritual rituals were conducted.

After mining commenced, all kainga were consolidated into four districts—Tabwewa, Uma, Tabiang, and Buakonikai—and each had specific rights to access water from certain *maniba* (wells) or *bwangabwanga* (water caves) and to terraces where young men were trained and rituals were conducted. In the early 1900s Tabwewa had eighteen kainga, Uma had twenty-three, and Tabiang had twenty-three, and of the two regions combined into Buakonikai, Te Aonanne had thirteen kainga and Toakira had ten. The head of each district could be male or female (although her eldest son or nearest male relative carried out her duties).[24] The head was not a chief in the hierarchical, Polynesian sense of the word.[25] He or she had limited powers, including the right to speak first, leading at meetings, and the expectation to have his or her opinion carry significant weight. All final decisions, however, were based on the majority's perspective and were a result of

"Tapiwa [Tabwewa] Natives—King's village—Ocean Island." Nei Teinemakin, the "old queen," is second from right, seated. Courtesy of the National Archives of Australia

extensive consultation and discussion. There were also key roles for district leaders that involved the welcoming of visitors and negotiating terms of trade, which Europeans would interpret incorrectly as binding for all villages. The photograph captioned by the Company as the "King's village," for example, was one such elevation of key representatives to the status of supreme authority.

Christian and Colonial Transformations

Important meetings were conducted in the mwaneaba, which also served as a space for performance, rest, and leisure. Songs and dances were important vehicles for preserving and transmitting knowledge as well as being modes of creative expression and entertainment. Many aspects of this culture and its associated practices changed after the adoption of Christianity, a process that began in 1885 and was cemented by the cultural, material, and economic changes brought by the mining industry in 1900 and by the establishment of a British colonial government. Gilbertese was established as the official language of the colony, and while Banabans already spoke a combination of Gilbertese and a more ancient Banaban language, this regulation further challenged the transmission of Banaban cultural knowledge and practices.[26]

Christianity arrived in 1885 in the persons of the Reverend Alfred Charles Walkup and a Tabiteuean Islander, Kinta, of the American Board of Commissioners for Foreign Missions (ABCFM). Kinta had been trained by another Tabiteuean, Aberaam, who in turn had been trained by a powerful Hawaiian missionary, aptly named Kapu, on the island.[27] Temaka Benaia writes that the Banaban ancestral goddess, Nei Tituabine, alerted the Banabans that "a most powerful God which she could see as a 'fire' approaching the island, was about to arrive." It is claimed she encouraged the Banabans to abandon their ancestral gods and to worship the new, most truly powerful god. Walkup's mission lasted until 1907, and Benaia asserts that by 1903 "Christianity was completely accepted by the Banabans."[28] Eventually the London Missionary Society (LMS) took over the missionary work, and after their relocation to Rabi in 1945 most Banabans joined the Methodist Church of Fiji with a smaller number converting to Catholicism. The training of Protestant teachers and pastors was the primary vehicle for Banaban education and thus their modes of leadership and resistance regularly took on a Christian tone and fervor.

Religious, cultural, and linguistic matters were of some concern for the resident commissioners who worked on Banaba, but they were of little priority for the Company. Ocean Island's global strategic value was clear to phosphate mining prospectors and investors, and matters related to the island were often raised and debated in the British Parliament. In the beginning, the venture was managed by the Pacific Islands Company (PIC), and then by the Pacific Phosphate Company (PPC) as one of many risky but often profitable European businesses in Oceania. An independent multinational body, the British Phosphate Commissioners, combining British, Australian, and New Zealand economic and political interests, took over the industry from 1920 to 1981.[29]

Displaced for the Good of Mankind

The Banabans protested mining and questioned the distribution of profits from phosphate sales early in the venture and for most of the twentieth century. Their efforts were futile: the resource was too valuable and even up until the 1980s Australian scientists were writing of the "magical" powers of superphosphate.[30] The following 1912 article from the *Sydney Morning Herald* well illustrates the debate as it played out in Australia:

Ocean Islanders: To Go or Not to Go? Bad Outlook for Natives

An acute situation over the land question has been created at Ocean Island, and probably never before have the interests of mining and agriculture so decisively clashed.

It has resolved itself into a fight for the survival or extinction of the phosphate quarrying industry at the island, either the phosphate industry has to go, or the whole of the population of the island, some 500, must be found some other abode.

The position of affairs at the island just now is unique in history.

The matter has an especial interest for the Commonwealth States, by reason of the fact that a good deal of the phosphate obtained from Ocean Island is converted into manure, which enter[s] largely into the economy of Australian agriculture, superphosphate being largely used in connection with wheat growing. The phosphate deposits at this island are enormous.

Effect of the Phosphate Industry

The phosphate can be found so frequently on the island that to get it out will altogether disturb the whole of the surface conditions of the place, and the natives are objecting to the inroads of the quarrying industry, realising that it means disturbing their possession.

A humane proposal is afoot to transplant the natives to another island in the Pacific, suitable for the purpose, in order that the valuable phosphate industry may go on unchecked, to the advantage of those industrially engaged in it, and of the people on the land in various parts of the world.

After Twelve Years

For some twelve years the phosphate deposit on Ocean Island has been worked, and exported to practically all parts of the world, and to Australia in particular. In the beginning, phosphate lands were bought very cheaply from the native owners; but some years after, when the owners of the land became dimly conscious of the value of their property, a higher rate was asked. When refused this higher price, the natives only sold their land under pressing need.

The Ocean Islander saw his lands and only means of existence gradually disappearing, leaving, instead of his palm and pandanus groves, worked out quarries. Foreseeing the inevitable end, the natives some time ago definitely refused to sell any more lands. A public meeting was called to discuss the matter with the native owners. The natives unanimously refused to sell any more land, declaring that the lands, and the palm and pandanus trees thereon were all they had, and they asked what they should do when the big steamers had carried away all their habitable land. There the matter stands awaiting adjustment at home.

Naturally some think the native owners are right, yet it is inconceivable that less than 500 Ocean Island–born natives can be allowed to prevent the mining and export of a produc[t] of such immense value to all the rest of mankind. The question is under the authorities' consideration at present, and the outcome is uncertain.

Suggested Remedy

The advisability of buying a small island, in the Gilbert Group and transplanting the Ocean Islanders has been discussed. The island—Kuria—even if it could be bought, is too small. To some the best way of solving the problem seems to be the purchase of a sufficiently large area of the best Crown lands available in the British Solomon Islands at a fair rate for the Ocean Island natives, on the understanding that when the advance of mining makes moving necessary (say in another generation) the natives are to emigrate to their new lands. Any native wishing to visit the land should be allowed to do so. The phosphate lands (some persons contend) should be bought at a fair price, and a fair royalty, fixed by Act of Parliament, paid the natives until the deposit is worked out.

As the annual payment of the character is almost nil, and the profit immense beyond most things in trade, it is thought that it should in no wise [sic] inconvenience the company, and would give the natives reasonable benefit from their property.[31]

The story reduces the Banabans' complex connection to their land to basic economics, and clearly the mining was not just for the good of "mankind" but for the profits of the investors. What kind of profit was the PPC making at this time? Macdonald writes that in 1906 and 1907 dividends of 30 percent and 50 percent, respectively, were paid to shareholders on a capitalization of £125,000. In 1908–1909 profits amounted to 455 percent on the 1907 capital, and dividends of 35 percent were paid. Between 1900 and 1913 the Company made profits in excess of £1.75 million and in the same period paid to the Banabans for land, trees, and phosphate less than £10,000.[32] The colonial administrators later established a trust fund for Banaban phosphate royalties, which they controlled and distributed, not in terms of individual landholdings but for the community's welfare as a homogeneous whole.

The clearly lucrative phosphate deposits, the highly developed mining infrastructure, and the Company town later made the island a target for Japanese occupation during World War II. Many Banabans and Gilbertese and Ellice Islander workers died under occupation, and the community was dispersed to prisoner-of-war camps in Kosrae, Nauru, and the Gilbert Islands. When the war ended, the *Triona,* one of four creatively named and lavishly outfitted Company flagships, collected all the Banabans and moved them to Rabi in Fiji. Rabi, or Rabe in Fijian, is an island that was lost to its Fijian settlers in a regional war involving the Tongan chief Ma'afu several decades prior to the Banaban settlement. The island was sold to the Australian Lever Brothers Company in the late 1800s, and Lever Brothers subsequently sold it to the Banabans. All transactions were conducted by the colonial administration, which paid for the purchase from the Banabans' trust fund, the earnings from mining managed by the British resident commissioner.

Lever Brothers was a large British company with significant copra trading and planting interests in the Pacific. It began as a grocery business, moved into soap manufacture, and then set up a vegetable oil mill and a soap factory in Australia in the late 1890s.[33] William Lever was a close acquaintance of the Pacific Islands Company founder John T. Arundel. At a critical juncture he had invested £25,000 in the PIC and bought its coconut plantations for the same price. This needed capital allowed the Company to improve its operations at Ocean Island significantly. Thus the later sale of Rabi by his company to the Banabans, brokered by the British government and the phosphate company, was no coincidence. The colonial administration, businesses, and missionaries were a labyrinth of intersecting political and economic interests and agendas. Many of the descendants of the Fijian Rabeans, who lost their island, live on islands surrounding Rabi and have maintained strong ancestral links to their home island. This has made for some very awkward interactions between Banabans and Fijians, and Rabi is thus a still-contested place with two displaced populations who call it home.

Relocating the Banabans to Rabi allowed the BPC unfettered access to all phosphate deposits, some of which were under villages, homes, and burial sites. On both Banaba and Rabi, the Banabans came to rely upon phosphate royalties and imported water, rice, canned goods, and other products, many of which were manufactured in Australia or New Zealand using the chain of agricultural commodities enabled by the phosphate fertilizer generated from their island. From the 1940s, by necessity, the community on Rabi slowly began to revive their traditional fishing skills and cultivated copra, kava, taro, and cassava.

Partial and Personal Truths

When I, a woman of Banaban heritage, began my research on Banaba in 1997 I was intent on writing about the injustices of the mining industry, as illustrated by the *Sydney Morning Herald* story, and about the effects of the displacement of Banabans to Fiji. Like many Banabans I was angry about this history for many years, and this was clearly reflected in my writing, which highlighted the *rawata,* or burden, and *kawa,* or pity, of Banaban history.[34] While anthropologists and historians have intensively tracked the histories of products, such as sugar, cotton, and bottled water, in our everyday lives we still rarely consider the labor, social upheaval, and loss supporting our consumption, needs, and desires.[35] Certainly few of us consider the phosphorus stories behind the food we eat, the clothes we wear, the milk we drink, or the grass beneath our feet.

However, while I combed through the archives of the BPC, it became clear to me that there were multiple, layered, and diverse experiences of the mining venture and the island itself. Banaba meant different things to different stakeholders, and the Banabans I found in the archives emerged not just as victims, but at times as agents of their own displacement. The stakeholders included not just indigenous Banabans, but the British administrators, the Australian and New Zealand company managers and investors, politicians in all three countries, Gilbertese, Ellice Islanders, Japanese and Chinese laborers, Scandinavian ship captains, the Australian wheat industry, the New Zealand dairy and beef industry, and a global fertilizer industry—and the list goes on. The fertilizer industry and most of the farmers frankly did not care where the phosphate came from. Their universe was governed by the price of both the raw materials and the manufactured superphosphate. The Antipodean exploitation and decimation of Banaba was now no less compelling to me, but the complexity of the story and the global significance of the phosphate rock were greater than I had imagined.

All this gave me pause and forced me to reconsider non-indigenous perspectives and experiences. Kirin Narayan's discussion of "how native is a native anthropologist?" particularly shaped my thinking at this stage. In her much-cited essay, Narayan argues that each anthropologist, native or otherwise, might be viewed in terms of their "shifting identifications amid a field of interpenetrating communities and power relations."[36] My initial engagement with the archival records had involved a search for "facts": What lands were surveyed? How many tons were shipped from where, on what day, and by which vessel? However the form and content of the archival records eventually adjusted my initial desire to just gather facts. Borrowing Donna Haraway's optical metaphor, I began to "diffract" texts and images.[37] In the field of physics, diffraction occurs when a wave of light encounters and bends around a small obstacle or when it has to pass through a small opening, resulting in a spreading of the wave. The nature of the diffracting object, too small to be seen by the naked eye, is illuminated by an observation of the ensuing diffraction patterns.

If we take a particle of lost phosphate as "the object," the stories or representations of it—published texts, memoirs, photographs, films, Company letters, colonial pamphlets—are analogous to the waves of light. The nature of their diversity, their scope or limit, and the major and minor characters they feature constitute the patterns to be observed or the pathways to follow. These are the patterns that tell us something about the diffracting object. So while I cannot directly track a single granule of Ocean Island, I can say something about the narratives, images, materials, and events that have emerged from its existence. Furthermore, just as the various stories constitute diffraction patterns, so too is the island itself diffracted across time and space. This Banaba could be mined forever, in more ways than one.

In my research I took this optical metaphor and visual approach quite seriously, and in the islands I produced fifty hours of digital video footage rather than a collection of fieldnotes. My notes came instead from archival readings, which were then set against the meticulously collected Company photographs that are now available through the National Library of Australia's search engine TROVE. The gaps between my observations in the islands, historical fragments from the archives, and the intensive visual collection resulted in an explosion of meaning and an eventual presentation of some of this diverse material in a constructivist fashion as a visual montage.[38] The montage drew attention to the connections and disjunctures between the multisited and multilayered Banaba stories.

In "Many Paths to Partial Truths," Elisabeth Kaplan challenges what she views as the isolation of archival practice from the broader intellectual landscape in which issues of representation, objectivity, and power are being debated:

> Anthropologists (just like archivists) have traditionally viewed themselves as disinterested selectors, collectors, and assemblers of facts from a transparent reality. But both actually serve as intermediaries between a subject and its later interpreters, a function/role that is one of interpretation itself. That translates into power over the record and how it is interpreted; and it points to where power is negotiated and exercised. This power over the evidence of representation, and the power over access to it, endows us with some measure of power over history, memory, and the past. While archivists and anthropologists may raise an eyebrow at the thought of their professions as powerful, the fact is that both are so deeply embedded in political institutions and societal frameworks that any residual claims of innocence and objectivity are completely unfounded.[39]

Kaplan's concerns resonate with those of indigenous communities, which often view library, archival, and museum collections with ambivalence. When I first began my research I would check out books on Banaba from the library of the University of the South Pacific, where dozens of Banabans have studied. I found the margins of library books about Banaba littered with responses from Banaban students. Harry Maude's, Arthur Grimble's, and Pearl Binder's texts displayed comments like "!!," "rubbish!," "no chiefs in Banaba or Kings!?," and "Grimble refused to find lawyer for Banabans." By contrast, there were no comments in Martin Silverman's 1971 ethnographic study, *Disconcerting Issue: Meaning and Struggle in a Resettled Pacific Community*. This I interpreted to mean that either his prose and symbolic anthropological approach were inaccessible (it took me several years to comprehend it) and/or Banabans liked Silverman.

Banabans are always interested in knowledge of their culture and history, and while few elect to do studies in the social sciences or humanities, they are always engaged in some form of interpretation of their past whether in the critical vandalism of library texts, storytelling around a kava bowl, creative choreography and performance, or the anniversaries of their December 15 arrival on Rabi. One clan spokesperson, Ken Sigrah, who eventually relocated to the Gold Coast of Queensland, joined forces with Stacey King, a descendant of Australian phosphate mining managers, to support the material and digital collection and dissemination of both historical and contemporary records of Banaba and Rabi.[40] I was inspired by my father, John Tabakitoa Teaiwa's, childhood stories of life on Rabi, my elder sister Teresia Teaiwa's initial research, poetry, and writing on Banaban politics and history,[41] and other stories overheard or performed at Banaban and I-Kiribati cultural events to similarly explore Banaban histories, in an institutional context.

I did most of my research in the era of Pacific studies "decolonization," when natives were writing back and challenging non-indigenous scholars and frameworks for their (mis)understanding of native histories and cultures.[42] This context also inspired a closer examination of land in the physical sense, since relations to place form the cornerstone of indigenous Pacific decolonization discourse. I asked: If, ontologically, land and people are the same in the indigenous sense, then what happens when *both* the people and the land are removed?

In addition to bringing the experiences of diverse mining stakeholders back into focus, the primary visual material in the archives also compelled me to pay more attention to the two-and-a-half-square-mile island itself. The Company had so meticulously chronicled, photographed, or filmed every centimeter of its industrial development that the records appeared cinematic. I had a fairly clear visual sense of the rise and fall of modernity on this tiny island in the very center of the vast Pacific.

"Development," of the economic and human variety, has been the most dominant framework shaping and transforming Pacific lives since their countries gained independence. With the current widespread acceptance of international development indicators, such as the Millennium Development Goals, it is even more so in the present. But as Arturo Escobar and other post-development critics have warned, the price of so-called development is often impoverishment or death, especially where the selling and degrading of natural resources are involved. Escobar writes of progress and planning in the developmentalist mode: "perhaps no other concept has been so insidious, no other idea gone so unchallenged."[43] The Banaban story shows clearly that economic growth and infrastructural development on an island are often devastating when shaped by foreign agendas and priorities.

Despite their historical centrality to global agriculture, Banaba and Nauru are not part of the well-researched cultural areas of Melanesia and Polynesia, which continue to capture the imaginations of anthropologists, historians, political scientists, writers, and literary critics. While culturally included, for geopolitical reasons they are usually omitted from the central and northwestern Pacific region described under the term popularized by Dumont d'Urville in the 1830s as Micronesia, or "small islands," in contrast to the "many islands" of Polynesia in the east and the "black islands" of Melanesia in the southwest. Transformed into an arena for the Pacific battles of World War II, most of Micronesia is currently dominated by the United States and is the focus of ongoing research on the impact of nuclear testing in the Marshall Islands, among other concerns, including environmental and heritage issues in Palau; the revival of navigation and sailing practices in Guam, the Marshall Islands, and the Federated States of Micronesia; and migration studies exploring the flow of Micronesian communities to the United States.[44]

Kiribati has recently become a focus of international research, popular media, aid, and foreign policy because of climate change. While parts of Banaba are over seventy meters above sea level, all other islands in Kiribati lie at just two meters above the ocean. Both Kiribati and Tuvalu are now seen, along with the Maldives and the Carteret Islands in Papua New Guinea, as being at the forefront of the global warming and sea-level rise debates. Kiribati, for example, has made moves to buy land in the northern part of Fiji to develop and potentially settle climate-change migrants. This development has of course raised questions about the need for I-Kiribati to learn from the Banaban experience.[45] This book thus contributes to a still small but expanding body of research and writing on the central Pacific islands and particularly the formerly British Micronesia, but I approach the area with a perspective very different from that of traditional anthropological studies.

Most of my father's family lives on Rabi in Fiji, not too far from the land the Kiribati government plans to purchase. Banaba was the home island of my paternal great-grandfather Tenamo and his mother, Kieuea. Tenamo had two children, Teaiwa and Aoniba. As is customary, Teaiwa was adopted out to relatives on Tabiteuea Meang (North) in the Gilbert Islands, where he lived in Utiroa village and married a woman named Takeua from Eita village. He was apparently unaware of his Banaban roots until he was recruited by the BPC to work in the mines on Banaba in the early 1940s. He was quickly identified on the island as kin and chose to stay with his Banaban family and cease working for the Company. Teaiwa and Takeua had a son named Tabakitoa, and he was adopted as a grandchild by Tebwerewa and Tebikeiti on Tabiteuea. In 1947 Teaiwa asked the couple to send Tabakitoa to join his family in Fiji, the new home of the Banabans who had been gathered up from Japanese war camps and moved to the South Pacific. My father, Tabakitoa, whose English name is John (a dual naming practice common at the time), then came to live on Rabi Island and was eventually the first Banaban to obtain a Fiji government scholarship to, ironically, study agriculture at the East-West Center and at the University of Hawai'i in Honolulu. There he met my mother, Joan Martin, who is of African American descent and the eldest daughter of Colonel John Thomas and Hestlene Martin of Washington, D.C.

Tabakitoa had nine brothers and sisters, and as the eldest and most educated he has been involved for much of his life with the welfare of Teaiwa's kainga, which now consists of over sixty children, grandchildren, and great-grandchildren, many of whom live at Tabona just outside the village of Tabiang on Rabi. At one time, phosphate royalties, distributed as annuities, helped to support the family but these were intermittent and quickly used up; most Banabans today face many basic economic challenges. After thirty years serving in the Fiji civil service, primarily as the permanent secretary (equivalent to a CEO) in the Ministry of Agriculture, from 1997 to 2000 my father was also both the chair of the Rabi Council of Leaders and the Banaban representative in the Kiribati Parliament. This provided me with my first opportunity to visit the now-remote and generally inaccessible "homeland."

One of the primary effects of phosphate mining has been the profound unraveling of kinship between Banabans and Gilbertese, today known as I-Kiribati.[46] As someone who is of both Banaban and Tabiteuean descent, I sometimes find myself in an awkward political position, seeking to spotlight the injustices of this history while still honoring my Gilbertese roots. While I strive to foreground historical complexity as signaled in or narrated by diverse sources, and to stimulate reflection on the relations between seemingly remote and insignificant islands and global agriculture, my position as a woman of I-Kiribati and Banaban descent inevitably has shaped the form and content of this book. I have been at times confused and exhausted by the far-reaching and never-ending nature of this phosphate story. In many ways I myself have been "consumed" by Ocean Island. Indeed, consumption is not just a central theme but an emotional ethos and motif in this work. A dictionary defines the word thus:

Consume

1. eat, drink, or ingest (food or drink): *people consume a good deal of sugar in drinks;* (of a fire) completely destroy: *the fire spread rapidly, consuming many homes;*
   use up (a resource): *this process consumes enormous amounts of energy;*
2. buy (goods or services);
3. (of a feeling) completely fill the mind of (someone): *Carolyn was consumed with guilt.* Origin: late Middle English: from Latin *consumere,* from *con-* "altogether" + *sumere* "take up"; reinforced by French *consumer.*[47]

The Structure of This Book

Aside from my own and others' obsessions with the island, in these chapters I explore the manner in which Banaba was fetishized, commodified, and consumed through a variety of interlinked and overlapping stories. The architecture of the book is shaped by one mode of storytelling from Rabi. Like most people in Fiji, Banabans tell many stories around the kava bowl. While still a ceremonial Fijian practice marking, for example, significant life events, the welcoming of and saying farewell to guests, and rituals for mending social rifts, kava is now consumed casually by many non-Fijians across the islands and especially by Banabans, who grow and sell their own Rabi brand. In many Pacific contexts, including in Kiribati, storytelling occurs with an audience of listeners patiently following the teller through his or her version of events. Around a kava bowl on Rabi, however, someone might start telling a story and then another person will interject with his or her version. Yet another person will jump in and very soon the story, after many twists and turns and jumping across time and space, will be claimed by many people, who often agree on the big picture but might disagree on the finer details with no satisfactory conclusion. They call this *tau boro,* meaning to take over someone else's conversation, or *anai boro,* stealing the ball or, literally, "give me the ball," as in the game of rugby when the ball swiftly moves through the hands of different players. For Banabans on Rabi, one story moves through the voices and perspectives of many people, and sometimes it is hard to pin down what really happened. Multiple perspectives are in circulation and up for debate without evacuating the weight and meaning of an event for those whose lives have been transformed by it.

The book is divided into three parts interrupted by ethnographic interludes reflecting on and recollecting key moments during my research process. Chapter 2, "Stories of P," describes the broader chemical and agricultural context, focusing on the effects of diminishing sources of phosphorus on global consumption and food security. In "Land from the Sea" and "Remembering Ocean Island," I explore Banaba's physical and conceptual consumption: the way it was mined, how it provided work for many, and the way it was a site of curiosity and entertainment for visitors and short-term residents. The stories of Banaba as depicted in a BPC film and the memories of white families and Gilbertese miners parallel the story of agriculture in Australia and New Zealand in "Land from the Sky" and the difficulties faced in "*E Kawa Te Aba:* The Trials of the Banabans." As Banaba has become a desiccated field of coral pinnacles, agriculture in Australia and New Zealand has thrived.

"*E Kawa Te Aba*" pays homage to Pearl Binder's passionately researched *Treasure Islands: The Trials of the Banabans* (1978). Here I explore the serious concerns raised by the Banabans as they began to realize they were not just losing their land and sense of efficacy, but losing out on the immense profits made from the mining. I delve into the dramas of the BPC and the colonial administration before and after World War II, ending with the well-publicized trial of the Banabans in Britain from 1971 to 1976. The documentary *Go Tell It to the Judge* and the Australian Broadcasting Corporation's *Foreign Correspondent* serve as critical resources for gaining a sense of the political and emotional atmosphere of that period. The Banabans were consumed with gaining independence from Britain and the Gilbert and Ellice Islands colony, and securing compensation for and rehabilitation of the devastated landscape, but while they gained global attention, they inevitably lost their cause.

"Remix: Our Sea of Phosphate" is a visual essay and play on the late prominent Pacific scholar Epeli Hauʻofa's "Our Sea of Islands," which reimagined the smallness of islands in terms of the vast ocean and flow of water that connects islands, peoples, and continents.[48] This chapter tracks the story as a remix of quotes, some of which appear in other parts of the book, and images highlighting the flow of phosphate into Victoria, Australia, through stunning photography, particularly by Wolfgang Sievers, exploring a Geelong processing plant owned by the Phosphate Co-operative Company. This visual essay was inspired by responses to the Banaban story presented at the "Media in Transition 5" conference at the Massachusetts Institute of Technology in 2007. In a gathering both celebrating and questioning the concept of appropriation and cultural remixing in cyberspace, conference rapporteur Suzanne de Castell responded to my presentation linking Banaban histories with those of empire, global economies, race, land, and oppression:

> Teaiwa's presentation on the physical removal of aboriginal islander land rich in phosphate which was "appropriated," [is] the most profound example of remixing I have ever encountered: where a two and a half mile island was stripped, the very grounds of a people's existence removed and relocated, to fertilize the grasslands of both new Zealand and Australia, to grow its lush, green pastures for other people's animal and food production. What I think we learn here is that we have to be very careful not to unthinkingly import to our attempts to rethink these new foundational ideas, assumptions, ideologies, conceptualizations, ways that continue to privilege world views and practices which have devastated other people in other places.

She continued:

> If we don't want a literal and superficial and enduringly oppressive epistemology of remix . . . , we need to go to the borders, limits, and edges to ideas whose deep roots challenge us to hold firm to our contexts and communities. We need these challenges from the borders and margins so an agenda of radical inclusion is in my view the most generative agenda for the future.[49]

"Coming Home to Fiji" is the interlude that disrupts this intensive focus on Banaba, an account of the period before a civilian coup in 2000 led by the self-proclaimed nationalist Fijian leader George Speight. This sets up the story of the Banabans living in the uncertain Fiji political context, where questions of citizenship and belonging, particularly for minorities, are challenging and stressful. In "Between Rabi and Banaba," the ruins of the home island continue to confound, inspire, and frame Banaban life as it unfolds in Fiji. Banabans' relations with I-Kiribati are constantly fraught and still in need of healing. This chapter is in many ways about Banaba's spiritual consumption, the way it functions as a sacred idea for many displaced Banabans, who cling to the dream of a distant homeland they can rightly claim. I interviewed Banaban teenagers in 2012, and in response to my question "What is your identity?" they were clear: "We are Banabans and we are Rabi Islanders. We are proud to be from Fiji but Banaba is also our home." I end this chapter with an exploration of my own family kainga in 2000, a hundred years after mining commenced on Banaba, and how the descendants of my Banaban great-great-grandmother Kieuea continue to carve out a creative existence on Rabi.

The images, maps, and diagrams accompanying the chapters are not meant to merely supplement and be subordinate to the text but rather should be read as an integral part of these diverse stories. The photographs provide critical views of dispersed but deeply connected sites linked through the phosphate industry and the chain of commodities that result from the mining of phosphate rock. Ultimately this book reconstructs and reframes Banaban histories by bringing the dispersed material of phosphate rock, and the home and landscape that once existed in the central Pacific, back into a dialogue with the people, their stories, and their experiences, and to situate all of that within the broader global context of agriculture and phosphorus security.

2   Stories of P

In this chapter I explore five stories of phosphorus and the phosphate compound from which it is sourced. What is phosphorus? Where does, in Dana Cordell's words, "humanity's addiction to phosphate rock" come from? How does it fuel essential food and commodity chains? And what does the possibility of "peak phosphorus" mean for the globe? How did Ocean Island—a landscape in which Banaban lives and practices were grounded and eventually disrupted and scattered—come to be made of phosphate? Why should indigenous Banabans today care about the science behind it all?

Global Phosphate

In 1938, with the United States just out of the Great Depression and on the verge of World War II, President Franklin Roosevelt spoke to Congress about the critical relationship between phosphate reserves, soil fertility, and agricultural security. He said:

> I cannot overemphasize the importance of phosphorus not only to agriculture and soil conservation but also to the physical health and economic security of the people of the Nation. Many of our soil types are deficient in phosphorus, thus causing low yields and poor quality of crops and pastures. . . . It appears that even with a complete control of erosion, which obviously is impossible, a high level of productivity will not be maintained unless phosphorus is returned to the soil at a greater rate than is being done at present. Increases by the addition of phosphorus to the soil must be made largely, if not entirely, in the form of fertilizers which are derived principally from phosphate rock. Therefore, the question of continuous and adequate supplies of phosphate rock directly concerns the national welfare.[1]

While from the 1930s to today the United States has continued to be a major global producer of phosphate, Roosevelt's presentation signaled the finite nature of supplies and the rapid loss of phosphorus from soils through erosion, leaching, and harvesting. Despite his plea for a national policy for the production and conservation of rock phosphate, a plea framed explicitly for the "benefits of this and coming generations," no such policy emerged.[2]

In 1959, in a rather different vein, the biochemist and prolific science fiction writer Isaac Asimov described phosphorus as "life's bottleneck": it is the ultimate limiting factor for life on earth, with no natural or synthetic substitutes. With a nascent sense of future problems to come from global warming, nuclear energy, and

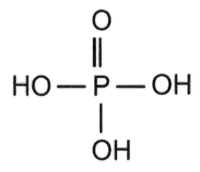

Phosphate in a stable phosphoric acid form, showing phosphorus bonded with three hydrogen and four oxygen atoms.

environmental pollution, Asimov wrote: "Life can multiply until all the phosphorus has gone and then there is an inexorable halt which nothing can prevent. . . . We may be able to substitute nuclear power for coal, and plastics for wood, and yeast for meat, and friendliness for isolation—but for phosphorus there is neither substitute nor replacement."[3]

What makes phosphorus so different, and why do we need it so much? Unlike the other essential elements—carbon, hydrogen, nitrogen, and oxygen— phosphorus cannot freely circulate in the atmosphere and is limited to circulation in the biosphere (the global biological system), the lithosphere (the earth's crust and upper mantle), and the hydrosphere (all surface water).[4] Elemental phosphorus, designated in the periodic table as P, is volatile and naturally locked away in a range of stable, benign compounds, some of which are deposited in the deepest trenches of the ocean, while others circulate through land and waterways. Phosphorus is essential to all living systems because a cell's growth, structure, metabolism, and reproduction depend on it. The stable compound phosphate consists of four molecules of oxygen (O) bound with phosphorus in a tetrahedral arrangement to make PO_4^{3-} (I will hereafter omit the valence electrons, for example, $^{3-}$). The stable form is the acid H_3PO_4. Human DNA, for example, is held together by long chains of phosphate, and cellular energy production and storage in both animals and plants are dependent upon the work of adenosine triphosphate. About 700 milligrams a day is required by the average adult, and 85 percent of the phosphorus in our bodies is stored in our bones and teeth as calcium phosphate with the remainder in soft tissues.[5]

Phosphorus is present in all living things, but by the time some foods are processed they contain very little of the element. The "phosphorus biographer," John Emsley, notes that phosphoric acid is added to Coca-Cola to give it a pleasant tang, and unlike citric acid it does not interfere with the taste of other ingredients. He tells us that polyphosphates make your supermarket meat tender and succulent, and cause bacon to shrivel up on contact with a hot skillet. Food addi-

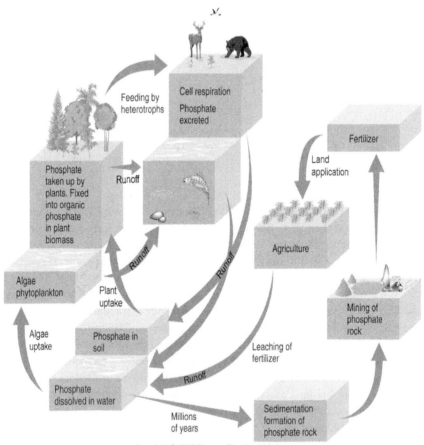

The phosphorus cycle, illustrating the flows between different phases.
Courtesy of Pearson Prentice Hall, Inc.

tives such as polyphosphates influence the shelf life and taste of the average store-bought cheese, hot dogs, cake mixes, frozen fish fingers, and non-dairy powdered coffee creamer.[6] Phosphoric acid is also widely used in detergents and pharmaceuticals, but its most prominent use is in fertilizers.

Phosphorus moves through the environment in three cycles, beginning with a long inorganic phase that creates deposits in the earth's crust. Millions of tons from the crust are released into soil each year, and from the soil millions of tons pass into rivers, lakes, and the sea as sedimentary, insoluble calcium phosphate.

This in turn is converted into phosphate rock as a result of geological pressure. Over millions of years these deposits are uplifted to form new land, and the cycle continues. The other cycles are much shorter and organic, moving phosphorus through living organisms via the food chain: the aboveground portion is relatively fast but slows down once the phosphate is in the less soluble and precipitated portion of the soil component, and it will take millions of years for it to cycle back to the surface when precipitated under the sea.[7]

In a natural state, phosphate rock has high concentrations of PO_4 in nodular or compact masses created from layers of an insoluble mineral compound called "apatite." The apatite in rock deposits can come from a variety of sources: it may leach out of limestone or other phosphate-bearing rocks; it may come from guano, that is bird, bat, or seal droppings and urine, on the surface; or it may develop from dead marine vertebrates that secrete shells of calcium phosphate ($Ca_3(PO_4)_2$) and from the bones of other vertebrates.

Feeding the World from Beds of Bone

There are a few competing genealogies for the identification of phosphate in its key mineral forms and its relationship to agricultural innovation. Richard L. Myers writes that in 1769 Johan Gottlieb Gahn and Carl Wilhelm Scheele showed that calcium phosphate ($Ca_3(PO_4)_2$) was found in bones, and they were able to obtain phosphorus from bone ash, while Antoine Lavoisier identified phosphorus as an element in 1777.[8] In 1799, Charles Darwin's grandfather Erasmus Darwin wrote *Phytologia; or, The Philosophy of Agriculture and Gardening* where he argued that both nitrogen and phosphorus were essential components of plants and absorbed through plant roots. He recommended that bone ash, manure, and compost be used to add these elements to the soil and that rock phosphate deposits be identified. However, it was decades before scientists agreed on the importance of phosphorus to plants. Indeed, writes Emsley, "It became apparent that phosphorus might even be *the* element that governed the fertility of the land."[9] In this period bone meal—a mixture of crushed and coarsely ground bones—was a popular fertilizer, and around 1840 the Duke of Richmond proved that the key ingredient of bone meal was not calcium, but rather phosphorus in its phosphoric acid form. It was soon found that the beneficial effects of calcium phosphate were sped up by treatment with sulfuric acid, and superphosphate fertilizer was born.

To make superphosphate, sulfuric acid (H_2SO_4) is applied to tricalcium phosphate ($Ca_5(PO_4)_3X$), a molecule bound up with an "X" which can, for example, be a hydroxide (OH), fluorine (F), chlorine (Cl), or bromide (Br). The combination of acid with rock creates a solution with soluble phosphate pentoxide, or phosphoric acid (P_2O_5), the key defining feature of fertilizer-grade phosphate rock. In the industrial literature, P_2O_5 is used to express the useful P content of "bone phosphate of lime," the common name for tricalcium phosphate.[10] The equation below shows the standard reaction for the conversion of solid phosphate into a liquid, or aqueous (aq), state using sulfuric acid (H_2SO_4), which is then dried into fine pellets for fertilizer and applied to soil.

$$Ca_3(PO_4)_2(s) + 2\ H_2SO_4(aq) \rightarrow 2\ CaSO_4(aq) + Ca(H_2PO_4)_2(aq)$$

At first glance, there seems nothing particularly exciting about exploring the chemical process that unlocks the phosphorus for human use. But the science writer Emsley has enlivened the story with a biography of phosphorus, exploring its discovery and use from ancient to contemporary times with extraordinary detail about its luminescent and explosive properties, and often dastardly applications.[11] Like many forms of knowledge, the study of its chemistry has created as many social problems as it has solved.

In 1840, the German chemist Justus von Liebig put forward his ideas on the "law of the minimum," likely formulated earlier by the agronomist Carl Sprengel, that the chemical processes in the soil were the basis of fertility, and influencing them would increase the productivity of the land.[12] Spurred by the English economist Thomas Malthus's population theory, which found that arithmetically increasing food production could not feed geometrically expanding human populations, "scientific" farming was conceived. Emsley writes, "Liebig's message fell on fertile ground."[13] Many of his original ideas, however, were inaccurate, and the practical improvement of soil fertility by the application of fertilizer was only achieved by John Lawes and Henry Gilbert in Rothamsted. From their work, the yield of a plot of land increased dramatically from what was possible in eighteenth-century farming practice and if matters were left "to nature."[14]

Animals preserve calcium phosphate in their bones and if left alone it will last millions of years after the soft tissue of the body has decayed. In the 1800s, as bone became a primary source of phosphate for fertilizer, even the fields of war were harvested, and graves across the continent were robbed to feed the superphosphate factories in Britain—a practice severely criticized by von Liebig.[15] The geological source of most global supplies of phosphate is still called a "bone bed"—ancient and fossilized versions of the calcium phosphate used in bone meal fertilizer. The urgent search for rock phosphate was a moral and practical step toward reducing the agricultural dependency on human and animal bones, and encouraging the use of natural manures, including human excrement, a practice still utilized in parts of the world today.

Superphosphate is phosphorus in a form readily absorbed by plants and is particularly necessary for strengthening roots in alkaline soil with a high pH (concentration of hydrogen ions) level. According to the Fertilizer Industry Federation of Australia, an organization established by the BPC and today representing a vast network of agricultural stakeholders, "plants with a severe P deficiency are generally stunted, develop slowly, lack vigour and have a lacklustre look about them."[16] Superphosphate still is a primary fertilizer used in Australia and New Zealand, along with nitrogen fertilizers, because of the nitrogen, phosphorus, and sulfur deficiencies in their soils. I was fascinated to learn that the initial process involved in sorting and separating the original rock into the ore most useful for fertilizer production is called "beneficiation." Everything else is treated as "waste."

The Rock of Micronesia

In June 2011 I had a meeting with a former student of my elder sister from Wellington. At the end of our chat she passed on a gift from my sister, which consisted of two items: a CD of original children's music, including compositions by my nephew in aid of the devastating Christchurch earthquake, and a T-shirt. The shirt was black and on the front it featured a green island with a fringing reef, a frigate bird, and some text:

BANABA

The ROCK OF MICRONESIA

$3\ Ca_3(PO_4)_2(s) + 6\ H_2SO_4\ (aq)$
$6\ CaSO_4(aq) + 3\ Ca(H_2PO_4)_2\ (aq)$

On the back, it said:

WEBRA

Wellington Banaba Rabi Association

The T-shirt is the product of the small but lively Banaban community association based in Wellington, the capital of New Zealand. Just a decade ago few Banabans and I-Kiribati groups were found outside the Pacific islands, but today there are enough numbers for organized communities to spring up in Wellington, Auckland, Melbourne, Sydney, Brisbane, and London. This Banaban community used the chemical equation (though all twos and fours should be in subscript for the equation to work) to convey that their land is now something other than an island.

This focus on the land itself, its chemical makeup, and its further manifestation as fertilizer is a relatively recent interest among Banabans, for whom understanding the transformation of the island and engaging with scientific and industrial interpretations of its value are necessary steps in the process toward healing, including the metaphorical recovery of the land and culture that have been lost. This means Banabans are also beginning to imagine the rock in a multiscalar and multisited fashion, from visualizing the island as a whole to imagining the fragments that emerge at various stages of the mining and industrial processes across time.

Superphosphate, so fundamental to the fertilizer industry in the twentieth century, was not widely available until the early 1900s. In the proceedings of the Seventh International Congress of Applied Chemistry in London in 1909, Hermann Voss, a principal analyst for the Pacific Phosphate Company, discussed the Pacific deposits and their importance to global agriculture.[17] He presented a table representing the known availability of rock in the 1890s that showed 200,000 tons available in France, 150,000 in Belgium, 50,000 in Spain and Portugal, 30,000 in the West Indies, and 25,000 in Canada for a total of 455,000 tons.

He then described the newly discovered deposits in America (Florida and Tennessee), Africa (Algeria and Tunis), and the Pacific islands, reestimating the world's production of phosphate with America topping the list at 2.3 million tons followed by Africa at 1.5 million. The Pacific islands—at 350,000 tons and just above 7 percent of the global supply—shared third with France. Belgium, the West Indies, Russia, Norway, and others made up the rest of production with a grand total of 4.8 million tons.

Voss argued that in many European countries the consumption of phosphates had increased by 100 percent, and if it were not for the newly discovered deposits in Africa, America, and the Pacific, "agriculture would be in a sad position for the want of fertilisers." He wrote that the deposits in Africa were of lower grade, containing only about 60 percent tribasic phosphate of lime, and that "it is therefore of the greatest importance to the future that very high-grade phosphate has been discovered recently on Islands in the Pacific and the Indian Ocean. . . . On Ocean Island and Nauru together, the quantity of phosphate has been estimated at about 50,000,000 tons."[18]

While prospectors and investors were celebrating their great Pacific find, geologists were not so certain about how the phosphate had been formed. Debates about the exact nature and source of the valuable rock were played out in various geology journals with little impact on the daily life of the Company, except when information was needed on new mining areas and deeper deposits. Geologists wanted to know more about how the island was formed, and miners primarily wanted to know what grade of rock they could access.

Two theories emerged in the geological and agricultural literature about the original formation of phosphate on Nauru and Ocean Island. The first suggested that phosphate was formed through sedimentation, "built up before the two islands were elevated above the sea level by a gigantic convulsion of the sea-bed. The fact that impressions of fish and fossilized shells, including conch shells, have been found among the Nauru deposits appears to lend weight to this belief."[19] The second proposed that the initial deposits on Nauru and Ocean Island were sedimentary but that for thousands of years after elevation from the seabed, the islands were resting places for seabirds. Their droppings collected on top of the original deposits and chemically combined with them to form phosphate rock. This second theory was supported by the fact that Ocean Island was once a nocturnal home for thousands of seabirds.

F. Danvers Power, a mining and metallurgical engineer, conducted the earliest detailed study of the geological makeup of Ocean Island beginning in 1901 and building upon work conducted by chemical analysts from 1900 onward.[20] Power's analyses would be the most cited by the Company and the commissioners for the next few decades though another geologist, Launcelot Owen, differed with him on some basic details of the origins of the island. They all agreed that Ocean Island was formed from an upwelling of the ocean floor upon which coral beds had developed over millions of years. The island was three hundred feet (eighty meters) above sea level at its highest point before mining removed the phosphate layers. This height considerably differentiated it from the low-lying coral atolls in the rest of the Gilbert and Ellice Islands group, many of which are just two meters above sea level.

Power believed that the central portion of the island, where the phosphate deposits are richest and deepest, was the center of an old lagoon. He also wrote that the island was submerged during the formation of the phosphate deposits, and chemically this would influence the nature of the phosphatization of the coral pinnacles to which the deposits are attached. Knowledge of the phosphate content of the rocks as one moves from shore to center was key to how and when the Company obtained leases from particular landowners. The Company mined the richest portions of the island in the middle, for example, in the 1960s and 1970s, when the Banaban landowners were no longer there.

In 1919 Power produced a booklet that further investigated the nature of the guano so key to the formation of phosphate rock.[21] He reported that birds that rested on the phosphate islands included sooty terns, mutton birds, frigate birds, and gannets. He reinforced that phosphates were deposited by animal and chemical means, with the former being guano (birds or bats) and the latter more ancient, maritime rock phosphates. Tern guano would yield between 72.49 percent and 79.21 percent calcium phosphate, while frigate guano produced between 81.91 percent and 84.34 percent calcium phosphate. He wrote:

> This is probably due to a slight difference in their food, for though the frigate-bird goes out to meet the tern as it flies home at night, and deprives it of its food, yet it also catches surface fish round the coast of the island, some of which, living largely on coral and seaweed are likely to contain more phosphorous in their composition than is required by the sea fowl, which get rid of the excess in the usual manner, with the result that their droppings are rich in phosphorous consisting largely of insoluble organic phosphates that are unaffected by rain.[22]

Launcelot Owen published his studies of phosphate on Banaba after spending three years on the island in the 1920s.[23] He similarly argued that the primary source of the phosphate was guano that was deposited on the dolomitized coral surface of the island over millions of years, which leached out in a solution that reacted with the coral bed, a bed that exists in various concentric circles, or terraces, from shore to center. This coral bed, he argued, was formed by "subaerial denudation," or stripping, with the guano developing in the post-Miocene period (after 5.3 million years ago). The reaction between the leached phosphate and the coral resulted in the buildup of a cap of calcium phosphate, the primary source of the valuable fertilizer. Owen agreed that the island was submerged, but not until after the guano was deposited. He argued that the richness of the rock in the center of the island illustrates that its primary source is from recent guano deposits and not older marine sources. He also contended that at some point since the cessation of the guano deposits, the island tilted on its axis, tipping it from the north-northwest to the south-southeast.

Phosphate is generally divided into two grades—rock and alluvial. The alluvial, as described by the Pacific Phosphate Company, was anything that got through a mesh screen measuring nine holes to the square inch. In the early days of mining, Owen argued against this nomenclature and called the alluvial "incoherent phosphate rock" and the other "coherent phosphate rock."[24] Samples from the deepest deposits taken in 1915 indicated a high concentration of phosphoric acid (40.18 percent) along with 87 percent tribasic phosphate of lime and small amounts of carbonic acid, carbonate of lime, organic matter, and water.[25] The percentage of phosphoric acid indicates the potential yield and its use value as fertilizer: the real potential of the rock for industrial uses. At that time and still today, the chemical analyses of Banaban rock reveal a relatively high, accessible, and therefore economically viable and lucrative percentage of P_2O_5.

Peak Phosphorus?

By the mid-twentieth century and with the advent of the Green Revolution, the potential yield of an average plot of land had increased exponentially along with dependence on costly inputs such as water, pesticides, fertilizers, fossil fuels, and new crop varieties. The most water- and energy-intensive practices are also the result of the current dietary preference for meat and dairy products, particularly in so-called developed countries. Today, it takes a ton of phosphate to produce 130 tons of grain, and about 170 million tons of rock are mined globally every year to keep soils fertile.[26] But phosphate is not easily accessed, and the known world supplies are finite.

In 2010 the International Fertilizer Development Center issued a report that had been commissioned to respond to rising alarm over the perceived limits of phosphorus for life on earth. The price of phosphate had spiked from US$40 per ton to US$500 per ton, and the perception of scarcity was at an all-time high. World trade today is dominated by the Moroccan state-owned company, the Cherifien Phosphates Board, with sales of US$6 billion in 2011. Morocco, China, South Africa, Jordan, and the United States now control the world's known phosphate reserves, with a staggering 70 percent of such reserves, including those in the western Sahara, controlled by Morocco alone.

The alarm was raised by passionate scientists, including Dana Cordell at the University of Technology, Sydney—a founding member of the Global Phosphorus Network. Her research in environmental studies, "The Story of Phosphorus," comprehensively places phosphorus within the broader context of its limited global supply. She also signals the ongoing lack of writing and public knowledge about this key mineral by stating, like others before her, "Without phosphorus, there would be no life on earth."[27]

Cordell has predicted that peak phosphorus production will occur around 2035 after which global demand will far exceed supply. Her research explores five aspects of phosphate security that extend beyond mere physical scarcity. She discusses the problems in the management of phosphorus throughout the entire food production and consumption system. Assessing global phosphorus flows, she finds that only 20 percent of the phosphorus in phosphate rock mined for food production actually reaches the food consumed by the global population due to substantial inefficiencies and losses from mine to field to fork. She also describes economic inequality: while all the world's farmers need access to sufficient fertilizers, only those with sufficient purchasing power can access fertilizer markets. Cordell further identifies institutional scarcity, such as the lack of governance structures at the international level to ensure the long-term availability of and access to global phosphorus resources for food production. Finally, she discusses geopolitical scarcity, reminding us that 90 percent of the world's remaining high-grade phosphate rock reserves are controlled by just five countries, some of which experience geopolitical tensions. This might limit the availability of phosphorus on the market and raises serious ethical questions.[28]

The prediction of a phosphorus peak produced more than a few media ripples:

Peak Soil: It's Like Peak Oil Only Worse

Peak Generation, May 12, 2010

Peak Phosphorus: The Next Inconvenient Truth

The Brokers, August 4, 2009

Might as Well Face It You're Addicted to Phosphorus

Climate Change: The Blog of Bloom, June 23, 2009

Peak Phosphorus Fuels Food Fears

ABC Science, August 5, 2010[29]

The size of phosphate reserves was reassessed in Steven Van Kauwenbergh's 2010 study for the International Fertilizer Development Center with slightly less alarming estimates.[30] Imminent predictions, he argued, were based on known or actively mined rock deposits—phosphate reserves—and did *not* account for the broader scale of phosphate resources in the earth's crust, such as unknown, lower-grade, and harder-to-access deposits. Van Kauwenbergh estimated 60,000 million metric tons (mmt) in reserves and proposed 460,000 mmt in resources with a note that many countries have been incompletely explored for phosphate. Many scientists, including Cordell, are arguing for the exploration of alternative methods of exploitation with the hope that future technological advances will produce new strategies for recycling industrial phosphorus or for accessing previously inaccessible sources from the sea.

However, Cordell's work makes no reference at all to the phosphate industry in the Pacific. The experiences of phosphate mining on Banaba and Nauru demonstrate the risks and ethical dilemmas inherent in such extractive industries. In these histories, as in others, the "good of mankind," the need to fuel and satisfy the consumption needs of the growing human population, is at stake. Future prospecting seems set to repeat past tragedies as the perceived broader good trumps that of the powerless few. This threat is very real and there are significant ethical implications for seabed mining, for example, particularly for Pacific island nations. What is pressing and relevant for agricultural and environmental scientists is the present and the future, rather than the past. The moral implications of mining, particularly for indigenous peoples, are inevitably subsumed by the geopolitical and practical needs of food security for the whole world.

There is little popular or scholarly discussion of the physical, social, or cultural impact of phosphate mining on the peoples, seascapes, and landscapes where reserves are held, especially when compared to studies of coal, gold, copper, and other minerals. Once a supply runs out, as is imminent on Nauru and Banaba, attention and research swiftly shift to other sites with abundant known or new sources. The focus of the slowly widening phosphorus debate is on the inefficient extraction and use of the resource, the lack of supplies, the pollution of treated lands and seas, and the need for innovative thinking for both environmental sustainability and food security.[31] But what does all this mean for indigenous peoples? The story of Banaba suggests some troubling answers.

Rock, Flow, and Ruin

In contrast to the science studies, the popular British journalist, novelist, and broadcaster Lucille Iremonger gave a lyrical and certainly cynical account of the formation of Banaba based on one of her visits to the island. Born in Jamaica in 1920, Iremonger received an M.A. with honors at Oxford, and in 1948 was awarded the Society of Women Journalists' Lady Britain trophy for the best book of the year for *It's a Bigger Life,* which chronicled her time in the Pacific as the wife of a colonial officer. No human, animal, or plant was spared Iremonger's sardonic wit. She wrote, "Every time anyone opened his mouth on Ocean Island the word 'phosphate' came out. In no time, and much against my will, I knew all about it."[32] Here is her version of what Company and other officials conveyed to her over cups of tea:

> Everyone knows how a coral atoll is formed. But until one has actually stood on one of them it is not particularly interesting to be told that billions of tiny coral polyps labour for billions of years making billions of cells, until one day a little peak of jagged coral pokes its head out of the water. That is the death signal for the coral polyps in the air, but the polyps in the water go steadily on. Some day a sea-bird alights on this new rock, and in time others nest on it, and in (a very much longer) time their droppings gradually begin to form a smooth soil on the surface. That is a coral atoll. Sooner or later the second great day arrives when a coconut gets washed up, and in no time at all the place is covered with coconut groves. It is only a matter of time after that to the approach of the white man in his topee and his crumpled white clothes, making a lot of bad jokes about the steady fall of coconuts and copra prices.
>
> To turn a coral atoll into a phosphate island a few more centuries must pass. Very likely it sinks into the sea, once or several times. This is not at all an uncommon habit among Pacific Islands. Falcon Island comes up for air every few years and disappears within a matter of hours. Sea water percolates through the birds' deposits, carrying phosphoric acid into the rocks beneath. These being limestone, the acid is automatically converted into phosphate of lime. You have only to treat this with sulfuric acid and, hey presto! Superphosphate! . . .
>
> The British Phosphate Commissioners had added their contribution of weirdness to ugliness. In the trail of their craggy diggings in the limestone bedrock they had left behind them strange shapes, ragged bumps, columns and protuberances of every sort. Row upon row of gnarled pinnacles of porous rock as tall as trees gave the place a look as of some mediaeval inferno. . . .
>
> For hundreds of thousands of years the slow process of making an island like this had gone on. It was slower even than one at first imagines, for there was never much bird life on it. Then one day a man struck his foot against a "coral" door-stop in a Sydney office, and phosphate was discovered. The life of a Pacific island was changed before the inhabitants knew anything about it. The natives became rich, and the island was destroyed.[33]

While both the Banabans and their landscape were uprooted and displaced, phosphate strengthened the roots of Australian and New Zealand agriculture, which provided essential commodities across the British Empire. If in our research into the effects of globalization, and on the movement of peoples and things, we do as the anthropologist George Marcus prescribes and truly "follow the thing," to track Banaban phosphate we would have to recover infinitesimal bits of phosphate and phosphorus from many a field, river, stream, and cereal bowl—and the bones and guts of birds, sheep, and children alike.[34] Records in the BPC Archives, for example, reveal shipments of Banaban phosphate sent as far away as Latvia, Lithuania, and Estonia. The chain of phosphate and phosphorus is endless; this is indeed one of those global flows, but "landscape" is not about to obtain the same status for articulating such flows as Arjun Appadurai's mediascapes, technoscapes, financescapes, ideoscapes, and ethnoscapes.[35] What is deterritorialized here is the territory itself.

The standard chemical reaction can also be imagined in the reverse, and we might consider another equation for Banaban rock, a kind of ontological linking of indigenous and industrial relations to land, resources, and mass agriculture:

$$\text{land/people} + \text{rock} + \text{technology} + \text{empire} \leftrightarrow Ca(H_2PO_4)_2 + \text{food} + \text{profit}$$
$$\text{[kainga] [te aba] [te rii]} \qquad\qquad \text{[fertilizer]}$$

The Pacific scholar Vilsoni Hereniko once wrote, "Our cultural identities are . . . always in a state of becoming, a journey in which we never arrive; who we are is not a rock that is passed on from generation to generation, fixed and unchanging."[36] There is a normative assumption in cultural and global studies and in anthropology that people, ideas, and things move, but not the physical land. Hereniko's rock was not from Banaba or Nauru. For there, on an island that was primarily made of solid phosphate, most rocks had a very great chance of moving and transforming into something else, but rarely as a destiny willed by Islanders. Banaban rock in both its creation over time and in its transformation through mining was never fixed, but was the result of deep and fluid processes. Banaban identity was and still is, from Rabi in Fiji 1,600 miles away from Banaba, embedded in that scattering of rocks. Hereniko continued, "After all, cultural identity is process not product."[37] If, ontologically, we follow an indigenous, place-centered logic, the landscape that shapes Banaban cultural identities is in process too.[38] A map of Banaba from the 1930s with several cartographic layers well illustrates the manner in which Banaba was remapped by the Company and the colonial administration so that new ideological, structural, and material systems were laid over, and eventually displaced or submerged, indigenous Banaban land tenure and sociospatial practices.

By 1980 it was estimated that the two-and-a-half-square-mile Ocean Island had been depleted by almost twenty-two million tons of rock.[39] What had taken millions of years to create, what had formed from the rubbing together of heaven and earth, was wiped out in just eighty years by the hands and machines of man. Many of those machines and most of the warehouses, crushing and drying plants, storage bins, tractors, and trucks still remain on the island in a state of ruin.

Ann Laura Stoler discusses how "to ruin," in the imperial sense, is an active and violent process. She writes, "In its common usage, 'ruins' are often enchanted, desolate spaces, large-scale monumental structures abandoned and grown over."

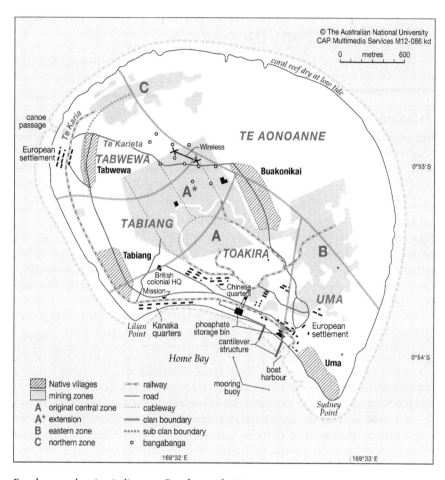

Banaba map showing indigenous Banaban and mining company
land divisions and infrastructure, 1930s. ANU CAP CartoGIS

But what is also of concern is what people are left with, what remains in the "after-shocks" of empire. She explains: "Such effects reside in the corroded hollows of landscapes, in the gutted infrastructures of segregated cityscapes and in the microecologies of matter and mind. The focus then is not on inert remains but on their vital refiguration. The question is pointed: How do imperial formations persist in their material debris, in ruined landscapes and through the social ruination of people's lives?"[40]

3 Land from the Sea

THIS CHAPTER EXPLORES life on the island as presented in Company documents and visual sources with a focus on the first four decades of mining prior to World War II. The BPC's archival textual and visual records are read both in terms of what they say or present and in terms of what they are missing: Banaban and other residents' historical experiences and contemporary realities. Nicholas Thomas discusses both the authority of dense, annotated archival Pacific histories and the turn, as seen in the work of the prominent ethnographic historian Greg Dening, toward a celebration of plural and diverse experiences. He argues that "histories do not merely differ and enrich knowledge through complementary diversity," but rather they "reflect interests in practical projects, in legitimizing or destabilizing; they entertain, and perhaps they perform some symbolic violence with respect to those who are spoken about but whose voices are absent."[1]

Stories gleaned from Company letters and diaries give a fragmented yet specific and usually authoritative point of view, while photographs with inadequate or brief captions beg a viewer to fill in the blanks regarding context. Documentary film and other cinema often attempt to present a total world for the viewer, but the Company film I explore here is an appropriately fragmented and hastily edited montage. These various Ocean Island sources and the kinds of global stories they tell offer particular, still-partial, and morally significant ways in which we might "know" the past. But as Thomas underscores, "history displayed might be harmless if it was evidently less persuasive."[2]

Kings and Phosphateers

Sir Albert Ellis is credited with discovering phosphate on Banaba in 1900, and he became the first phosphate commissioner for New Zealand in 1921. In 1962, a decade after his passing, the minister of agriculture, B. E. Talboys, wrote the following tribute:

> Of Sir Albert Ellis it could be truly said that he became a legend in his lifetime. He was a pioneer who had the satisfaction of playing a long and active role in the administration and growth of phosphate manufacture. Even a man of Sir Albert's foresight could not have predicted the present New Zealand use of a million and a quarter tons of phosphatic fertilisers and mixtures containing phosphatic fertilisers annually, when he discovered the high-quality rock phosphate deposits on Nauru and Ocean Islands at the turn of the century.[3]

Ellis was one of many Australian, English, and New Zealand men who, not unlike their religious counterparts, were preaching the virtues of capitalism and commerce and spreading industrialization throughout the South Pacific in the late nineteenth and early twentieth centuries. They were professed Christians as well and viewed their economic activities as directly connected with the inevitable task of bringing civilization to native populations. These men built the Pacific Islands Company, the Pacific Phosphate Company, and the now-iconic Pacific companies of Burns Philp, the Colonial Sugar Refinery, Lever Brothers, the British Phosphate Commissioners, and many other plantation, mining, manufacturing, shipping, and trading ventures. Maslyn Williams and Barrie Macdonald called those in the industry "the phosphateers," and titled their book accordingly: "This history is dedicated to the many thousands of men and women who, through their enterprise, skills, labour and patience over eighty years, helped to develop a unique institution."[4] The imagined audience is clear, and former employees of the Company aided in summarizing and organizing archival records during the authors' extensive research.

In 1897 Ellis's employer, the London-based firm John T. Arundel and Company, with offices in Australia and New Zealand, transformed into the Pacific Islands Company with interests in guano mining, coconut plantations, and the copra trade. The staff, including Ellis, his father, George, and his brothers James and George, regularly searched for Pacific sources of guano and phosphate. In 1899, Ellis and a Company manager, Henry Denson, figured out that a large rock, which had for years propped open a door in the Sydney office of the Company and had previously been classed as fossilized wood, was made of pure phosphate obtained on Nauru.[5] Since the island was at the time a German territory, the politics of looking for phosphate there were not favorable, but Ellis and Denson reasoned that nearby Ocean Island might be of similar geological formation. In early 1900 Ellis, another employee, James Mortensen, and an assistant, A. G. Naylor, were sent on a prospecting trip.

According to Ellis, the parting advice from the PIC management was, "Those Ocean Islanders are hard cases. You take your rifle and revolver with you, and as soon as you get on the beach show the natives you can use them."[6] An extract from Ellis's diary as he approached Banaba reads:

> May 3rd 1900. Arrived Ocean Island at daylight; steamed round to the King's village at West end of Island; canoes came off bringing King and Chief. Supercargoes started trading with the natives for sharkfins, vegetables, fruit, curios, etc. Proceeded round to the village South end of Island. Mr. Mortensen and I went ashore with the King and Interpreter and proceed[ed] inland about 1½ miles; sank several holes, getting depth of 3 feet of Alluvial Phosphate with Rock [Phosphate] mixed up. Found that most of the pillars of rock described

A piece of the phosphate doorstop on display in the Museum of
New Zealand Te Papa Tongarewa. Photo by Nicholas Mortimer

by Mortensen were hard coral rock and valueless, but that among them were
large boulders of phosphate stone; saw at once that the deposits are very valuable. Returned to village and opened negotiations with the King, Mr. Mortensen
conducting the business. King said would require to refer the matter to a chief
on the steamer.

After having lunch at the Teacher's house, we went aboard the vessel with the
King, and after a good deal of talk, the latter agreed to our working the Phosphate deposits at a yearly rental of £50. He and the Chief signed the Agreement,
*as his authority is undisputed, it was not considered necessary for any of the na-
tives to sign.* The King and Chief were firm however, that our prospecting party
must not stay at the Southern village, but must go round to the King's village;
this owing to there being considerable rivalry between the two places, it being
said that the Teacher at South village was trying to undermine the King's authority.[7]

These passages mark an agreement that has been lamented by Banabans ever
since. While there were clear systems of genealogical precedence and rights, there
was never a "Banaban king." The rivalries that Ellis appears to have exacerbated
are between the villages of Uma (spelled Ooma in the archives) and Tabwewa,

which represent two different ancestral clans; the Tabwewa line is the genealogi-cal elder. Clans belonging to Tabwewa enjoyed certain cultural privileges accord-ing to a system of rights distributed among all the kainga groups on the island. As Martin Silverman notes, the two divisions of Tabwewa, Te Karia and Karieta, in addition to setting the timing for or opening certain rituals, operated as distri-bution centers for persons, things, and certain "new" items. One of these was the right to board new vessels and to greet visitors, a right reinforced by the ances-tress from Beru, Nei Anginimaeao, in her division of Banaba.[8] Ever since the so-called king, a representative of Tabwewa named Temate, mistakenly signed away rights normally held by individual landowners, the right to meet and greet visi-tors has been a sore point of contention, including on Rabi today.[9]

It is worth examining Ellis's agreement on behalf of his employers, the Pacific Islands Company, which is also reproduced in whole in Williams and Macdon-ald's book.

> Ocean Island
> 3 May 1900.
> An agreement made this day between The Pacific Islands Company, Limited, of London, England, and of Sydney hereinafter called "the said Company" of the one part, and the undersigned King and Natives of Ocean Island (Paanopa) for and on behalf of the entire population of Ocean Island hereinafter called "the said Natives" of the other part—
>
> 1. The said Natives concede to the said Company the sole right to raise and ship all the Rock and Alluvial Phosphate on Ocean Island for and on account of the said Company.
> 2. The said Natives agree that the said Company shall have the right to erect buildings, lay tram lines, make roads, build jetties and shipping places, or make any other arrangements necessary for the working of the Phosphate de-posits, also to bring labourers from other countries for the purpose of carry-ing on the aforesaid work.
> 3. The said Company agrees not to remove any Alluvial Phosphate from where Cocoanut or other Fruit-Trees or Plants cultivated by the said Natives are growing but to have the right to remove any non-fruit bearing trees which may interfere with the working of the Phosphate deposits.
> 4. The said Company agrees to keep a store or stores on Ocean Island where the said Natives may buy goods at prices current in the Gilbert Group and shall purchase from the said Natives Cocoanuts, Fruits, Vegetables, Fish, etc., at prices current in the Gilbert Group, the said Natives agreeing that the said Company shall have the sole right to keep stores or trading stations on Ocean Island.
> 5. In consideration of the foregoing privileges the said Company agrees to pay to the said Natives at the rate of Fifty (£50) Pounds per annum, or trade to that value, at prices current in the Gilbert Group, payable half-yearly.

6. This Agreement to be in force for a term of Nine hundred and Ninety-nine (999) years.

> THE PACIFIC ISLANDS COMPANY LIMITED
> per Albert F. Ellis
> TEMATI King of Ocean Island
> His X mark.
> Witness E. RIAKIM.
> KARIATABEWA Chief
> His X mark.
> Witness E. RIAKIM
> Witness to all signatures
> J. MAKINSON.[10]

After securing what he assumed was unfettered access, not just to phosphate but to trade on the island, Ellis swiftly made plans for transport. On May 4, 1900, he wrote:

> Friday Rain squalls during night and today; moderate breeze North East; reef fairly smooth. Decided to shift camp, present locality not being suitable. Pitched tent close to beach; King made a present of a native hut, which was carried down bodily, and placed close to tent. . . . With three Ocean Islanders I went right inland to summit of Island, about 1½ miles and probably 300 feet high; found Phosphate Rock and Alluvial everywhere. The center of the Island is a Tableland, and is practically covered with Phosphate Rock; many native walls were seen composed entirely of this stone, mostly in lumps for immediate shipment.[11]

One person's "wall," one of the carefully constructed terraces that dotted the island, is obviously another's "lump for immediate shipment." The cairns on the coast and in the center of the island were not mere "walls." Banabans had built terraces and platforms, some several meters high, from coral and phosphate rock, using them for specific purposes from housing to sacred ritual sites. Maude and Maude write, "The people of Mangati—the fierce people— . . . form the division of Te Karieta or Upland folk . . . [and] lived on the uplands above the present village of Tabwewa and in their territory may still be seen the cairns of rough stones which local tradition states to have been connected with the fire-worship of the autochthones."[12] This refers to the practices of the oldest settlers of Banaba prior to intermarriage with migrants from the west, who brought deities such as Auriaria and Nei Tituabine and, more recently, Nei Anginimaeao and her brothers from the Gilbert Islands. These genealogies and the rights associated with them began to unravel as Ellis and his colleagues followed their own protocols for negotiating mining rights and broke the established channels of communication and decision making.

In order to legalize and protect the rights of the PIC, Banaba was incorporated into the British Protectorate of the Gilbert and Ellice Islands in 1901. This meant that the island now required a colonial representative, and Ellis soon found himself dealing with various resident commissioners, who were responsible for native welfare. It became fairly awkward having to explain how the Company obtained its rights via the one-sided contract in the first place. In 1902 the Pacific Islands Company became the Pacific Phosphate Company and in 1903 the Company's representatives created a new arrangement, this time with landowners, called the "phosphate and trees purchases"—deeds that ran for between five and ten years. This recognized Banaban ownership of both the surface and mineral rights in the land and also required the Company to constantly negotiate with individuals, rather than approach "the natives" as a corporate entity.

On November 19, 1909, while being harassed by the resident commissioner, John Quayle Dickson, Ellis wrote to Alfred Gaze, the representative for the Pacific Phosphate Company in Melbourne, explaining why new contracts were required:

> Re. Original Agreement with the King of Ocean Island, and Phosphate & Trees Purchase Agreements.
>
> The first named was for the general right to work the Island. I had to obtain this right from somebody; the Island didn't belong to any civilized Government, so I could only deal with the native King. The authorities at Fiji had been previously informed of my intention to visit the Island and negotiate for the Phosphate deposits, and they saw nothing to prevent my doing so. The Phosphate & Trees Purchase Agreements made subsequently with the individual landowners, directly compensated them. The King of the Island couldn't sell the Phosphate or "all the Cocoanut, Pandanus and all other trees" as they weren't his; they belonged to each individual landowner, who presumably *has* the right to sell them.[13]

The rest of Ellis's letters in the archives are consumed with justifying the Company's requirements with respect to both acquiring enough land for mining and constructing the original agreement with the supposed "king." He points out that in the original document the Company agreed not to remove any phosphate where cultivated plants grow. This, therefore, excluded most areas where pandanus plants appeared (in Ellis's eyes) to grow wild. This tactic of defining certain areas as cultivated and as noncultivated lands was a technical tool often wielded by the Company and not without some commercially convenient assumptions about the "primitive" Banabans. On Ocean Island, when there has been enough rain by central Pacific standards, pandanus, almond, and coconut trees grow abundantly. In the Gilbertese language there are no less than three hundred identifiable species of pandanus.[14] There was nothing wild about the tree or the Banaban and Gilbertese attitude toward it.[15]

Ellis begins a section of a 1909 memorandum with a report on a proposal to level some of the pinnacles opened up by mining in order to facilitate the replanting of food trees. From the perspective of the present, we know that such activities were never carried out and were part of the reason that Banabans sued the British government and the mining company in the 1970s. Decades earlier, however, Ellis stated authoritatively:

> The patches of Pandanus and Cocoanuts away from the village are very badly cultivated, or else not at all, owing to the inherent laziness of the natives; the consequence is that the dead leaves, grass and weeds accumulate to such an extent that they constitute a great danger as regards fires. In drought times the Island has frequently been swept by fires, previous to the advent of the Company—and since operations were started, there have been numerous serious fires, some of which would have swept the Island, but for the Company's labourers being put on to beat them out. These fires have damaged the food trees much more than the Company's operations have, and they could be avoided if the land is kept in better order.[16]

The very next section says that leveling the pinnacles would be unfeasible and that trees will grow better if they are left alone. Ellis is inconsistent in his recommendations though consistent in his authoritative and definitive tone. Sometimes he seems to express concern for the natives' welfare, and other times he advises action that would benefit only the Company. He is also extraordinarily exasperated with the fact that the Banabans are not always eager to work for the Company. In the same memo Ellis writes:

> (b) It can hardly be said that the purchase of Phosphate and trees is tantamount to purchasing the land, I think. The natives are quite aware that each block reverts to them after the Phosphate is worked off. . . .
>   d) It is certainly hoped that the Government *will* help us to secure land when needed; we haven't had much assistance in this request of late. It is however useless to rely on the Banabans for working at the pinnacles or anything else which requires much exertion.[17]

In spite of the Banabans' ability to often thrive, and in adversity still survive, on a tiny piece of phosphate rock with limited flora and fauna in the middle of the vast Pacific for over two thousand years, the stigma of indolence sticks to Banabans to this day. They are even characterized this way by other Pacific Islanders who themselves have suffered from the "lazy native" labeling since Europeans first entered the Pacific. While Ellis's tone makes sense given his work as a prospector in the early twentieth century, it points to his even grander role in retirement as the phosphate commissioner for New Zealand. Ellis committed his life to extracting as much phosphate as the Company needed for fertilizer manufacturers and farmers in New Zealand and Australia, and indeed more than enough for a healthy surplus to feed the global trade. From the moral and economic perspective that still marks development discourse and policy today, such "productive" agricultural industries are seen to be much more valuable than the unproductive and "less civilized" activities of a small number of indigenous peoples.

While engaged in the mining activities on Nauru and Banaba, the Company continued to hunt for other islands in Fiji and the Solomons that might contain similar phosphate deposits. In particular, they looked for alternatives in case trouble should arise on Banaba; there were many worries that the Banabans would discover what kind of deal they had been inveigled into. If Ellis was confident of the agreement with the king in 1900, he was much less so in 1909. He wrote, "Though the King of Ocean Island, and subsequently all the Four representative chiefs agreed to our working the Island under an annual payment of 50 pounds per annum, they didn't for a minute think it would be possible to export so much Phosphate as we have been doing, and therefore require so much land." With the ground beginning to disappear from beneath homes and ancestral lands, the Banabans became alarmed. He went on, "If we were to limit our payments to the 50 pounds per annum, the Ocean Islanders (and others as well) could with some truth say that we took advantage of their ignorance and bound them down by a hard and fast agreement, when they had no adequate idea what they were getting themselves in for."[18]

These were prescient concerns, because it did not take much longer for the Banabans to realize they were losing not just their land, but their sovereignty and a fair share of the mining profits. The majority of the mining income and taxes were being paid to a communal Banaban fund, to the protectorate, then to the colony of the Gilbert and Ellice Islands from 1916, and individual landowners were actually getting very little.

After a long and distinguished career, Albert Ellis passed away on July 11, 1951, and the last I heard of him during my archival journey was in a 1948 speech I found in the Maude and Maude Papers in Adelaide. He was erecting a memorial on Rabi in Fiji marking the Banaban arrival in 1945. As sure of himself as ever, he proclaimed to the new Rabi Island Council,

> Now I would like to tell the Council a little about the phosphate. The white man goes to Nauru and Banaba and takes away plenty of phosphate. What does he do with it? He puts it in a machine and then puts a very strong acid on it and that makes it good to put on the ground. When that is done everything grows very well, the sugar cane and the wheat and the grass for the cattle—every kind of food. That is good for the white man but it is also good for all the other people too. The rice, sugar, tinned beef and flour and other kinds of food which have been grown with the phosphate come back, come to Rambi. To work the phosphate is good for the white man and good for the Banabans. I am an old man but I am very glad to be doing useful work with the phosphate because it is good work for the white man and good work for the native too.[19]

Visualizing Ocean Island

> What renders a photograph surreal is its irrefutable pathos as a message from time past.... What is surreal is the distance imposed, and bridged, by the photograph: the social distance and the distance in time.[20]

The visual anthropologist and filmmaker David MacDougall has discussed the debates in anthropology over the place of visual knowledge and documentation and the regular critiques of its scholarly standing. He argues that this critique is one of fear rather than indifference: "the photograph is . . . too engaging, for it draws the viewer into an interpretive relationship that by-passes professional mediation."[21] In other words, far from "vision" being a transcendent masculine metaphor, an excess of "the visual" problematizes the idea of a single and definite truth for any given object, in line with Donna Haraway's argument about situated knowledges.[22]

In the basement of the Burwood office of the Melbourne Archives sits what must surely be one of the most complete photographic documentations of the material and certainly "industrial" history of a Pacific island. When we look at a photograph, we often apprehend the whole but presume a meaning suggested by the caption, if one is available. I would temporarily ignore any captions so that while turning pages of Company photograph albums, the visuals came to life with a cinematic effect. I experienced every possible view of the two-and-a-half-square-mile island, including zooming into each rock, tree, wheel, buoy, wheelbarrow, and wave. When coordinated with my contemporary knowledge of the now-defunct industry and life on Rabi, this experience became one of diffraction and remix: every photograph generated a potential storyline that overlapped with the edges of another storyline centered on a newspaper fragment, a letter, a face-to-face interview, a coral pinnacle, or a moment on a canoe.

Hundreds of images covering almost eighty years of mining begged for reflection on how one "knows" the past. As Susan Foster writes in *Choreographing History:*

> In their movements, past bodies also rubbed up against or moved alongside geological and architectural constructions, music, clothing, interior decorations . . . whose material remains leave further indications of those bodies' dispositions. . . . these partial records of varying kinds remain. They document the encounter between bodies and some of the discursive and institutional frameworks that touched them, operated on and through them, in different ways. . . . A historian of bodies, approaches these fragmented traces sternum leading, a sign . . . that his or her own body is seeking, longing to find, the vanished body whose motions produced them. . . . This historian's body wants to consort with dead bodies, wants to know from them.[23]

Although my concerns did not approach Foster's imagined archival necrophilia, I did start to ask questions and imagine the moving bodies of those freeze-framed in the past. How *did* these people walk past each other? How did their muscles feel at the end of the day or at dawn? How did a grown native man feel when a white man called him "boy"? Did his chest tighten, his throat close—or did he smile and do as he was told, and then curse the Europeans later? Did he go home from the mines with a really bad cough from all that phosphate dust? How many died from respiratory infections? Where was that wheelbarrow before it got to Ocean Island, and who constructed it?

As if to support this type of questioning, I soon located several BPC cinematograph films that had likely not been viewed since the decade of their making. Of particular interest were four reels on Nauru and Ocean Island, some in color and others in black and white. In this section, I describe vivid scenes from an eighteen-minute film labeled *A Visit to Ocean Island and Nauru*, which features a Company ship named *Triaster*. While the title indicates a visit to both islands, the tape only contained the portion on Ocean Island.[24]

The films were stamped, rather vaguely, as being from 1951 to 1971 so we could not really tell when they had been created. I sent off copies to two former residents, Ray Dobson in New Zealand and Mary Zausmer in the United States, who had both lived on Ocean Island between 1950 and 1951 and who generously shared their written memoirs of that period. Ray and Mary both agreed that the film was probably shot pre-1950 and probably before World War II and the Japanese occupation. They noticed, for example, that the buildings were different from the ones they remembered from their time on the island. This makes sense because much of the industry was destroyed during the war and rebuilt rapidly in 1946. The BPC itself demolished most of its mining facilities to prevent the Japanese from using them, and they in turn destroyed some buildings during air raids. Dobson also pointed out that during his stay on the island the main store was called the "trade store," while in the film it is called the "general store." Most significant to both Dobson and Zausmer was that in this footage Chinese laborers are shown working in the fields. After the war they were mostly employed as "skilled" laborers and not as fieldworkers. It seems likely, then, that the films were from the late 1930s or, at the very latest, just before the Company evacuated in 1942.

The BPC had commissioned the building of several grand Company ships, all named "Tri" for the three partner governments: *Triona, Trienza, Triaster, Triadic,* and *Tri-Ellis* after Albert Ellis. According to Williams and Macdonald, the first ship, *Triona*, was named for Ocean Island ("o") and Nauru ("na").[25] There were two ships named *Triaster*: the first was the commissioner's original motor vessel, launched in March 1935, and the second was built in 1951, launched in 1955, and sold to Nauru in 1970.[26] In describing the events around the advent of war in the Pacific in 1940, Williams and Macdonald also mention that the first *Triaster* was sunk on the morning of December 8, 1940.[27]

All four films were silent with intertitles that framed various scenes. While this meant that the master narrative of conventional documentary often provided by voiceovers was missing, the intertitles spoke volumes about how the BPC wished to depict the island to its stakeholders. Whether because the camera operator or the editor was inexperienced or because the Ocean Island conditions were logistically challenging, in most of the scenes the camera jerks along, the picture flickers, and the frame cuts rapidly between shots. There was also a good deal of dust, hair, and other bits of fluff caught in the film, which still appear in the transfer. The editing of the footage resulted in a montage-like product with few long takes. Throughout the film, if one watches carefully, one can see the jump cuts and multiple perspectives of the same space, event, or action. Sometimes the camera is on a moving boat with other boats revolving in the space around it; the result is a spinning frame that heightens the frenetic pace of the industrial action.

The sequences were organized linearly as "a visit" with the common arrival and departure scenes. Unlike arrivals on other islands, however, there are no greetings from the local people. This is very important given that the Banabans still lived on the island at the time. None of the rights outlined in their oral traditions—the rights to greet visitors, to collect food, and so forth—appear to be in practice. The Company and the British colonial administration have claimed the island as their domain and established new authorities and protocols, and the presumably Australian, New Zealand, and British visitors and new residents arriving on the *Triaster* are greeted by other white folks.

All the films have common features, including an overview of the mining process from extraction to crushing to loading, and snapshots of the social and commercial life on the island. Some scenes include "the natives," but there is no specificity about which natives, and none of them appear to be Banaban. The footage is constructed as a promotional film to illustrate the productivity and harmony of both the industry and the nonspecific but racially diverse and segregated community.

Touring the Island

After a brief flicker of the label "Kodak Safety Film"—an improved nonflammable film stock launched in the 1930s—the first two intertitles appear: "A Visit to Ocean Island and Nauru," followed quickly by "Leaving for the islands" and a shot of a steamship being loaded with cargo. Passengers in warm traveling clothes and carrying luggage ascend the gangplank, and the frame cuts to "Shipboard sports en route." Young white men and women in summer clothes play deck quoits for barely five seconds when the screen proclaims "Arrival at Ocean Island." We see what appears to be a low-lying mound hovering on the surface of the sea. In a matter of seconds we have traversed the Pacific Ocean from a port somewhere in Australia or New Zealand to Banaba. There is a pan of the island from west to east, and while the landscape is dominated by the mining town, the southeast corner is a cluster of coconut trees and thatched houses. There is a flurry of activity as a surfboat approaches on a rather choppy sea with Islander boatmen balancing nimbly at its prow while the ship's crew prepares to anchor.

When Ellis first arrived at Banaba in 1900 he mistook the first men who approached *The Archer* by canoe to be the most important men on the island. Just three decades later, "Doctor and officials board ship" instead. This is followed by a jerky left-to-right pan of the entire island, and then "Passengers disembark and are welcomed on arrival." Two identical pans of the same people standing at the wharf are awkwardly cut together here, suggesting that either we are watching a rough cut, the editing was done by a semiprofessional on basic equipment, or it was meant to be artistic.

The first of these rapid shots has a dog moving in the left corner toward the greeting crowd, many of whom are carrying parasols. The camera operator has obviously arrived on an earlier boat as the frame cuts to an approaching rowboat, oars fanning out in synchrony from its sides. The frame then jumps to the oars held vertically in preparation for landing. We see the phosphate cantilever in the background just before the passengers ascend the steps at Home Bay, led by a little boy wearing a big white hat. To the left of the frame and the mainly female greeters is a row of bare-chested island men in *lavalava*, looking suitably subservient.[28]

What follows are further "arrival" shots: Europeans in a motorcar, and then three native porters marching in a perfect row enter the frame carrying suitcases on their left shoulders with their right arms swinging in unison. A sense of homogeneity among the Islanders is immediately established along with an atmosphere of service and proto-military precision. We arrive at a modern bungalow surrounded by green shrubs with bright red flowers, and a white woman greets each of the passengers with a handshake or a kiss. There is a brief cut to the porters arriving with the suitcases, and then we move into the interior of the house. Things appear to be most civilized with everyone sipping from cups of tea. Much of this is indecipherable when the film is watched at normal speed, but when I slowed it down I discovered that the last shot, which had previously appeared dark and fuzzy, was of a piano.[29]

The "Staff Residences" are impressive as the film moves to a sequence of shots of concrete buildings, the bright red and green foliage, a large water tank, and some of the smaller, wooden staff quarters. A native in a more formal lavalava and a white shirt climbs a coconut tree in the foreground as laborers hover and a white man descends the steps of another building in the background. The film then cuts to a wide shot of a large house raised on stilts with three people sitting on chairs just below it. A close-up reveals a white man and two white women sitting comfortably while a native woman in a *muumuu* stands to the right of the frame. The man beckons to the standing woman with his left hand and holds a pipe in his right. She moves closer, carrying a small container that she shows to one of the women. This scene cuts to the next title: "Stone marking Sir Albert Ellis original camp site—in 1900." A young Islander strides into the frame from the left and places his hand on a rock with a plaque mounted on the front. We see his lips move as if he is reading the plaque. We do not know if the man is Banaban, Gilbertese, or Ellice Islander, but the entire scene displaces him, a possible "native" from the very place now claimed by this memorial. The camera reveals its proclamation:

THIS STONE MARKS THE CAMP SITE
OF A. F. ELLIS WHEN FIRST PROSPECTING
THIS ISLAND IN MAY 1900. HERE THE
BRITISH FLAG WAS FIRST FLOWN

It is obvious that someone told the man to walk up to the rock and read the words, but since we have just witnessed an arrival scene of white visitors one has to wonder why one of them was not used in this brief staging. The island now appears to be in total possession of the Company; it is as if Ocean Island history originated with Albert Ellis's arrival, and, importantly, we have a "native" to attest to this originary event.

The film then lurches from a few very long to some very brief scenes accompanied by awkward intertitles. Watching it from our visually saturated culture of the present without any background knowledge of Banaban history, we might find the scenes boring or even slightly exasperating. Views such as the next shot of "Home Bay," with an aerial perspective of the industrial activity, seem to prepare us for something but then end peremptorily after just fourteen seconds. Apparently, the camera operator zoomed about the island as if he were using a still camera, collecting shots here and there.

We then move to "Stores and Recreation Room," which begins with the arrival of a tram carrying three white men in white outfits. They sit on comfortable seats with lots of room for at least ten more passengers, while six times as many island men stand crowded on a platform behind them. One of the "natives" raises his hat to the camera. They disembark, and the film moves to a large building labeled "General Store." We briefly see the inside of the building, which is filled with shelves of goods while prospective shoppers lounge near the counter. This is followed by one of the more interesting shots of the road through the main town with pedestrians and bicyclists all moving past and away from the camera.

The "BPC Ocean Is. Office" is revealed: a massive, white, two-story building sporting balconies on both levels. But then we're whisked back to the scene at Home Bay, where the ship is now "Discharging Cargo." The surfboats and launches create quite a bit of traffic between the ship and the dock, and we see that the cantilever is used to facilitate the arrival of goods as well as the discharge of phosphate. A pulley lowers a steel bucket filled with sacks to a mobile platform, and

Albert Ellis memorial stone on Banaba, 2000. Photo by Katerina Martina Teaiwa

workers push it along to train carts. The harbor is a grand scene of industrial and commercial activity with the ships seeming to signal that progress is here to stay. We see closer shots of the *Triaster* and a slew of rowboats forming a living chain of activity between the ship and the shore.

The film reveals the operation as a remarkable technical undertaking. The people who set out to mine, process, and ship phosphate brought to it their experience with shovels, brooms, and wheelbarrows in the guano trade and then succeeded through years of improvisation and at great distance from the nearest workshops or suppliers to build up an industry that was "ultimately to replace an army of boatmen loading a maximum of 2,000 tons a day, with cantilevers each of which could pour directly into the ships' holds at 400 tons an hour." This was seen to be particularly remarkable from an engineering perspective because "beyond the islands' fringing reef the sea-bed plunges into thousands of fathoms. No anchorages exist and the immense chains used to serve what are reputed to be the deepest moorings in the world reinforce in the imagination the hazards which sent ship after ship to destruction on the reefs."[30]

We know in the early days that many ships ran aground, moorings came unhinged, yards of chain were lost, and some ships had to be loaded or discharged while they were under way. Many Pacific Islander workers were killed as a result of such hazards. We know the weather was often challenging and, according to Ellis, "there would be a daily parade of four or five large vessels in front of the settlement, with signals flying 'When will the weather moderate?' or phrases to that effect. Such congestion of tonnage naturally was not conducive to obtaining the low freight so necessary in the phosphate trade."[31]

But when the weather was accommodating and ships were waiting, things happened—loading and unloading—at an extraordinary pace. What the Company called the "Kanaka" laborers—the Gilbertese and the Ellice Islanders—worked the mines and crewed the lighters or surfboats with an agility and prowess that was greatly admired by the Europeans, all without safety gear of any kind. While racial and Company hierarchies are clearly represented in this film, a sense of extraordinary competence in a challenging environment is also achieved.

Mining the Rock

From the water, we are beamed back to the land and to "Phosphate Fields. Mining Phosphate." In this period there were two methods of obtaining rock; the first was a mechanized contraption, a "grab," with metal jaws that swung back and forth between the face of the rock quarry and the transport containers. The camera observes this from above the mining field and then relocates to the level below for the second method: workers armed with picks and shovels scrape the rock into baskets, which are then dumped into one-ton bins. Ominously, none of the men have protective footwear or headgear, except for slight protection from the sun. The Company seems to have capitalized on the fact that island men prefer to work without shirt or shoes. They all, however, appear to be working happily as the film cuts to a wide shot of another part of the field, which is starting to resemble the "moonscape" for which both Nauru and Banaba are now famous.

We see a group of Chinese workers, who are considerably better dressed than their Islander counterparts, wearing broad hats and shoes. These men are throwing rocks into the waiting bins, which are then launched through the air via a grab-and-skip system to discharge the rock into a vibrating hopper. The hopper spits out the rock into the one-ton train cars, which are then "conveyed by narrow guage [sic] train to the 'Crushing and Drying Plant.'" This train runs on a track that cuts through a field of pinnacles, a reminder that the surface of the land once rested at the tops of those coral rocks. The rather clumsy editing of this footage only serves to heighten the very act of removing land as we are jerked to disparate spatial perspectives of the moving train cars. The rock is then offloaded in a series of shots that simply repeat the dumping motion of the metal car. Inside the phosphate crushing and drying plant, the dryers spin and then the dried rock is "conveyed to Storage Bins to await shipment." Mountains of finely crushed rock rise like pyramids from the bin floor as dust continues to fall from the discharging pipes. Sunlight pours over the shoulder of a Chinese mechanic, creating a melancholic mood.

We then move to "Loading Phosphate to Ship," and the conveyor belt streams upward carrying its load along the inside of the cantilever. Guided by the hands of waiting workers, two mobile nozzles, which look rather like nipples, pour the rock into baskets arranged compactly in a boat. A man is engulfed in a blast of phosphate dust as the film cuts to a long shot of the traffic between the waiting ship and the collecting boats. There are two almost identical pans between the ship and the cantilever. The activity beneath the cantilever seems to require almost cat-like agility as some workers scale the chains between the various levels of the structure and others balance on the heaving boats, holding them steady beneath the nozzles and directing the nozzles into the baskets. The next series of shots is a montage of spinning images as the camera is balanced on another boat trying to take in all the action while moving around the working men. Nothing is stationary—the camera, the sea, the delivery activities. Everything seems to be moving in different directions at different speeds relative to the camera. The collecting vessels are connected by lines of rope and are tugged by a motor launch to a giant black and red ship looming above the scurrying workers.

Watching this footage conjured up images of ant colony hierarchies and their relentless lines of labor between food and the nest. I imagined the thousands of workers as soldier ants, the BPC ships and phosphate commissioners as the queen ants, and Australia and New Zealand as two giant nests. I thought of Gilles Deleuze and Felix Guattari's descriptions of the rhizome as a network of subterranean

"Ocean Island—Lower levels—Nearly worked out—Pick lying in bottom of hole—
Coral pinnacles to right and left of picture—Phosphate deposit (light coloured) in the
background—Very good country—Ooma—September 1910." Courtesy of the National
Archives of Australia

stems, swarming rats, or burrows and concluded that Banaban land *is* a rhizome: "any point of a rhizome can be connected to anything other, and must be. . . . A rhizome ceaselessly establishes connections."[32] Banaban phosphate does this in the mining and the movement of the rock; in the dust that floats off across the ocean, is breathed into the lungs of a Gilbertese worker, or is caught in the handkerchief of a white woman disembarking from the *Triaster* to visit friends on Ocean Island; and in the mechanical spaces of the watchful camera eye. The "hair in the gate" that appears in several of these old shots may be lines of "phosphate in the gate."[33] What was probably intended as a fairly simple expository film on phosphate mining may be read as the lines of Banaban land, lines of rocks, lines of narrow gauge trains and conveyor belts, lines of motor boats connecting to lines of ships, lines across the Pacific Ocean, lines of superphosphate sacks, and lines of fertilizer falling from the bellies of crop dusters.

Between the launches and the phosphate boats, there is a brief glimpse of a man calmly paddling an outrigger canoe among all the mechanized activity. The camera is then repositioned onshore between the concrete flanks of the cantilever, which temporarily frames the scene. The nipple/nozzle analogy is lucid from this point of view. The film then zooms back to the agile workers in shadow under the gigantic structure, the phosphate journey to the ship, and finally a basket of phosphate's rise and fall into the hold of the vessel. While things are so busy, so active, and so industrious the dark bodies, the lavalavas, and the handwoven phosphate baskets belie the universal claims of progress. The camera has called attention to the very anonymous labor exploited by the industry and the very visible, racialized hierarchies of work and play. As organized as things look, the reality was that over the life of the industry, hundreds of workers died on the island from a variety of respiratory ailments and other complications, including pneumonia and what the BPC archives regularly recorded as "consumption."

"Native Welfare"

The work section of the film concludes, and as if to answer questions on the treatment of the workers, we now enter the "native" portion of the film. The "natives" are not Banabans but are still portrayed as a homogeneous, and somewhat well-provisioned, group. The "native lines" are rows of wooden structures for housing both married and single workers. There is a brief shot of a man singing with a ukulele as smiling men in the background tussle to get into the frame; this is followed by a shot of two men carrying a large fish between them. According to Macdonald, in the 1930s the government insisted that one-third of Gilbertese workers be accompanied by their wives, a policy that helped to maintain good labor relations.[34] We do see women and children in the distance, but the next pan frustratingly concentrates on the buildings rather than the Islanders: their heads are left bobbing in the lower left-hand corner of the frame. For a couple of seconds there is the one and only shot of an island man speaking animatedly to someone behind the eye of the camera. Of course, we cannot hear him.

The "native" laborers are portrayed as both content and subservient to the whites. A subsequent shot shows two white men relaxing and chatting on a veranda while two "native" servants stand silently by with hands behind their backs. But then, as if to ameliorate the racial hierarchies, the next title proclaims "Native Police." Lines of Islander men with bayonet-tipped rifles march across the frame. Two of them pose for the camera; one of them is Fijian.

The sequence on "Native Dancers" included the most awkward and engaging scenes for me. Whereas previously, we could not tell who were Banabans or Gilbertese and who were Ellice Islanders, from the costumes and choreography I *know* that this group is from the Ellice Islands. While the actual sounds of their performance could not be captured by the camera, they sing away with passion. A close-up of a line of dancing women shows two Ellice women who look like sisters.[35] This is followed by another woman dancing madly for the camera, which illustrates how clowning is a very big part of Gilbertese, Banaban, and Ellice Island performance.[36] The film switches to various performing bodies, and the last shot in this assemblage is a close-up of two men singing and dancing, their bodies rising and falling with a bend of the knees, arms reaching forward and to the side, moving to the beat of music we cannot hear.

The next intertitle proclaims "Native Fishing," and we are presented with a long shot of a canoe at sea with a large fish trap on board. The two fishermen return and unload their catch, and a young girl carries the enormous fish trap on her shoulder. Two women carry the fish on a basket hanging off a pole between them as two more women stand in the background; one scratches her tummy. Her left arm moves around in a circle on the left side of her stomach, and her dress moves with it. It is such a normal gesture in what is being rigidly portrayed as an extremely exotic scene. We are then presented with a basket of dead fish.

The film moves along to show us the very modern "Native School," and to me it seems much more modern than the ones that now exist on Rabi over seventy years later. Schoolboys line up for inspection by a native teacher; they are homogeneous in their white *sulus,* all with brown skin and black hair. We see how obedient and disciplined they are as they stretch, bend, stretch, bend, and bow. I recalled my years in primary school in Fiji: standing arms akimbo, then arms straight, while a prefect yelled: "At ease! Attention!" A European figure on the left observes this display before we are hurtled onto the sideline for a few brief seconds of a "native" cricket match.

To assure viewers that all the natives are well cared for, we visit the "Native Hospital and Baby Welfare Clinic." A health attendant checks the lungs of a worker, and the camera pans around the hospital complex. A "native" doctor washes his hands; another binds the foot of an injured worker, who smiles with gratitude.

An assistant puts eye drops into another worker's eyes, reminding us of the scene beneath the cantilever with dust flying everywhere. The BPC is saying: we really look after our workers. Following this, we momentarily see the very separate "European Hospital" for ten seconds, but the privacy of the European patients is not compromised.

Following this rosy view of island health, we move to "Island Recreation and sport," and I recalled this:

> The commissioners have done all that is possible to make life pleasant. On each island is a tennis court well lighted by electric arcs, facilities for cricket, football, halls for cinema and other entertainments and all the essentials of a happy, social life. Mr. Cozens is himself an enthusiast at swimming and he says that on a Sunday at Ocean Island as many as 40 men and 10 ladies have been seen diving at the springboards or sporting in the ocean.... The homes on these islands are of the modern bungalow type with electric lights, ice chests and appointments which are suited to a warm climate. Mr. and Mrs. Cozens will return by way of Sydney and they will be happy to find themselves once more in their healthy island home.[37]

There are indeed healthy bodies diving, springing, swinging, and frolicking everywhere in Home Bay. The harbor is so deep it makes the swimming experience that much more pleasant, its depth enticing the many intrepid divers. The European visitors to Banaba enjoy golf and a friendly round of doubles tennis before it's time to depart. In the 1970s, the golf course was the last area to be mined. The Company must have weighed recreational needs against mining the valuable rock, and at least temporarily, recreation won.

As the film ends, the white visitors crowd into the rowboats once more with the "native" oarsmen, who are ready to return them to the waiting *Triaster*. A couple of the women have parasols to ensure full skin protection from the hot equatorial sun. We ascend the gangway, and in a shot looking from the ship down to the rowboats we see one man holding a woman's elbow to prevent her from pitching forward. Moving bodies, hats, dresses, and white suits fill the frame, and before you know it anchors are away and the *Triaster* is off.

* * *

The film compresses years of cultural, political, economic, and material transformation and in eighteen minutes shows how Banaba has become Ocean Island, a phosphate mine, a town, and a place of work and leisure, overwritten by industry and commerce; indigenous spatial and emplaced meanings and practices are evacuated with each shipment of rocks.

The Company's zeal for visual documentation of the industry in both still photos and films resonates with Susan Sontag's critique of tourism and photography: "photographing something became a routine part of the procedure for al-

"*Triona* under cantilever," 1957. Courtesy of the National Archives of Australia

tering it."[38] Subjects often appeared to be posed in "typical" native occupations while in reality, the very agents who employed the cameramen were rapidly altering the indigenous economic and social landscape. As Sontag writes of early amateur photographers in the United States: "faced with the awesome spread and alienness of a newly settled continent, people wielded cameras as a way of taking possession of the places they visited."[39]

But unlike America or Australia, Banaba was never envisaged as an enduring settler colony. For the white residents, it was very much a temporary experience since neither the Company nor its employees ever had any intention of making Banaba a lifelong home. This is not to negate the intense feelings of nostalgia that many former residents still have for the island. Their physical possession, however, was irrevocable since it is impossible to replace the missing land that has been permanently consumed through agriculture. And until funds are found to rehabilitate Banaba, the imprint of the industry remains in the relics of its buildings, machines, water tanks, empty swimming pools, and the dilapidated cantilever that still stands in Home Bay.

PART II
MINE/LANDS

This land is mine land
it used to be our land
from tabiang to tabwewa
from buakonikai to uma
birds made this land for posterity

This land is mine land
it used to be our land
but then we leased it to greedy miners
who only saw it as something called phosphate
and used it for their own prosperity

—Teresia Teaiwa, "Mine Land: An Anthem"

4 Remembering Ocean Island

> Stories are told, and should be told, simply because storytelling is a good thing
> to do—but particular stories are never innocent of wider agendas.
> —Nicholas Thomas, *In Oceania*

THERE IS A significant and growing interdisciplinary literature on storied landscapes, places, spaces, and memories with scholars engaging and weaving a variety of textual genres from memoir and autobiography to film and interview. The
motivation for much of this work stems from a critique of the metanarratives of
the nation-state and of prominent and privileged actors who have erased or submerged the lives and voices of everyday people, including women, workers, children, slaves, and indigenous communities, often described in postcolonial studies as constituting the "subaltern."[1]

Jennifer Shennan and Makin Corrie Tekenimatang's *One and a Half Pacific
Islands* is this kind of important project. Inspired by Adam Manterys's collection of 101 stories from among 733 children who arrived in New Zealand in 1944
as orphans from Poland,[2] Shennan and Tekenimatang's book gathers the stories
and memories of 68 individuals—children, elders, teenagers, scholars, elected
leaders—who speak of two home islands and of Banaban life in Fiji on the sixtieth
anniversary of their landing on Rabi. These views are complemented by those of
a select number of Banaban elders and colonial and Company officials and their
families.

Memories of Banaba, particularly from the perspective of former European
residents, have helped me to accept the plurality of colonial and Company experiences and perspectives. The views and goals of Albert Ellis, for example, were
very different from those of the folks hired to work in the pharmacy or the general store. Furthermore, the quotidian experiences of any accompanying family
members, especially the experiences of women, were rarely told. Here, I relate
three particular stories since, aside from Mary Hunt's writing, they are not accessible in any published form. These stories exist as situated knowledges, articulated
from different lived contexts but all related to the same landscape. Compared to
the BPC Archives in particular, these memoirs illuminate the lives not of phosphateers or industrial "heroes" per se, but of men and women whose relationship

with the island was less privileged and more fleeting. Furthermore, when compared with the Company films and official histories, they provide far more ethnographic detail and a vivid sense of the everyday cross-cultural experiences of white folk on Ocean Island.

Mary Hunt's Story

Mary Hunt (née Robertson), the wife of a former PPC employee, was from New Zealand and transcribed her stories in Tauranga between 1945 and 1950.[3] Her family then self-published some of her writing in 1999. Shennan and Tekenimatang also published an extract from her memoirs, so where possible I have tried to highlight some of her other experiences. Her memoirs exhibit a stream of consciousness in which there is a marked oscillation in time and place between there (Ocean Island, the past) and here (New Zealand, the present), structured by preoccupations with the relationships between "civilization" and the "primitive."

Mary was born on March 22, 1883, and married Henry Hunt in 1906, and they settled in Christchurch, New Zealand. Henry was a plumber whose business had gone bankrupt and while Mary was visiting family in Dunedin, Henry wired that he was leaving to visit his family in Melbourne. She joined him there with their son, and after five months gave birth to a daughter. Mary recounts that two weeks later:

> Dad came home from work one night and asked did I know where Ocean Island was, I had never heard of it, so he went round to his people's place to enquire there, but no one had ever heard of it either. However the next day he used his dinner hour to go to the office mentioned in the advertisement for a plumber to go there, and when he came home that night, he said he was leaving for the Island in a week. He was told at the office that it lay in the tropics, that he would be able to hang his hat on the equator, and that was about all he knew.[4]

Henry went off, and after two months Mary joined him via the ship the *Sildra*. She writes:

> Two extremes of life mix on Ocean Is. On one hand are the primitive dwellings of the native Banabans, Banaba being the native name, a few pandanus posts supporting a palm leaf thatched roof with a few mats spread on the ground, and in striking contrast the comfortable dwellings of the European residents, with the electric power for driving machinery, and supplying light and ice, a good telephone service, recreation rooms, libraries, locomotives and large steamers at anchor, in fact in a small way all the bustling activity of civilisation.[5]

Having had no idea what to take to Banaba "except something light," she landed on the island to find to her surprise that "living conditions were of a very high standard, that the people there dressed much better than the average Melbourne citizen, and I thought I was going to a half-civilised sort of place."[6] Even in these very early stages of the mining, the island was already a "civilized" place for Europeans although, she hints, not necessarily for the other segregated communities: the indigenous Banabans and the laborers from other islands, China, and Japan.

She seems to have anticipated greater privation and hardship from the outset and was surprised that the Company put her up in Sydney in one of the best hotels, where "I was able to get my baby washing etc. done alright."[7] There is a sense of being well looked after by the Company. They provided everything for Mary and her son and daughter, including hansom cab transport between the hotel and wharf. The *Sildra* had a Norwegian captain and a Chinese crew, all of whom took a liking to her son. She wrote that whenever one of the crew would pass him on deck, they would give him a Chinese coin, "so he had quite a collection of them which he kept for years."[8] She enthused about the trip and in particular the excitement of witnessing a "burning mountain in the sea," apparently a volcano emitting smoke and then, after dark, great flames of fire shooting up. As she approached Ocean Island, Mary thought it looked like a "sugar bun," a deliciously Eurocentric confection in contrast to the island's more common depiction in Company terms as "oyster-shaped" with the phosphate likened to a hidden pearl.

Henry Hunt was sent to Ocean Island to put in a new sewage system. This is rather ironic given that Banabans living on the island today are using the beach to relieve themselves. Henry would carry the pipes across the reef, cementing them to the coral at low tide, while "native boys" would dive under the water to fix the chains to the coral below. Mary writes that the "boys" worked so fast that Henry did not believe they had done a good job. Two escorted him below, one holding onto each arm, so he could see for himself. A disparaging suspicion of "lazy natives" pervades her narrative, even when it is confounded. "The native Banabans were allowed to work for the Company whenever they felt inclined, but only a limited number of them ever felt inclined. They lived the same kind of life as the Maoris [*sic*], never working, always laughing and very happy."[9]

Mary and Henry had a nice, new, cool house sheltered by a coral pinnacle. Most of the furniture was provided, along with the coal, wood, and electric light, while a kerosene lamp was used after the electricity shut off at 10 PM. She writes:

> Of course practically everything we ate came out of tins—fruit, vegetables, meat, milk, butter, etc.—but we did get some fresh food at times, for whenever a steamer came from Sydney, which was once a fortnight, sheep were brought up, and when killed and dressed and cut up, were distributed among the white people free of charge. I can remember getting a leg of mutton about every six weeks or so, and in between times, other joints. . . . A cow was kept on the island somewhere. I never saw her but each child was allowed one cupful of milk, so I always got a very welcome pint each morning.[10]

Mary's memoirs suggest that almost everything was provided for them: ice to keep the food cool, a basket of free fish each morning, and a boy to clean and fill the lamp. By contrast, Banabans had to buy food from the Company. Mary did not even have to do the laundry since another boy collected Henry's suits and the towels and sheets every Monday for washing. Again, her suspicions about lazy natives are confounded. Mary writes that she could not believe that the "native" women got anything done: they seemed to have so much fun while handwashing, and managed to do that and the ironing too. She would sometimes bargain for limes and eggs with Banaban children. They would ask for AU$4 for half a dozen limes, but "one would beat them down till they would go away quite happy with a piece of cake of soap or anything handy."[11]

Most people got up at 5:30 AM for tea and were working by 6 AM. Mary noted that there was neither a dawn nor a twilight: the sun comes up and goes down swiftly on the equator. She suggests a disciplined daily routine: breakfast at 8, lunch break from 11 to 1 PM, and work stopped at 4. At home, the European men had a combination of a saltwater shower to clean off and "condensed water" to rinse. Water had to be conserved, and during the year the Hunts lived on the island, it rained only once but "it was torrential while it lasted."[12]

Contrary to other observations from that time, Mary wrote that there were only cockroaches on the island, no birds or "creeping things," although she later mentioned hermit crabs. Every evening, she said, hundreds of hermit crabs came up from the reef. There were so many that their shells tinkled as they bumped each other. In the dark, they "made an eerie sound." She did see one pet Banaban bird, likely a frigate bird as per Banaban custom, chained to a stake, which she thought was cruel.[13] Of the Banabans, she wrote:

> Some of the women were very good looking, especially the young girls with such perfectly shaped hands and lovely teeth and hair. There were large black butterflies with a bright purple spot on each wing, and the young girls used to tie one end of a piece of cotton round the body, and the other end to their hair and with these butterflies flitting round their heads, and a red hibiscus in each ear they made a pretty sight.[14]

While walking through native villages, Mary observed the abundance of sewing machines. Each person seemed to have one, she says, which is an important indicator since sewing machines are a luxury on Rabi today. Mary had a "girl" from Tarawa to do housework, whom she described as both thorough and slightly ignorant. Apparently the young woman once squirted two-thirds of a bottle of kerosene through her mouth to fuel Mary's precious copper boiler, which was soon wrecked.

A woman's, and more specifically a mother's, perspective adds new quotidian information about life on the island that is absent from the literature authored by men. Mary observes that native women washed their children by placing them between their legs and squirting them with water out of a coconut shell after warming it in their mouths. They would then dry the children with the blade of a palm. She wrote that sometimes families would bathe together in the sea, and the father would catch a small fish and give it to his child to suck like a lollipop.[15]

She wrote about how the Europeans would travel between Ooma (Uma) and Tapiwa (Tabwewa) on a trolley pushed along by two or four "Kanakas," rowing them in unison like boats. She wrote: "After having a year of Melbourne's slow old cable trams, it was indeed a thrill to be driven along at such a speed."[16]

For Mary, life on the island was pleasant, never dull, and far above her expectations. She and her son even learned to speak "the Banaban language," but her happiness ceased once Henry got malaria and dysentery. The climate apparently suited European women, who had a life of relative leisure, rather better than it suited the men, who had to work in the hot sun all day. Nevertheless on key holidays no expense was spared for the British population. On New Year's Day in 1910 the Company threw a carnival presided over by Albert Ellis that featured the following menu:

SOUP

Consommé in Cups (Cold)
Giblet

ENTREES

Lamb Cutlets and Peas
Salami of Duck
Fricassie Chicken

POULTRY

Boiled & Roast Fowl
Roast Goose
Roast Duck
Roast Turkey

FISH

Boiled Salmon & Tartare Sauce
Prawns in Aspic

JOINTS

Roast Haunch of Mutton & Jelly
Boiled York Ham

VEGETABLES

Baked Potatoes
Boiled Potatoes

"Mrs. W. Going for Joy Ride," 1920s. Courtesy of the National Library of Australia

Haricot Verts
Peas

SWEETS

Xmas Pudding
Almond Blancmange
Macédoine of Fruit
Victoria Sandwich
Port Wine Jelly
Ice Cream
Chocolates

Unfortunately, Henry's childhood emphysemic cough became worse, probably from all the mining dust, and they left the island in March 1910—in a hurry after a drunken doctor diagnosed Henry with consumption. Mary writes, "I was very, very sorry to leave, life had been so pleasant for me, more so than in any other place I have ever lived in before or since."[17]

After living for several years in Queensland, Australia, Mary and Henry returned to New Zealand in May 1920. Writing from New Zealand after World War II, she noted that all the Banabans had been transported to "Rambi" in Fiji.

William Ray Dobson's Story

William Ray Dobson, who goes by "Ray," lived in Redcliffs, Christchurch, and for three years we chatted via email about his time on the island. He sent me his memoirs, "On Banaba (Ocean Island) in the Central Pacific 1950/51," where he speaks of how he first heard of the island in 1949 when working in a pharmacy in Dunedin in the South Island of New Zealand. One issue of the *Pharmacy Journal* offered a position as a "dispenser and hospital assistant" on Ocean Island in the Central Pacific. He writes, "Not knowing where the island was I went to the public library and found that it was a small island just south of the Equator noted mainly for its deposits of guano. With visions of swaying palms and sandy beaches I decided to apply. Incidentally the salary offered was quite good and the conditions excellent . . . no income tax, free house and all meals supplied."[18]

Ray didn't get the job, but the BPC kept his file on hand. Five months later they contacted him urgently, offering him the job. Apparently the Australian pharmacist who had been contracted was an alcoholic and "was helping himself to Tincture of Orange which is 90% ethyl alcohol." All the memoirs indicate that the rate of inebriation on the island was relatively high. Williams and Macdonald, in their analysis of a report from 1905 by a Company manager, Harold Gaze (Alfred's son), wrote that liquor rations were actually established to placate workers and to stamp out any tendencies toward unionization on the island. The result was that almost all the rations fell into the hands of the hard drinkers, who would orchestrate a regular "Saturday evening binge."[19]

Ray joined the *Teviotbank* in Dunedin, which stopped at Auckland on its way to Ocean Island. It was a pleasant trip; they each had a cabin to themselves, and "we dined at the Captain's table and did nothing all day while having the run of the ship. We spent many happy hours in the wireless room chatting to the radio operator and the junior officers and sunbathing."[20] When Ray arrived, the Banabans had been removed but there were Gilbert and Ellice Island workers, Chinese mechanics from Hong Kong, and European overseers from Australia and New Zealand. He said the Company had started an apprenticeship system for men from the Gilbert and Ellice Islands colony, who were trained as electricians, carpenters, and plumbers to eventually replace the Chinese.

Ray worked in the hospital with an Australian doctor, Maurice Ingram; a senior registered nurse; and ten orderlies for the men's wards and ten nurses for the women's. There was also one special orderly for the European ward farther down the hill from the main hospital, and one for the Chinese ward across the main road. The hospital, like the housing, was clearly segregated. The head orderly was Alessana Seosi (an Ellice Island name), and there was a head nurse named Ute. A nurse named Nei Tiri (a Gilbertese name) did Ray's washing for a small payment so he could avoid the starchy style of the official BPC washers.

Ray described the hospital in detail, including the dispensary, operating theater, laboratory, and darkroom. He learned basic laboratory analysis and how to assist as an anesthetist while on the island. Ray's assistant was a young man called Cheong Ken Yu from Hong Kong, who "had grown up under the Japanese occupation there, somehow found his way to Ocean Island and was determined never to return to Hong Kong. He was universally well liked, bubbling over with cheerfulness and always helpful to everyone. He spoke his own brand of Gilbertese and English but seemed to be able to make himself understood by all."[21]

Ray wrote that people on Ocean Island worked for five days and a half with Saturday afternoons and Sundays off. Most of the Europeans were Australian, so cricket was regularly played on the sports ground at the very top of the island. They made the pitch out of concrete with coconut matting, but "the outfield was rough and littered with small lumps of coral. If a ball was hit into the pinnacle everyone had to search for it." Ray remembered being on a BPC team that got sorely beaten by a team of policemen: "In fact one burly sergeant made more runs than all our team put together."[22] Policemen on the island were usually Gilbertese and Ellice Islanders with a European commander, and in the early days there were Fijian policemen as well.

Ray's memoirs bring to life some of the archival photographs and material relics I have seen on the island. I had noted the floodlights on the tennis courts, because they seem so weirdly modern among the silence and dust of the dead town. In his time, Ray wrote, tennis was played at night on a green concrete court to catch whatever breeze was blowing. The BPC club was called the Ocean Island

Tennis Club. Even more interesting was the Rifle Club. When I was on Banaba in 2000, the manager's wife told me a strange story of a gun that had shot a man instead of the chicken it was pointed at. I was previously unaware that guns were allowed on the island outside of the police force.

According to Ray, the rifle range was in the northern part of the island. Sunday mornings were rifle range days: the men would "pile onto the back of a truck, thrust our bottles of beer into a tub of ice and off we would go. Lunch was supplied by the mess which meant we could spend most of the day on the range."[23] Australians and New Zealanders in those days apparently were not straitlaced Christians like the old men of the Company, Gaze, Ellis, and Arundel. One can imagine all the Islanders faithfully at church on Sunday while the European men drank beer and shot ex-army 303s all day long. Apparently the shed the men used to shelter in between sessions was a favorite molting spot for scorpions, and any new club member would find one next to him on his first day. Ray goes on to talk about the golf course:

> Some golf was played on a very primitive course of about 9 holes. The balls had to be painted yellow or red so they stood out against the background of white coral. I can remember my assistant, Cheong, painting these gold balls for the doctor and others. He would pour the paint into the palm of his hand then rub the ball between his hands. An excellent method of painting but it left his hands rather sticky.[24]

Saturday nights were apparently big gambling nights for the men, led by "the Aussies." They played games like poker, pontoon, solo whist, and two-up. Two miners acted as bookies for the Sydney races, and there was another for Aussie Rules games in Melbourne, which Ray joined in.[25] Twice while he was there they had a gambling night for charity with lots of games, including a "penny to pound raffle" and roulette.

Junior staff members had dinner in the singles mess, which was staffed by a Chinese chef and his assistants, an Australian manager, and Gilbertese and Ellice waiters. Ray's most memorable dinner was one in which "Millionaire's Salad" was served. Each coconut tree was numbered and plotted on a map of the island. However, "sometimes it became necessary to cut down one or more palms to open up an area for mining. In these cases compensation had to be paid but the growing tips were saved and great was the competition for this delicacy."[26] Apparently the manager had secured some of these "hearts of palm" for one special dinner. The most profound thing about this salad is that its uniqueness relies on the death of an entire coconut tree. There isn't any substitute for that ingredient.

While the food might have been good, until 1951 Ray was usually "bored and spent most of the time . . . reading, writing letters or studying Gilbertese." Then an influenza epidemic came in from Hong Kong and spread swiftly across the island. It hit the Islanders the hardest, and they had to erect two new temporary wards at the hospital. This kept Ray busy for two weeks and even halted the mining. Overseers with no jobs became orderlies, filling in for the sick Islanders. Ray had to improvise on drugs, creating five-gallon kegs "filled with my special mixture which contained anything I had in store. It tasted vile but was greatly appreciated as the general opinion seemed to be that anything as vile as that must be good."[27] After running around for ten days the epidemic ended, but Ray finally caught the flu himself. The description of an event like this is a grounding contrast to the healthy, happy, and productive workers illustrated by the BPC archival films.

Ray ended his memoirs with three stories. The first was the tale of a staff member and his wife who had been murdered. The investigation included taking fingerprints from their house, which were found to match two Chinese men, who were then taken to Fiji for trial and hanged. I wonder about this incident. Since most households had both Chinese and Islander help, how did they connect such fingerprints to the actual murder? Ray does not mention what connection the men had to the murdered Europeans, and for most of his time on the island, the murdered couple's house remained unoccupied.

The next story was his recollection called "The Recruit." This was the period in which one of the BPC ships would go around the colony and return laborers to their home islands while recruiting new workers. The policy of the colonial office was that a certain quota from each island had to be filled to spread around the income from waged labor, otherwise the Company would have contracted men just from one or two islands. The ship would also go to Hong Kong to return the Chinese workers, and the Europeans would often place large orders for camphor chests to keep their clothes safe from insects. The Islanders preferred plain ones, while the Europeans preferred carved and decorated chests. Ray wrote, "The small boxes are long gone but I still have the large ones and, 50 years later, the odour of camphor still lingers."[28] He unfortunately lost all the other materials he collected from the island, including photographs and embroidered pillowcases made by the nurses. These pillowcases are still valued gifts today in Kiribati, Tuvalu, and Rabi.[29]

Ray's final story was about a young Gilbertese man named George, who was his chief apprentice. George was Catholic and asked Ray to take photos of the Catholic church at Tabwewa. He agreed, and since George was learning to become an electrician, Ray took the photos in exchange for a light box with which to print his negatives. This was made with the help of a carpenter, who used discarded bits of wood. Ray later gave it to George, who had become interested in photography by the time Ray left the island. The Catholic church that George wanted memorialized in a photograph still stands today—probably the best-kept building on the island. Ray then left Ocean Island for a job in Moshi, Tanganyika, at the foot of Mount Kilimanjaro.

Mary Zausmer's Story

Ray sent me his memoirs along with those of a woman named Mary Zausmer. Mary was born in Canada to Australian parents, and she and I spoke regularly via email about her long and adventurous life. She was married three times; her last husband was Eddie Zausmer, a Jewish electrician from Brooklyn. Her stories are written with many cultural references to her life long after Ocean Island, but they are also written in that imaginary "ethnographic present." Here I consider an excerpt titled "Ocean Island, Paradise of the Pacific."[30]

Mary's father lived in Australia and Buenos Aires before he met her mother in Perth, where she was working as a nurse in a veterans' hospital. They had one son and first moved to Canada and then California, where her second brother was born. The Critches returned to Australia in 1938, but the parents died in their mid-fifties. After the eldest son also died, Mary and her remaining brother returned to North America in 1955; she currently lives in Tacoma, Washington. In 1950, Mary married Horace Rogers, known as "Blue," a surveyor, and they lived in Bomaderry, New South Wales.

Mary's writing style is lively and full of humor, and no amount of paraphrasing can capture it well. She starts off talking about a man named Noel Frye, who had been a surveyor for the BPC on Ocean Island:

> He said that since his departure they were still looking for a replacement. Noel intimated he had resigned after becoming infatuated with Queenie Wills, the chief accountant's wife, a beautiful half-caste with four young daughters. Harry Wills was a tall, muscular man supporting 250 pounds of determination and Noel weighed about 140 pounds carrying his golf clubs. When Tommy Muir, the assistant island manager, tactfully suggested Noel might not wish to renew his contract, he immediately agreed.[31]

The image of a tall, muscular accountant and a spindly surveyor definitely inverts the commonly held ideas of western masculine types and had she kept writing, Mary might have gone on to literary fame. In 1950 she joined the *Triona* in Newcastle for the journey to Ocean Island:

> When the other passengers came on board and day of departure arrived, an energetic little tug towed the *Triona* out into the deep-water channel. I asked Ian Smith, the first mate, who was leaning over the rail supervising operations, "Why do we need a tug? Couldn't they just put the engine into reverse and back out?" "Because a ship is not a bloody ice cream wagon," he said with his heavy Scots accent.[32]

Once the tug cast off its towing cables they moved off at nine knots. Mary describes the journey as rather tumultuous, especially on her stomach: "it was like being in a washing machine at a laundromat." After this unpleasant oceanic experience Mary decided to stay on Ocean Island forever, or until they put in an airstrip. She shared her cabin with the wife of a colonial government official in Tarawa and remembers that the woman said they would have five-course dinners and would pass the port wine to the left in accordance with British tradition.

When they finally reached the island, launches arrived with husbands greeting their children and wives. Mary said her husband was wearing an outfit of white twill shorts and a starched short-sleeved shirt with knee-high stockings. "We were soon climbing down the ship's swaying ladder held in place by a grinning Gilbertese who casually kept one large foot on the ladder and the other on the launch as it rode up and down on the ocean swell."[33] On land Mary noticed the white and brown children diving off the sea wall just below the huge dust-covered processing plant. Blue pointed out "Ooma Point" to Mary as they left the harbor by jeep, heading to their new home on the windward side of the island in an area called Bukentereke.

Mary noticed that the "native" families lived in large huts with "a steeply pitched thatch roof with low, overhanging eaves and walls of woven pandanus set on a floor of coral sand." She remembers a Gilbertese woman in a red and white lavalava who strolled along the track and waved to Blue. "As physical examples of the human race, they seemed vastly superior to the average white man and woman," she wrote. They drove past a white church with a tall steeple, which had been built by the London Missionary Society (LMS). Blue explained to Mary that "[every] three months, immediately after the natives were paid, the god-botherers, as the Aussies called them, arrived in their sleek schooner from Tarawa. . . . Later, our houseboy explained that if he did not contribute to the 'el-em-ess,' God would punish him and his family in the Hereafter—salvation on a cash basis."[34] The LMS laid the foundations for what eventually became the Kiribati Protestant Church, and Mary's houseboy, an Ellice Islander named Taamo, sang the Lord's Prayer in Latin for them at dinner, followed by "a rich baritone version of *You are my Sunshine,* a favorite song among the natives."[35]

Mary and Blue lived in a house called the "Wireless House" after its original use. It had louvered windows, a front veranda, a kitchen, and in the back an enormous concrete water tank. From her descriptions the island seemed to have enjoyed a good spell of rain: bougainvillea, coconut trees, pumpkin vines, banana trees, and pandanus were in abundance. She noted everything from the water tank to the geckos as well as the employees' handbook, which listed the furniture in the house as follows:

1 dining room table and 4 wooden chairs
2 Rattan armchairs
1 double bed, mattress, 2 pillows, 1 mosquito net
1 chest of drawers

1 breakfast table and 2 chairs
1 electric stove
1 refrigerator[36]

Like other Europeans, Mary's life on the island was materially comfortable. A Company employee would take her shopping order, and it was delivered promptly the next day. At first she drank the water from the taps in the house and was soon spending most of her time in the bathroom. She talked to the Company doctor, whom she called "Les" Ingram, about her problems and he laughed, "No one has lived in the Wireless House for two years, so next week we'll pump out the water tank and the problem will disappear." Mary wrote, "After removing the skeletons of a few rodents, the tank was filled with fresh water that had come from Melbourne as ballast. I was glad the problem was solved so easily because no one likes to have dead animals in their water supply."[37]

When Mary lived on the island there were Australians, New Zealanders, two Scots, Chinese, Ellice Islanders, Gilbertese, and the English resident commissioner and his wife. She said that the young native children, who were called "piccaninis,"[38] attended classes with the white children. These were the children of "houseboys" and "wash janes" or "housegirls."

In Mary's story she relates that the English resident commissioner and his wife had been transferred from Nairobi, and "they gave the impression of much preferring the Kikuyu tribesmen to the uncouth Aussies." Mary was very critical of the British colonial representatives on the island. She describes the husband as overly nostalgic about English colonial superiority and his wife as disdainful of the Company. She recounts one amusing incident:

> On the occasion of the King's Birthday celebration this dream team once sent out invitations to the senior staff and when the guests began arriving they found the absent minded couple tucked in for the night under the mosquito net reading three-month old copies of the *London Times* with a chilled martini pitcher on the floor. . . . Rising nobly to the occasion, the mem-sahib said, "Ah, yes, the King's Birthday. Quite. The boy will get you a drink, and we'll be with you in a moment."[39]

The main transport on the island was an old World War I ambulance driven by a man named Telly, short for "Telephone."[40] There were several Company jeeps but only two private cars, both of which had been badly dented from being swung onto a barge from the ship's hold. Alcohol was regulated on the island: the whites were allowed one quart of beer per day and a bottle of gin a month. However, according to Mary, more was consumed, and every three months the brand of beer was changed to avoid arguments. Foster's from Australia was a favorite with everyone.

In the same flu epidemic described by Ray earlier in this chapter, Taamo, Mary and Blue's houseboy, died. Their next houseboy was Nukai, who was Gilbertese. He was paid £2 out of the £12 that Blue earned per week. Mary would communicate with him "in gestures, broken English and kitchen-Gilbertese." Life seemed to have been amiable on the island, and Mary talks about how Islanders would bring the whites gifts and entertain them with songs and dances. While "the Aussies" were known not to like the natives, who she says called them "boongs," they seemed to be respectful of those who worked at Ocean Island.

Mary wrote that life was generally peaceful and the wives supported each other, the way they might in the Australian outback. The whites were allowed to bring pet cats to the island but not to take them back. One time, two cats who had become feral raced into her house and fought to death under her bed. Nukai then picked up "the loser," walked through the pinnacles to the ocean, and threw it in.

Mary and Blue were eventually invited to the house of Harry and Queenie Wills, the Gilbertese woman with whom Noel Frye had fallen in love. Queenie's father was a Swiss trader who owned a shirt factory in Tarawa. Because Harry had married "a native" (albeit an educated "mixed" woman), he would not be promoted in the Company. They had four daughters, all blonde, who entertained the guests with a song called "Goodnight Irene, Goodnight." They also often sang what Mary called "Maori's Farewell" to send off people who were leaving for Australia.[41]

The "Tri-ships" would come in for a load of phosphate about every six weeks, and this was always an occasion for the Company employees. They eagerly awaited mail, newspapers, and magazines and enjoyed greeting and bidding goodbye to their neighbors, as portrayed in the archival films. As Mary watched people get used to living on the island, she said that they developed a "who cares" or "akia kaak" approach to life. I think she must be referring to the phrase akea te kanganga, which means "no problem" in Gilbertese and is similar to sega na leqa, which suggests the cavalier approach to life in Fiji.

Mary records six weeks of heavy rain in December one year. It was so heavy that people were stuck in their houses, and some seemed to develop "cabin fever." She recounts a story of two men who lived in a bungalow together and who were quite different in personality. One man was very neat, the other very untidy. During this rainy period, while inebriated, they decided to saw their lounge in half so each could have his own territory. The rain then plunged through the roof and damaged everything. The Company immediately shipped them back to Australia.

Given the size of the island, the BPC did all it could to maintain peace and security. Sports and recreation became key tools for achieving this, including the establishment of an outdoor movie theater that impressed all but the Chinese workers, who were not so keen on English films. Elderly Banabans, however, fondly remember these entertainments since they were few and far between on Rabi.

People especially liked action films about cowboys, and Mary said that Nukai was convinced that these films represented real life in Australia and America. Mary remembers a "terrible period," however, when they were sent an eight-week supply of "weepies," all starring Margaret O'Brien.[42]

The wives on the island would have elaborate tea parties and even doughnut parties, all served up on good chinaware. Mary's specialty was pie made from pumpkins, which she says the Japanese planted on the island during the occupation in 1942–1945. Mary was good at sewing and had a machine imported from Kowloon, where many of the products like chinaware, chests, and furniture originated. On weekends they had something called "Sunday Morning Drinks," which started at ten and went from house to house as long as liquor was supplied. Afterward, she writes, "The furry mouth lasted until Tuesday."

Mary describes in detail a forty-two-year-old man named MacRobert, or "Mack," who was the focus of a number of women's affections. He was a former Shakespearean actor from London and the manager of both staff housing and the singles' dining room. According to Mary he was gay, and although Australian men normally did not tolerate his "type," he was so kind, gracious, and competent that everyone liked him. Mack's stint on Ocean Island was apparently the result of the lack of demand for theater actors, thanks to the advent of television and film. Mary wrote that the single white women—at any one time the Company allowed only three: the nurse, the schoolteacher, and the office stenographer—would lavish their attentions on Mack, which sometimes made other men jealous. She said the women were hoping for "an immaculate conversion with a happy-ever-after ending."[43] According to Mary, Mack never made moves on the men and thoroughly enjoyed the company of women. She writes that the women, herself included, were ignorant about homosexuality in the 1950s.

Mary and Blue's marriage eventually deteriorated on the island, and after his two-year contract they parted ways in Australia. Her memoirs are lively, reflecting her vivacious personality and open-minded world view. Mary wrote with great detail and intensity about people and places, bodies and clothing, personalities and hang-ups. She wrote of scorpions and caterpillars, rats and feral cats and weevils. These are the daily details and the embodied experiences usually left out of Company records and history books like Williams and Macdonald's *The Phosphateers*.

One of the most interesting connections between Ray's and Mary Zausmer's stories is the Wireless House, which appears on the map in "Stories of P." It had been empty for so long before Mary and Blue moved in because it was the same house in which the European couple had been murdered. Mary thought a native had been convicted of the crime, while Ray wrote that it was two Chinese mechanics. People would casually ask Mary if she had any blood stains on her walls. She was confronted by this legacy one day after she asked Nukai to chop some pumpkins for scones. Nukai later walked out of the kitchen toward her with a crazed look on his face and a carving knife in one hand. Mary, ever observant, writes, "My first surprise was that Nukai was left-handed." He then fell to the floor and later was diagnosed with the same terrible flu that had afflicted many of the Islanders. When Mary wrote her memoirs forty-five years later, she still had the same ivory-handled carving knife, "although the handle has yellowed somewhat."[44]

Laborers' Views

When I traveled to Banaba for the second time in 2000, an I-Kiribati woman named Roruama, accompanied by her husband, Baekanebu, and another man, Martin, sang a folk song that is well known throughout Kiribati. The lyrics convert the hard work, the tensions of racial divisions, and even the longing for home into the golden idyll of a Pacific paradise. No one is sure who composed the song, except that it emerged from the labor experiences on Banaba, which is why much of it is in English (the recurring Gilbertese line can be translated as "The people [the Islanders], the white people, they are happy"). I made several inquiries about it, and the New Zealand artist Robin White said that it was one of the first songs she learned on Tarawa in Kiribati, where she lived for seventeen years as a Bahai missionary.

> On the beach, on the streets of Banaba
> I'm in the shadows of a golden dream
> When I'm watching the boys and girls playing
> Happy working for the BPC
>
> Lovely beach, lovely place of Banaba
> *Aomata, I-Matang, a kukurei*
> Everybody, including myself
> Happy working for the BPC
>
> When the sun's going down
> I'll be alone
> Thinking of my homeland far away
> But the moon shining bright on the ocean
> Makes me happy forever more
>
> Lovely beach, lovely place of Banaba
> *Aomata, I-Matang, a kukurei*
> Everybody, including myself
> Happy working for the BPC
>
> When I go out to sea in the night time
> I can see all the lights in a sitting line
> understanding the lights are calling:

back to shore
have a bath
go to bed

Lovely beach, lovely place of Banaba
Aomata, I-Matang, a kukurei
Everybody, including myself
Happy working for the BPC.

Various newspapers and magazines offered regular stories about life on Ocean Island and Nauru, but we get very little sense of the experiences of the Asian or Pacific Islander workers signaled in this song. In 1929 the *Auckland Star,* for example, ran the following:

Like an Oyster: Lonely Phosphate Islands/ Deepest Mooring in the World

Natives and Chinamen

On Ocean Island the output is from 180,000 to 250,000 tons per year, which is larger than in former years. Some 600 natives and about the same number of Chinamen are employed and in addition there are about 100 European officials. Mr. Cozens says the Chinese are good workers. The rock is blasted and dug out from the quarries and sent by cars to crushers and driers, from where it is shipped in bulk.[45]

Initially, the recruitment of Islander laborers to work on Banaba was difficult for the Pacific Islands Company. Banabans did not want to work in the mines, and according to Ralph Shlomowitz and Doug Munro, Gilbert and Ellice Islanders preferred to work at Fanning and Washington Islands on coconut plantations.[46] Those who were initially recruited often did not want to return for a second contract because they were satisfied with the money earned after the first two or three years. The populations of these islands were also quite small and could not fulfill all the needs of the massive and labor-intensive industry on Nauru and Ocean Islands.

In 1920, for the available pool of about 1,500 men, there were many alternative sources of work, so the Company made up the necessary numbers with Asian workers. Between 1905 and 1920 on Ocean Island they used Japanese workers, who were known as "mechanics" (skilled tradesmen) and "coolies" (unskilled laborers). The Company would pit the ethnic groups against each other, and according to Shlomowitz and Munro, "In 1911 . . . the use of Japanese boatmen was seen as a corrective to the Kanakas who consider they cannot be replaced."[47]

After 1920, when the BPC was established and following several labor disputes with the Japanese recruits, the Company switched to Chinese workers from Hong Kong. From then on Ocean Island had a mix of Chinese, Gilbertese, and Ellice Island laborers. The Chinese, however, were usually segregated from the rest of the community. According to Mary Zausmer, during her time on the islands they spoke Cantonese and pidgin with their employers and were all single men on five-year contracts: "Ardent gamblers, they spent their leisure hours playing fan tan and sometimes lost all the money in their account, then from necessity signing on for another five year term rather than go home empty handed."[48]

There were also great tensions between the Chinese and Gilbertese groups, and Macdonald describes one particularly violent clash in the 1920s: "an incident arising from a Chinese washing his clothes in drinking water set aside for Gilbertese soon escalated in a general Chinese attack on Gilbertese labourers, retaliatory stoning of Chinese by Gilbertese and full-scale riot[ing] after which weapons ranging from nail-studded pieces of timber to broken bottles were seized by police."[49]

In his faithful combing of the BPC Archives, the reasons for the dislike between the groups was described by Macdonald as primarily cultural with the Chinese looking down on the Gilbertese for their *lack* of culture, and the Gilbertese resenting this and looking down on the Chinese as physically "puny men." There was also anger over "Chinese attempts to seduce Gilbertese women."[50] The above-mentioned riot was not the first between Gilbertese and Chinese workers, and we may never know exactly how their differences played out on the ground. Today there are many people of Chinese heritage on Rabi, on Banaba, and throughout Kiribati, including among my father's family on Tabiteuea.

The Gilbertese men were primarily recruited from the southern part of the group, which is prone to drought; this was a major inducement for employment in the phosphate industry. The numbers of Ellice Island recruits increased in 1936 when an influenza epidemic resulted in a quarantine of the whole Gilbert group.[51] Each ethnic group was basically given a different job: Asians filled the ranks of skilled labor, including carpenters, mechanics, boat builders, and cooks; Gilbertese worked in the phosphate fields; and Ellice Islanders crewed boats. The boatmen and miners, however, often did both jobs, depending on when ships arrived for loading.[52] In their economic overview of the Nauru and Ocean Island labor trade, Shlomowitz and Munro are critical of this stereotyping of ethnic groups as suitable for one job over another. Indeed, the racial separation of employees on the island did not make for the best working relations between them, despite the Company's attempts to ease the tensions through sports and recreation.

Moreover, such divisions were not just between Europeans, Asians, and Islanders but were between Islanders themselves, as we will see. The Gilbert and Ellice Islands were governed together by the office of the British Western Pacific High Commission as a protectorate in 1892 and a colony in 1916. The Ellice Islanders all had to learn Gilbertese, the official language, along with English. Ellice Islanders had light brown skin while the Gilbert Islanders from the more exposed northern environment were darker. In the films the Ellice Islanders were labeled "natives," and it was their bodies and faces that were privileged over Gilbertese or Banaban ones. There was a racial hierarchy with Europeans at the top and Gilbertese at the bottom. Part of my task after exploring the Company archives in Melbourne was to talk directly to some of the men who had experienced life as laborers on Banaba. I was interested not just in the work they did and their attitudes toward the Company and the Europeans but their relations with other workers.

The following memories of Banaba were all collected on Tabiteuea Meang (or "Tab North," as it is called) during a five-week visit in March–April 2000. I lived at an old convent in the village of Tanaeang with two nuns and a postulate: Tina Mangarita, Tina Maria, and Nei Aom. My father had arranged for me to stay at the convent, partly because I have many relatives on the island and my elder sister's visit several years earlier had caused more than a few family disputes over the right to host her. Our grandmother Takeua, from Eita village, was dearly loved and the elders had not seen her since her departure in 1947. Hosting relatives and special guests is a precious right in the Gilbertese custom, so I stayed with the nuns to prevent conflict and that way all my relatives could visit and I could make overnight trips to each of their homes.

While it is an ancestral home for me, I also chose to visit Tabiteuea because Williams and Macdonald had written of a 1961 labor strike led by Tabiteuean workers. The strike is said to have been sparked by the harsh language of one Gilbertese overseer relating to Gilbertese workers, but it soon escalated to include a number of different grievances and the man's European superiors, who also liked to use harsh language.[53] Even today Tabiteueans are known to be, to use a popular phrase, "hard-core." Back then, they were seen as tough, they carried knives, they were proud, and they were known to have strong magic. My grandfather Teaiwa, recruited from Tabiteuea to work in the mines in the early 1940s, had all these traits in spades.

The Company had always had problems finding Gilbertese to fill positions of authority because of the egalitarian code that frames Gilbertese social life. Everyone is equal; no one is above anyone else, but you always respect the elders. Thus, being promoted over your fellow Gilbertese is always risky, and the same usually applies on Banaba and Rabi today. The BPC approached the 1961 strike in the light of a 1948 strike, also led by Tabiteueans, after which, Williams and Macdonald claim, no Tabiteueans were recruited for years. Contrary to this, I found at least three who were living or working on the island in the early 1950s.

I interviewed the men who were now unimwane, or elders, with the help of a translator named Temakau, a former seaman, or kaimoa, now a teacher at a primary school in Tauma. He had several mechanical and electrical skills, which the nuns valued, and he would come over to fix the solar panels at the convent where I was staying. After I discussed my project with him, he introduced me to his relatives Teweia and Ntongantonga, who also worked on Banaba. Later, in Fiji, I sat down with my father and we went through each of the taped interviews. The following account is derived from our discussions, my father's translations, my mother's transcriptions, reviews of the tapes, and my own memories of sitting with the men on the island.

Stories by Enere, Booti, and Temokou

I met Enere, Booti, and Temokou at Booti's house in Tanaeang. They lived near each other and I thought it might be a good idea to hold one group interview in a more formal manner, given my gender and the age difference. This proved to be problematic for a number of reasons. Enere and Booti had worked on Banaba from 1947, while the youngest, Temokou, worked from 1970 to 1979. I asked Temakau, the translator, to ask each of them the same series of questions, and we went around in this highly unproductive and awkward way for two hours or so. I was a young woman, who all of them knew was also Banaban and Tabiteuean, and yet I did not speak to them in Gilbertese. I was also asking them to objectify and comment upon a past some decades gone. They thought it quite strange that here I was on Tabiteuea, my ancestral island, and all I wanted to talk about was Banaba. Their recountings were not so expansive because I had structured the meeting as a series of questions and answers rather than as an informal conversation. There was also a reluctance to talk over each other, and a low energy level and circumspection prevailed. However, once the formal part of the meeting ended, the stories began to flow.

Booti sat cross-legged to my right with one knee against a rolled-up foam mattress. He described working in the mines and would often mime the actions with his upper body. He'd pretend to lift a rock or use a shovel and then point up to the ceiling, his eyes following his finger as if looking up at a skip above what they called the bwangabwanga, which literally means "hole" or "opening," but also refers to the water caves.

> I nako ni mwakuri i Banaba n te ririki 1947. . . . [Pauses] I mwakuri n te tabo ni koroka ma n akea bwaira ni mwakuri ae ti na otanganaki iai man bubun te tano ke bwakabwakan atibu nako nanon te bwangabwanga, are ti keniken inanona. . . . [After questions are directed to Enere and Temokou, he continues] I teirake ni mwakuri ni ukebwau moa, niman te tia koroka nakon ruaiua te kaa. . . . eaki raoiroi te tabo ni mwakuri ao kabonoike ibukin bubun te tano . . . au ururing ibukin Banaba. . . . [He thinks for a minute] te aba ae rangi ni kananoanga ngkai.

> I went to work on Banaba in 1947. . . . I started in the mines and we worked with no protective clothing against dust and falling rocks in the mine. . . . I started on contract and later on regular hours. . . . When I did contract work five of us were required to fill nine carts. The workplace was unhealthy be-

cause of the dust from phosphate rock. . . . My memories of Banaba? . . . It's a very pitiful sight now.[54]

Enere sat to my far left, leaning against one of the corner posts. He had thick, large glasses perched on his nose, which were secured by a string around the back of his head. He was a natural storyteller and would often mimic the way people talked with great facial expressions. He would reply *akea . . . akea . . . akea* ("no," "none," "naught," "zero") to many of the questions and then proceed to tell a long and interesting story.

> I kan nako Banaba ibukin tangiran te batika, te tienti ao te kani maiu raoi. . . . I moana au mwakuri n 1947. . . . I mwakuri moa n te tabo ni koroka. Bon te mwakuri ae rawata te mwakuri anne, ao imwina I a manga mwakuri n te power-house. E aki kanganga ngkanne au mwakuri n te tabo anne. Bwa are kanga ai te tia kabeabeanaki ngai. . . . Bwa ngkana e kangai te mataniwi, karaoa aei, I karoia ana te baei, I anaia. . . . Ai bon arona nako naba anne . . . ara mataniwi bon te I-Matang, ao e aki kumeira bwa ti ngkana e kabeabeanira ao ngkanne ara mwakuri bwa ti na karaoia are ti tuangaki. . . . E kananoakawaki uringan Banaba n aron raoiroin aona ngkekei ma taran aona ngkai. . . . Te aba ae uruaki aona man tara ni kananoanga.

> I wanted to go and work on Banaba to buy the good things of life. I worked there in 1947. I just worked in the mine. That was hard work. Later I worked in the powerhouse, and work there was easy because I was merely doing what I was told to do. When the boss says do this, I do it, take this, I take it . . . so the work was easy. . . . Our boss was a white man . . . he didn't bother us that much. . . . My memories of Banaba . . . it is really sad to think just how beautiful Banaba was then compared to its present state. . . . it is degraded and damaged.[55]

Temokou's memories of Banaba were clear and detailed perhaps partly because he had been there more recently than the other men. He first worked in the phosphate warehouse and then at the cantilever, which had by then acquired a long swinging arm that deposited the phosphate directly into the hold of the waiting ship.

> Ngke I moan roko i Banaba ao I mwakuri n te umantano. . . . Iai bwai ni mwakuri ibukin kamanoan te ubu man bubun te tano ao ti katabuaki ni benira ibukin ae e kona ni bae beem n intinin bwai ni mwakuri ao ko kona ni kabuanibwai ngkanne. . . . Bon iai tuua ibukin tararuan maurin te tia mwakuri . . . iai naba ara mataniwi ae bon te aomata[56] ao teuaei, e rangi ni kairimatoa ao a maiti taan mwakuri ae kabaneia. . . . [When asked about accidents or problems for workers, he said] I uringa naba ae a maiti taan mwakuri aika bwaka n aoraki, aika ikoaki iaon te mwakuri n aiaron temanna ae moanaki n te kako are e wintiaki nako aon te booti. Teuaei e bwaka i tari ao e aki roko n te reke rabatana. . . . te bwai ae titiku n au iango ao I aki kona ni mwaninga bon raoiroin ma tikiraoin aon Banaba ngkekei mani kabotauaki ma ngkai. . . . a bon bane n turanako

bwain aona n aiaron te kantiriwa, auti ni maeka umantano, motoka ma bwai
ni mwakuri mitiin. . . . E rangi ni kananoakawaki ururingan Banaba.

When I first went to Banaba, I worked in the phosphate warehouse. . . . we
were required to wear protective clothing like face masks, and we were not allowed to wear lavalava as this could easily be caught in the machines and en-
danger safety. . . . there were safety rules which we were required to follow at
the workplace. . . . We also had a boss who was Gilbertese who was very strict
and hard on us. . . . [Later] I remember a number of people who got sick, there
were also fatal accidents in the workplace. I remember while the ship was unloading cargo onto a dinghy a man was knocked by the winch into the water
and his body was never recovered. . . . What I can't forget about Banaba? . . .
how good and modern the facilities were then . . . how all those have become
dilapidated. . . . it is so sad.[57]

In general all three men felt that the BPC was a good employer and that, despite the hard work, life on Banaba was easier than life in the village back home.
Contrary to Shlomowitz and Munroe's observations for the 1900–1940 period,
they said that men were always willing to be recruited for work on Banaba.[58] It
enabled them to buy things like bicycles, sandalwood chests from Hong Kong,
chinaware, kitchen utensils, te booa (a type of tobacco), clothing for special occasions, and European food items. They also knew that Banaba now lay in a ne-
glected state and recalled fondly the earlier days of its prosperity.

Concerns about pay, work conditions, skills, and safety were central to the
racial divisions between the Europeans, Asians, and Islanders and between the
Islanders themselves. As mentioned earlier, the Gilbertese were at the bottom of
a perceived racial hierarchy in the first few decades of the industry, which was
compounded by their physical location in the bwangabwanga, or mines, and their
hard labor and intensive work. The following anecdote was related in response to
a question about both spiritual experiences and relations between workers.

Enere remembered something that had happened to a young Ellice Island
woman named Pesiki in 1947. According to his version, she and her sister went
walking one day and one of a group of Gilbertese men resting by the side of the
road called out "aura taura," which literally translates as "your light is shining,"
meaning "you are beautiful." Pesiki turned around and snapped back, saying, "E
aki bo tau te betin ma te bata." Enere called out, mimicking Pesiki, "No comparison
can be made between the basin and the pot." This veiled speech hid a powerful
insult. Interpreting Enere's story, Temakau said that because the Gilbertese men
worked in the mines under the hot sun all day long, they were very dark-skinned.
By contrast, these Ellice Island women were fair-skinned, and so the woman insulted him by saying, "Your skin is so black, don't think you can talk to us!" My
father had heard a similar version of this incident, further recalling that there was
a song describing it, part of which went as follows:

Te betin te kuro	The basin, the pot
E aki botau	It's not the same
Bwa i buretireti	Because I'm so ugly
Bwa I batangoingoi	Because I'm so black
Kabarai buren au taeka nako	Forgive the mistakes of my words[59]

After Pesiki insulted the group by the roadside, the man who had called out the compliment vowed revenge. He was very hurt by her words and approached two Tabiteueans to help him. These men were renowned for their ability to cast spells and, as mentioned, Tabiteueans in general were known to be powerful. The playing field at the top of the island near the hospital where the village of Bua-konikai once stood was known as Maraen te Tabiteuea (the Tabiteuean marae, or communal space),[60] marking yet another cartographic stratum of knowledge and identity on this already deeply layered landscape. The men agreed to punish Pesiki for deriding the dark skin of the Gilbertese men. They lit a fire at Maraen te Tabiteuea and effected a spell that, Enere said, caused Pesiki to lose her mind. One day soon after the incident, she walked down the road and tore off all her clothes. She often ran around naked after that and was never cured.[61]

Temokou recalled a time of unrest on Banaba in 1978–1979. This was during the period when a group of Banabans were repatriated to the island to "occupy" their land. Other members of the Banaban nationalist movement, which wanted independence from what was about to become the nation of Kiribati, accompanied them. Temokou remembered that the Banabans bombed key phosphate installations despite the efforts of the Gilbertese police to stop them.[62] He also mentioned that my grandfather Teaiwa and grandmother Takeua were on Banaba between 1975 and 1977. I did not know that Teaiwa returned to Banaba at all until Temokou told me this story, which my father later confirmed. I wondered how my grandmother felt about the divide and the violence between the Banabans and Gilbertese in that period. She died in 1978 on Rabi as she was preparing to return to Tabiteuea for the first time in forty years.

Teweia's Story

I arrived late at Teweia's house on the back of Tina Mangarita's motorbike, apologized profusely for my tardiness, and we made our way to his small house. He was far less concerned about the time than I was. Unlike many of the other houses I had visited, Teweia's was on the ground and had walls made from the mid-ribs of the coconut palm. I had become accustomed to climbing up to sit on the raised floor of a mwenga, or house, but at his house we had to duck down and sit on the sandy floor.[63]

Like my grandfather Teaiwa, Teweia Intiua is from Utiroa village on Tabiteuea Meang. When I interviewed him in 2000 he was seventy years old. Teweia knew

Teweia Intiua in Utiroa village, March 2000. Photo by Katerina Martina Teaiwa

my grandfather well but did not know of Teaiwa's parents. He particularly talked about what a good fisherman and diver Teaiwa was, especially when using "traditional" methods. Teweia had been much younger than my grandfather but avidly followed the older man around.

> I rangi ni kinaa Teaiwa bwa rarou ngke I roko mai Kosrae. . . . Te ikawai riki ngaia nakoiu bwa e a tia ni iein ma Takeua ae natin Kabuabwai ao tao uoman natia, ma I ti uringa Terianako ae e mena irouia. . . . I aki ata natia ane Tabakitoa ae e atongaki bwa e mena iroun tibuna Tebwerewa I Terikiai. Eng, I rangi ni uringa Teaiwa n te tai anne bwa kanga te aomata ae aki rau arona ao e mamanging, ma te tia akawa ae koro arona . . . e rangi n rabakau te akawa ae te taumata, ao I nanako n akawa ma ngaia n te kawa are Kabuna.

> I knew Teaiwa well. He was a close friend after I came back from Kosrae. He was much older than myself and had married Takeua, the child of Kabuabwai, and they had two children, one was Terianako whom I used to see with her parents and the one you mentioned, Tabakitoa, who lived with Tebwerewa in Terikiai, I did not know. . . . Teaiwa then as I recall was rather unsettled and he drank. . . . However, he was a good fisherman particularly with the *taumata* style of fishing, using a fishing line and a pair of goggles.[64] We used to go fishing in Kabuna [the southern end of Tab North].

I then displayed some of the old BPC mining images for Teweia on my digital camera, and he immediately became excited. He recalled that he went to Banaba with his parents when he was about eight years old; his father had worked on the island as a telephone operator. His recollection was that living conditions were poor. He said they had no furniture, they had to collect their own firewood for cooking, and when people were sick it was a big expedition to carry them to the hospital since there was no ambulance and a general lack of medical equipment. He said that pregnant women in particular struggled in these conditions.

While Gilbertese and Banaban women probably knew how to facilitate home births, there were colonial regulations regarding such things. According to Williams and Macdonald the baby welfare clinic was established in 1937, just before Teweia lived on the island.[65] Families were brought over as nuclear units, and the extended family or village members who would normally be available to help out on such occasions would have been absent. One can imagine that simply plonking Gilbertese and Ellice Islander families together on one island would not have resulted in a fluid redistribution of social roles and relationships. People would have created new relationships that varied considerably in degrees of rapport.

Teweia enjoyed playing with other Gilbertese and Ellice Island children, but they all had to live in separate ethnic quarters. During World War II, his family was forced by the Japanese to go to Kosrae, where they lived for about three years. After what he called the "American liberation," his family returned to Tabiteuea.

In 1954, Teweia returned to Banaba to work as a cable operator. He wanted to save money for a bicycle and a sewing machine, which were prized possessions on Banaba and in the Gilberts. He also said that while working conditions were very bad for the miners and some men had been injured by falling rocks and carts, he wanted to be able to "eat what white men eat."

Teweia described in detail the movement of the phosphate from the grab at the rock through the aerial cable-and-skip mechanism. He reflected on the fact that some sections of the fields were mined with a grab and others by hand. He described how each system had a number, "kaeboro n tai akekei tai n te tai arei . . . iai number teuana, te skip number teuana . . . ao number uoua te skip e naba" (at that time the cables . . . here was cableway number 1, skip number 1, and skip number 2), and then how he would shift from operating the cable to driving a motorboat containing baskets of phosphate, which were then dumped into the holds of the ships. Like the others, Teweia called the rock not te aba but te tano: sand, soil, clay, or ground.

Teweia remembered various grievances about food rations, pay, and the lack of Company information about safety and working conditions. He talked a lot about how they were never allowed water or te mwangko, the cups for drinking, while working in te bwangabwanga, inside the mines. His stories shifted back and forth between when he was on Banaba as a child and as an adult worker. They were punctuated by sections of intense detail as he described the mining operations and then shifted to more hazy and general reflections on life before and after the war. I think that the details about the mining operations were stimulated partly by the videos I showed him and partly by the fact that it was such long and monotonous work that it would be hard to forget. But on many other topics, he would stop and we would sit in silence until he mumbled, "I mwamwaninga" (I forget).

In writing we often leave out the things we forget or don't know, preferring to present as authoritative an account as possible. This is apparent in the memoirs of the Australians and New Zealanders. In most informal oral accounts, stories are inflected with the very process of remembering. In between verbal utterances there are silences, pauses, furrowed brows, heads down, which suddenly rise when a memory or image leaps back into consciousness. When I asked the specific question "What do you remember about the island as a boy?" Teweia reflected for a moment and then exclaimed, "Te mwakuri!" (The work!).

He worked for the Company for eleven years and left in 1965.

Communities of Memory

The contexts in which I collected and now re-present the stories of Banaba from the BPC films in chapter 3, the Australians and New Zealanders through their memoirs, and of the Gilbertese men through oral interviews are obviously very different. It was much easier to describe and reflect upon the films and written memoirs; historians have long favored textual over oral historical accounts, though not always cinema. The interviews with the Tabiteuean men occurred in a highly charged, intersubjective situation. First and foremost, the men were interested in who I was by descent; why I was so incompetent in the language (and by implication their culture); how I had received such a high educational standing at such a young age; and why at twenty-five I had no children. Apparently I was too young to have an advanced Western education but too old in terms of childbearing.[66] The women were often concerned with similar issues but even more so with the size and shape of my body. They concluded that I was skinny (by I-Kiribati standards) because no one loved me enough to feed me enough. I didn't have the heart to tell them that my weight had more to do with the effect of the local water on my stomach.

Each of the interviews involved a long discussion about my grandfather Teaiwa, grandmother Takeua, great-grandfather Tenamo, or all three of them. This usually took place before anyone wanted to talk about phosphate. Teweia and Ntongantonga, for example, spent more time talking about Tenamo and Teaiwa than about their work on Banaba. Ntongantonga also told me amazing stories of his experiences in the war and of friendships with African American soldiers. Throughout my stay on Tabiteuea, people always assumed that I was on the island to learn

"Phos[phate] Fields," 1920s. Courtesy of the National Library of Australia

more about my family. For some reason, actually learning something about my genealogy had not been at the forefront of my mind in preparing for the research on Tabiteuea and Banaba. A friend of my grandmother showed up at the convent twice to patiently inform me of my various ancestors and about the lovely woman my grandmother was. I began to understand that being Banaban, like many others with parents and grandparents from other Gilbertese islands, was to be connected deeply to even more homelands.

The story of Ocean Island is, in one sense, a sad but typical story of imperialism, colonialism, and environmental exploitation and devastation. But in another sense, there is nothing typical about a two-and-a-half-square-mile hub of intense industrial activity surrounded by thousands of miles of open sea. The stories of the diverse communities created on Banaba to support the mining industry are unevenly sedimented into this landscape given the short contracts and high turnover of staff. More than a few Company employees and their families are buried in the Banaba Cemetery, which is still divided by that racial colonial logic into native, European, Japanese, and Chinese burial grounds.

The Gilbertese men remembered Banaba in pragmatic ways with a few laments about its state in the present. It was primarily a means to a material end, and though they made many good friendships along the way, they were not overly romantic about their experiences. The Europeans, perhaps with the exception of the spunky Mary Zausmer, were more or less nostalgic for an island "paradise."

My personal memories, while just as fleeting, are informed by personal, cultural, and academic contexts beyond the island and phosphate history, including the decolonization movement within the field of interdisciplinary Pacific studies.

The people and events brought together by the BPC, while engaged in seriously exploitative industrial and colonial pursuits, also formed a kind of imagined community that lives on. Over the eighty-year life-span of the industry, people from all over the world were born on, lived on, passed through, or passed away on Banaba. An online community run by a descendant of BPC managers, Stacey King, and her Banaban partner, Ken Sigrah out of the Gold Coast of Australia, attests to this.[67] People are constantly writing in, saying they were born on the island, and does anyone remember so-and-so from 1962, 1933, 1907, and so forth. It was through social networks like this that the now-defunct Banaban Heritage Society, a kind of social, historical, aid, and development club of former Ocean Island residents, was formed out of Queensland, Australia, in the 1990s; it has now been reconstituted as the website Abara Banaba.[68]

Most people who share a common memory of Banaba—Australians, New Zealanders, British, Gilbertese, Ellice Islanders, Chinese, Japanese, and Banabans themselves—have not interacted with each other face-to-face, but at some level feel attached to the same island and to the diffuse community that emerges from it. The mining venture itself has not been visibly preserved as part of the national historical landscape of Australia and New Zealand; there are no public memorials of the British Phosphate Commissioners or anything to do with Banaba or Nauru, for that matter, aside from "Phosphate House," which once graced Collins Street in Melbourne, and the various "Nauru" buildings, towers, and houses that previously existed from Melbourne to Honolulu.[69]

How does one write about such an ethnically, geographically, and temporally disparate Ocean Island community, or even call it that? My analysis is based on the very juxtaposition of multiple memories, stories, and events. As Liisa Malkki has written, "Who one is, what one's principles, loyalties, desires, longings, and beliefs are—all this can sometimes be powerfully formed and transformed in transitory circumstances."[70] We know that Ocean Island mattered for governments, for investors, for fertilizer manufacturers, for farmers. But it also mattered for mining laborers, boatmen, plumbers, medical officers, administrators, and their spouses and children, all of whom temporarily called the island home.

Sydney Point and Lillian Point on Ocean Island were named after the daughters of the first Pacific Phosphate Company manager, John Arundel. Lillian's memoir was reproduced in Shennan and Tekenimatang's people's history and is a colorful ethnographic account of Banaba in 1906. Women talked to other women, and they noticed what children and babies were doing. Lillian spent long periods with Banabans and made good friends with them, particularly "the old Queen," Teiene-

makin, an elderly female figure who was obviously prominent and i...
was rarely mentioned in the male-dominated Company or historical l...

A poem written by a friend of Lillian Arundel illustrates the now wel...
lished trope of European longing for an island paradise despite the context o...
ropean colonial and capitalist exploitation and environmental degradation. Th...
well-traveled Lillian described the Banabans as living with "freedom, romance...
and beauty unequalled in any other part of the world."

Ocean Island

In a far and distant country,
On some dark and dreary day,
You'll recall to mind the sunshine
In an island far away.

When you see the ferry's headlights,
As they play across the Bay,
"It reminds me of the island
And the flying fish," you'll say.

When you hear a distant trainload
Rush along its iron way,
You will say it sounds like breakers,
Like the darling surf at play.

When the dead leaves round are falling
As you gently through them tread,
You will dream of swaying palm-trees,
Hear them rustling overhead.

For the rustle of the palm-trees
In the memory lingers long,
And the sound of dashing water,
You cannot forget its song.[72]

the Sky

stories without knowing how to read our landscapes

Pasts to Remember"

As EPELI HAUʻOFA suggests, a reading of our landscapes and seascapes—spaces that are the products of multiscalar processes in both contemporary and deep, geological time—is necessary to better explore our Pacific histories. For many Pacific scholars, such as the late Hauʻofa, Albert Wendt, and Anne Salmond, history and a sense of temporality were not just limited to archival texts, or to the last century or two, but rather extended tens of thousands and even millions of years across time in embodied and material forms. We can expand Hauʻofa's proposal to include our reading and framing of the contemporary stakes of globalization and the intense interconnectivity of the twenty-first century. This requires material, corporeal, grounded, and symbolic readings across disciplinary boundaries, geographic areas, and temporal contexts.[1] Furthermore, to truly acknowledge diverse ontological realities, we need to acknowledge that in indigenous epistemologies and ontologies, poetics are never just poetics.

In this chapter I move from an exploration of the representations of social life and work on Banaba to tracking and understanding phosphate, including its transformation from rock into fertilizer for consumption in Australia and New Zealand. That fertilizer, the superphosphate that transformed Australian and New Zealand land, is te aba.

The Phosphate Flyers

In August 1916 the *New Zealand Farmer Stock and Station Journal* ran a story by Albert Ellis on the discovery of phosphate and declared that if they "could get something of that kind in New Zealand it would be better than all the gold mines in the country."[2] The industry was a complex chain linking the mining company on Ocean Island, on Nauru, briefly on Makatea in French Polynesia, and, later, on Christmas Island in the Indian Ocean with the shipping, stevedoring, fertilizer manufacturing and distribution, aerial topdressing, farming, and food exporting across two distinct creations of the British Empire—the Dominion of New

"Crop Dusting Plane Eric Lee Johnson," 1958. Courtesy
of the Museum of New Zealand Te Papa Tongarewa

Zealand, established in 1907, and the Commonwealth of Australia, established in
1901.[3] In historical literature and popular writing these two nations have been referred to as "the Antipodes," a geographic and familial designation for their location on the opposite side of the earth from the "mother" country. The genealogy
of the British Phosphate Commissioners, as a joint enterprise of these three developing and deeply linked nation-states, thus constitutes an imperial formation
of a particular sort, involving multiple kinds of colonial kinship, settler coloniza-
tion and indigenous dispossession, innovation, transformation, destruction, and
very specific commodity and service chains.[4]

In a 1959 New Zealand documentary titled *Land from the Sky*, the pilot of a
Wanganui Aero Works Cessna adjusts his helmet as a tractor discharges its load
into the hold of his craft. A fine white powder floats through the air and up the
driver's nostrils as the pilot prepares for takeoff. In a few minutes the plane taxis
and lifts to soar above the Wanganui hills. It dips and rolls over Aotearoa, giving new meaning to the island's *Māori* name, Land of the Long White Cloud, as
the pilot releases a trail of white dust from the back of his Cessna.[5] The particles
hover and then settle over what many hope will soon be green paddocks and pastures. Below the pirouetting plane, two farmers take a break against a perimeter
fence and survey the landscape:

FARMER 1: They've done a hundred tons this morning.

FARMER 2: Mmm, about a thousand acres.

FARMER 1: Place is looking pretty good

FARMER 2: [As he opens a packet of cigarettes] We've both come a long way, haven't we? I'll soon be running twice the number of sheep up here. You know it's wonderful what topdressing has done for the hill country.

The scene switches dramatically to a far less fertile period in New Zealand history. Rain is beating down onto soil that appears to fall away from the roots of a tree desperately clutching the edge of a crag. The voiceover belongs to one of the farmers:

When I think what it used to be like. Half the hill farms in the country were bad. Rough, dirty, worn out. They were deteriorating everywhere. The pasture'd thinned. It didn't have any roots any more to hold it together.

[Sound of thunder, flash of lightning, then rain, shot of sodden sheep blinking in the rain. A farmer on his horse dismounts to examine the ground]

After the rain I'd find the evidence I'd dreaded. The signs [that] the farm which had to support us all was on the move. And mind you, I'd seen what had happened to other places. The hill country was falling apart.

[Eerie, sad music]

The early settlers felled the bush and burned it. The ash fertilized the hills for a time, but now the land was exhausted, finished. And here we were stuck with it. Everywhere, waste and destruction; the topsoil was sliding down off the hills.

And then we began to lose the lush valleys too as they began to fill with silt.

In 1947 the New Zealand government determined soil erosion to be a major national problem and set up a committee under the Soil Conservation and Rivers Control Council to discuss the matter. The narrator of the documentary provides the commentary: "They investigated, and they talked. You know. And finally it all led to something like this":

COMMITTEE MEMBER 1: Fertilizer would grow grass on the hills and hold them.

COMMITTEE MEMBER 2: How are you going to get the fertilizer up there?

COMMITTEE MEMBER 3: It's too steep to do it with machines.

COMMITTEE MEMBER 4: Spread it by hand.

COMMITTEE MEMBER 5: What, on fifteen million acres? [Laughs]

COMMITTEE MEMBER 6: Could we . . . drop the stuff down. Spread it from the air?

[Laughter]

The scene switches to a mechanic fixing a tractor. He talks about how everyone had employment problems at the time, how they were restless, and how everything was "crook." He talks about how a chance meeting in a bar changed his life. Over a beer with a man in military uniform, he agreed to go see "how things are set up in peacetime." The mechanic, who turns out to be a former member of the air force, traveled to a base where the air force was "making a test for the soil conservation boys.... Apparently, some bloke thought that fertilizer could be spread from a plane. And he'd persuaded the council to take a gamble. And he'd risked six hundred quid to prove it." The council put their faith in getting phosphate onto the hill country, and an engineer explains: "We rigged up this hopper, and we're putting it into the bomber so we can get the stuff up into the air."

In September 1948, agricultural scientists working closely with the air force successfully developed a method of delivering phosphate fertilizer to previously inaccessible lands in the New Zealand hill country. The aerial topdressing industry began with old Tiger Moth planes and former World War II fighter pilots delivering some sixty tons of phosphate a day across thousands of acres.[6] Soon it was possible to deliver half a million tons a year to over four million acres of farmland, using a low-flying method that followed the contours of the hills to give an even spread. The mass distribution of fertilizer not only created vegetation on previously eroding lands but dramatically escalated the levels of production for New Zealand sheep and cattle farms. Aerial farming rapidly became big business.

Since I had first encountered the BPC images in the Melbourne Archives I had been thinking about a visual project that would juxtapose images of mining on Banaba with farming in both New Zealand and Australia. Geoff Park, a senior staff member at the Museum of New Zealand Te Papa Tongarewa, pointed me in the direction of a man named Les Cleveland. Cleveland was a political scientist, photographer, and musician who had arranged a song called "The Phosphate Flyers" in 1956. The experiences of the men who worked with phosphate in New Zealand are comparable to those of the men who worked in the mines.[7] While they were spatially different, both kinds of work were very dangerous. The men who worked in the topdressing industry distributed the phosphate while flying above the earth, while the men on Banaba who extracted it worked up to a hundred feet inside it. Both types of laborers were involved in transforming lands that belonged to indigenous peoples, whose lives were irrevocably disturbed and transformed by British subjects.

According to Geoff Park, "The Phosphate Flyers" was a very "blokey" (or macho) song, which he remembered listening to on the radio as a child. Les Cleveland wrote to me to say that he had arranged the music for a song written by a New Zealand poet called Joe Charles. In the 1950s, they had worked together on a series of radio presentations that included Charles's poetry. Cleveland and Charles had compiled rural folk songs, and some of these had been turned into popular national ballads.[8] It is worth reproducing most of Cleveland's letter to me, which included the lyrics of the song:[9]

> I enclose the text of "The Phosphate Flyers" as sung on the recording.... It relates to the early phase of aerial topdressing in NZ when a lot of ex wartime pilots were earning a precarious living in backcountry flying.... A hopper was inserted in the back seat to hold a load of phosphate. The pilot flew low over the hillside under treatment and released the stuff at the right moment. A similar technique was used for crop dusting. Later, Cessna aircraft were used. A network of airstrips was established in the NZ hill country and used for fertiliser dropping as well as for venison recovery. This involved picking up deer carcasses shot by meat hunters and flying them to locations where they could be processed for export. I once shared the cabin of a Cessna with the pilot, seven deer and my rifle and pack. Takeoffs were the most exciting part as we were seriously overloaded.
>
> The song can be understood as a piece of occupational folklore which describes the dangers inherent in this kind of flying. (There was a considerable accident rate). Hence "The Phosphate Flyers" is a cautionary tale about the risks of sitting close to a petrol tank with an engine up front and a load of superphosphate behind you. But it is also a tribute to the occupational skills required in this high-risk activity with its anticipatory reference to space travel.

The Phosphate Flyers

I was drinking beer in Sullivan's bar
With a chap called Black Billy Joe,
Just listening to the gas and gab
Of the boys just back from the show.
A lanky leathery sheepman,
With a voice both loud and coarse,
Said, I saw the whole darned outfit,
But I never saw one horse!

A lot of hacks and ponies
Bred for show and sport,
But a horse, with guts and gallop
There wasn't a likely sort.
And the riders? Well I ask you!
You should have seen the sights—
With fancy pants and bowler hats,
Bow ties and all that skite.

Where are the boys they used to breed,
That like their horses rough?
A moke that couldn't buck them off
They thought was ladies' stuff.
Here Black Billy Joe stuck in his oar,

He used to be a Jock once—
A bullock-busting side showman
Who knew the buck-jump stunts.

He said, I've ridden some horses
And a few bad bulls beside,
But I'll tell you chaps there's just one thing,
One thing, I'll never ride;
And that's these aerial topdressing planes—
The modern youngster's hack—
You wouldn't chase me into them
With a shotgun up my back.

I tell you, chaps, it takes a man
To be a phosphate flyer!
I don't like these blessed hencoops
Made of calico and wire,
You can't get in the flaming things
Without a mighty squeeze
Sitting on a petrol tank
With an engine up your knees,

And half a ton of "super"
Sitting bang right on your neck.
You don't find enough to fill a sack
When the boys have a wreck!
And the way they throw things about—
It makes you dizzy to look,
They make a spry young sparrow-hawk
Look like a barnyard chook!

And another thing I'll tell you—
And you know you can't deny—
If ever those brilliant scientists
Make a rocket that you can fly,
And shoot it up to the moon and back,
Or twice as ruddy far,
There'll be more young bucks to fly it
Than flies around this bar.[10]

"Britain's Outlying Farm"

The film *Land from the Sky,* which features many of these phosphate flyers, was a reenactment of the 1948 topdressing innovations and was filmed for public broadcast on New Zealand television. Since British settlement from the 1840s, agriculture was the most important political and economic focus of New Zealand's development. In a collection called *Environmental Histories of New Zealand,* the chapter "The Grasslands Revolution Revisited" by Tom Brooking, Robin Hodge, and Vaughan Wood features a poster from a 1946 edition of the *New Zealand Journal of Agriculture* that, in their words, characterizes New Zealand as "Britain's Outlying Farm."[11]

It is hard today to imagine New Zealand as anything other than green and fertile. This fecund New Zealand is the centerpiece of the nation-state's global branding, making it an ideal choice for eco-friendly tourism, rugby World Cup matches, and the "middle earth" setting of Peter Jackson's *Lord of the Rings* trilogy (2001–2003). But the early British settlers actually found the landscape not so green and quite hostile to their constant domesticating efforts. Holland, O'Connor, and Wearing write: "Away from the Canterbury Plains, there was little soil ready for the plough, and in many parts of the colony wetlands, dense forests, fast-flowing rivers, steep hill and mountain country, and unseasonal weather compounded settlers' difficulties."[12] Due to the availability of capital and livestock, New Zealand was seen to be suitable for wool production, and there was a constant search for more suitable pastoral land. The New Zealand landscape and climate, like the *Māori*, were seen to be wild, and so early colonists did their best to transform their settlements into tranquil gardens, or "Edens in the Antipodes," bringing in new "trees and shrubs, herbs and grasses, flowers and vegetables, birds and mammals . . . insects and fish" from their temperate origins.[13] According to Holland, O'Connor, and Wearing, by 1860 there were 2.5 million sheep, and the grazing preferences of the livestock dominated settlers' approaches to the land.[14] This had a devastating effect on the native ecosystem. It is in this harsh New Zealand context that individuals such as Albert Ellis and many other key movers and shakers in the phosphate industry were bred.

The founder of New Zealand's Reform Party, William Massey, also known as "Farmer Bill," who served as prime minister from 1912 to 1925, was key to securing Ocean Island and Nauru phosphate for his country.[15] He was a conservative who supported farmers and rural development, but clashed with miners and waterfront workers. Massey University, with three campuses in Palmerston North, Auckland, and Wellington, is named after him and originally had a focus on agricultural science. It is no coincidence that Barrie Macdonald, who has been prolific on the politics of phosphate and New Zealand–Pacific relations, taught there for many years.

In a 1962 tribute to the Pacific phosphate mining industry, B. E. Talboys, then minister for agriculture in New Zealand, wrote:

Phosphate has always been New Zealand's most widely used fertiliser. Our dependence on phosphatic fertilisers is such that only in a few areas can crops or pastures be grown without them. It is impossible to estimate where our agricultural economy would be today without the use of phosphate to augment

soil fertility. Certainly livestock farming based on grassland, as we have it in New Zealand, would not have developed so rapidly or so intensively without this vital aid.[16]

In spite of the fact that the majority of the populations of New Zealand and Australia have been urban and coastal since the advent of British colonialism, agriculture and relations with the landscape are still central to their national identities. The ideal Antipodeans are very "blokey battlers," doing it tough and persevering in a challenging, usually rural environment. The 1840 Treaty of Waitangi, New Zealand's founding charter, which lays out a set of agreements between the British Crown and *Māori* tribes, foregrounds these relations to land. While there are clashing interpretations of the treaty, with *Māori* in particular arguing that their rights are rarely honored, it sets the terms of reference for New Zealand as a bicultural nation.[17] This bicultural element is integrated structurally in many contexts, including education, health, government, media, and everyday language. Most businesses and public radio and television have a policy of using basic Māori phrases and greetings, such as *kia ora,* which can mean several things, including "hello" and "be well." More recent migrants to New Zealand, including Asians and Pacific Islanders, must position themselves politically and socially with respect to this bicultural code, even though it is unevenly honored and even though *Māori* still struggle for their cultural, land, and water rights.[18]

Tributes to agricultural history are visible in key New Zealand public institutions, including galleries and museums. For many years, the Museum of New Zealand Te Papa Tongarewa in the capital city of Wellington enshrined farming in the form of a permanent exhibition called *On the Sheep's Back.* This emphasizes that the story of agriculture usually begins with sheep, cattle, and farmer, rather than with the land or soil. Figures such as Albert Ellis, the New Zealand phosphate commissioner from 1920 to 1951, who constantly focused on the soil, have faded from the landscape of New Zealand history. An avid writer who regularly disseminated his views, Ellis maintained a consistent focus on phosphate as the solution to all farming woes:

As an instance of what has happened with great numbers of farms we may turn to the pumice area where only a few years ago many thousands of acres were considered useless for farming, the soil being singularly deficient in humus and stock liable to "bush sickness." The same area now contains hundreds of prosperous dairy farms, and there is still ample scope for further development. Briefly, the transformation process is to clear and plough the land and then give it a heavy dressing of superphosphate, about nine cwt. per acre. This speedily develops a remarkable growth of clover, which in its turn stimulates useful grasses. The land is then ready for the dairy herds, and its occupation combined with annual topdressing result in a comparatively rapid development of humus. It is doubtful if the dominion's pastures ever looked as well as they did last season.[19]

While the iconography of aerial topdressing is a key symbol of agricultural heritage, the fertilizer that regrew and multiplied farm productivity is viewed as but one of many factors, rather than the primary one, as it was in the minds of the phosphateers. Furthermore, the histories of the source Pacific nations are seen as tangential and mostly irrelevant. However, compared with Australia, New Zealand provides far more details to the public on the centrality of phosphate through a number of sources, such as a permanent video and costume exhibition in the Museum of New Zealand Te Papa Tongarewa (featuring aspects of my research) and an online education resource funded by the government, *Te Ara: The Encyclopedia of New Zealand*.[20]

Over half of the main themes of the encyclopedia are engaged with the land and sea, and every theme foregrounds a *Māori* perspective. In a section called "The Settled Landscape," readers can learn how the first Polynesian settlers brought their own new crops, such as kumara (sweet potato), taro, and yam. Rongo, or Rongomatane, was the god of agriculture and protector of crops, as well as the god of peace.[21] These *Māori* histories are compared with those brought by the *pakeha*, or white settlers. Sydney Parkinson, an artist on Captain James Cook's voyage to New Zealand, remarked in 1769: "The country about the bay is agreeable beyond description, and, with proper cultivation, might be rendered a kind of second Paradise."[22] The cultivated rural landscape, "a middle landscape," not unlike Tolkien's "middle earth," was the ideal choice between the European city and the barbaric bush.

In several sections authored by Arthur Duncan, the encyclopedia website brilliantly tracks the origins of phosphate from animal bones and sedimented rock, detailing its transformation with sulfuric acid to superphosphate. As long as the soil has enough water, the fertilizer "increases the strike rate of seedlings, stimulates root development and flowering, and improves plant growth."[23] Compared with many countries in the world that now rely on nitrogen-based fertilizers, New Zealand, due to the nature of its soil and its deficiencies in both sulfur and phosphorus, continues to consume superphosphate in significant quantities.

The significance of phosphate for the agricultural development of both Australia and New Zealand cannot be understated, but while it was an important building block, the shifting political and economic priorities and the nature of the global phosphate trade point to the risks inherent in depending on such a commodity. In 1962, Talboys wrote:

> The superphosphate that we manufacture locally from Nauru and Ocean Islands rock phosphate accounts for 90 percent of the total fertilisers used in New Zealand. When this supply was cut at the source during the Second World War, New Zealand was reminded sharply and unpleasantly of her reliance on Nauru and Ocean Islands. Because our primary industry is so closely linked with our national welfare, the whole nation, and not just our soil, was affected by this threatened phosphate famine.[24]

Unfortunately, as on Banaba, the intensive use of fertilizer in New Zealand has also damaged the environment, contributing to widespread erosion and the pollution of waterways in some areas. One source describes it as an "ecological disaster."[25]

The manner in which their land and its transformation into fertilizer in other countries is imagined by Banabans is signaled in a reflection by a member of the Banaban Dancing Group, which visited Rotorua, New Zealand, in 1976 when a Rabi contingent was included in the Festival of Pacific Arts, a regional gathering of Pacific nations, states, and territories to celebrate traditional culture and the arts. Kaiao Borerei wrote: "While on a bus trip through the nearby countryside, we saw an aerial topdressing plane putting fertiliser onto a farm. The bus driver told us it was superphosphate from Ocean Island and that made us feel sad and stirred our hearts. It seems that some of Banaba is in New Zealand."[26]

The Better Farming Train

As phosphate was being distributed across the New Zealand hill country by air, the Better Farming Train was traveling along a vast complex of rail tracks, distributing jute sacks of phosphate across Australia by steam. In the 1920s a new rural education initiative received wide press: "There will be no mistaking the 'Better Farming' special train when it leaves Melbourne for a tour of Gippsland on Monday. Painted a bright yellow, the train carries its name in bold black letters along the sides of two carriages. It was being assembled yesterday in the Jolimont yards."[27]

According to the Victoria Department of Primary Industries, the Better Farming Train steamed out of Melbourne for the first time in October 1924 bound for Gippsland in the very eastern corner of the state.[28] The train operated within Victoria, and at the time and for years later the states had incongruent tracks, which greatly hampered interstate rail services, including the transportation of phosphate and processed superphosphate. New South Wales adopted the European standard gauge of 1435 mm, Victoria and South Australia built with the broad Irish gauge of 1600 mm, and Tasmania, Queensland, Western Australia, and parts of South Australia used the narrow 1067 mm gauge.[29] A former Ocean Island resident commissioner, Edward Eliot, wrote in his 1938 memoir: "The Australian railways are still the laughing stock of the world."[30]

The Better Farming Train, however, was impressive. Its engine towed fifteen carriages, which were painted bright orange, not yellow. Each carriage was fitted out with agricultural displays: pigs, cows, poultry, bees, dairy utensils, potatoes, bacon, tobacco, manure, fodder, and pasture samples. The train also carried a range of "expert lecturers" to speak about the displays. This public education scheme was developed in cooperation with the Departments of Agriculture, Railways, Education, and Public Health and aimed at improving farming techniques and raising agricultural production. The train made at least thirty-eight tours of rural Victoria between 1924 and 1935, and each tour visited ten regional centers, with one day spent at each center. Upon arrival at a station, the train was prepared

See the
BETTER FARMING TRAIN

at

A WONDERFUL EXHIBITION ACCOMPANIED BY EXPERTS
TO HELP THE FARMER, — AND LADY DEMONSTRATORS
IN HOUSEHOLD AFFAIRS TO ASSIST THE FARMER'S WIFE.

INCREASED PRODUCTION, REDUCED COSTS, FARM EFFICIENCY, IMPROVED STOCK.

VIC. RLYS.   Poster No.154.

"See the Better Farming Train," ca. 1935. Copyright Percy Trompf
Artistic Trust. Courtesy of the Josef Lebovic Gallery

for exhibition: cattle were walked out into the yard; the sides of the pig truck were let down to enable farmers to view the animals; pasture plots were lowered to the platform; and the display carriages were opened to the public.[31] A series of lectures on subjects relevant to the area were then conducted:

> Demonstrators showed how superphosphate could improve pastures. Lecturers discussed varieties, diseases and cultivation of tobacco and potatoes. In Gippsland, dairy officers demonstrated milk testing. A popular display in most centres was the "women's branch." Lectures and demonstrations were given about infant welfare, cooking and clothing design. Mothers brought babies for examination by the nurse. "A box of samples including aprons, knitted frocks, embroidery and riding pants aroused a great deal of interest" as did demonstrations of "simple cooking with special consideration to dried fruits, soups, casseroles, re-cooked meats and pastry making."[32]

It was reported that between five hundred and two thousand farmers and townspeople attended the exhibitions at each center. The train thus served as a traveling agricultural and home economics school, an "experimental farm on wheels and a chance for a day out."[33] It was presented as a novelty and a spectacle and attracted many people who might not otherwise be interested in attending lectures or courses. "So eager was one woman in Gippsland to view the train that she rose at 3.30 AM in order to milk the cows and get the children ready. She then drove over thirty miles to visit the Better Farming Train."[34]

In her novel *Everyman's Rules for Scientific Living,* Carrie Tiffany writes about life aboard the Better Farming Train as it wound its way around Victoria in the 1930s. The men tell farmers about new, better, scientific ways to increase their production, and the women tell wives how to become better home economists. Aboard this train is Tiffany's protagonist, Mr. Petergree, an expert in superphosphate. He is able to tell any man exactly where a sample of soil comes from by tasting it. Many challenge his skills, but he can identify a sample even when he is totally drunk and when the soil has been mixed with foreign elements to trick him.

Tiffany's narrator and soon to be the wife of Mr. Petergree, Jean Finnegan, says:

> The soil and cropping wagon is a relief. It has been newly added to the train for our tour into the wheat growing districts of Victoria. The wagon's glass-roofed—all sunlight and air and waving plants, a greenhouse on rails. We walk down the aisles as if down the middle of a field parted by God. The wheat in the good field on the left is tall and vigorous, the stems reaching out to touch our skirts; on the right just a few dry sticks poke from the soil.
> *The soil is hungry for phosphate—use SUPERPHOSPHATE,* says the sign. There can be no doubting the magic of it.
>
> Mary Maloney explained superphosphate to me like this: "It's an earth mineral, a powdered earth mineral, the best ever discovered, and it makes you light up."

"How do you mean?"

"Well . . ." Mary's words were unsteady. "I'm just telling what I heard, not what I've seen, but when you touch it in the sack or on the ground it makes you glow like there's a light inside you. Dad heard of a bloke down at Drouin who spread it in the morning and woke up in the night with his hands all alight. They found him in the dam next morning, stiff with cold."

Sister Crock said his death was clearly a case of poor farm hygiene. But I rolled the strange new word around on my tongue—superphosphate, super-phosphate, superphosphate.[35]

Even in the agricultural context, supposedly governed by scientific and prag-matic principles, superphosphate took on a mythical quality, especially for rural communities. Ellis and others in the New Zealand context certainly walked a fine line between science and magic when lauding the power of superphosphate to transform previously "unproductive" lands. Australian newspapers were con-stantly likening it to gold and praising its extraordinary qualities. A monograph on phosphorus produced by the Centre for Resource and Environmental Studies at the Australian National University in Canberra unequivocally stated in its in-troduction: "Superphosphate might as well be termed the magic dust of Austra-lian agriculture."[36]

In Tiffany's novel, however, the application of superphosphate does not do much for the drought-stricken country, and the farmers end up losing everything, along with their faith in science. Australia, like Banaba, is regularly prone to pe-riods of devastating drought. When I moved to Canberra from the United States in 2007, there were vigorously patroled water restrictions in the eastern and south-ern states on everything from gardening to washing your car. Many houses dis-played signs that said "tank water in use" or similar so their neighbors would not report them for water infringements. Having your own backyard pool was not something envied but was frowned upon. Many households in Victoria intro-duced miniature hourglasses that you could hang over your door to keep time for a three-minute shower. Ironically, water in Australia, similar to Banaba, is the real factor defining survival.

In the service of further proposed technological innovations, the Better Farm-ing Train made another brief appearance in print in the July 20, 1939, issue of the *Argus*. Above an ad for bottles of Pimm's Cup, it stated:

There was no reason why the State Electricity Commission should not have a carriage on the Better Farming train to advocate the use of electricity on farms, said Mr. N. C. Harries, one of the Railways Commissioners, yesterday. The train which was operated by the Railways Department in conjunction with the Agricultural Department, had, unfortunately, not run since 1937, and no plans for its future operation had yet been considered because of the depart-ment's financial position.

Although the train ceased operation, by 1940 the industry was humming along with other new and exciting developments. That year, the BPC constructed a new office block at 515 Collins Street in Melbourne. The building with the inspired name, "Phosphate House," was designed by Rae Featherstone, who later became the first staff architect at the University of Melbourne, and was the subject of many an architectural magazine story, apparently a perfect example of the new, modern, art deco style.[37] In time, 515 Collins Street became a focal point of agricultural business, housing livestock marketers such as Macarthur and Macleod Pty., Ltd., and, most significantly, the Australian Dairy Produce Board and the Victoria section of the Australian Wheat Board. Macarthur and Macleod would regularly post reports on sheep sales, highlighting the recent market movement in "fat sheep," "fat lambs," and "store sheep."[38]

When I spoke to farmers from Burrumbuttock—a farming region of New South Wales just north of Victoria—about superphosphate decades after the Pacific supplies had ceased, the heyday of farming had similarly diminished and there was far less mystique around the fertilizer. The farmers, one of whom was in his seventies, recalled the trips to the station to pick up their jute sacks of phosphate, sacks, they remarked, that "probably came from Bangladesh," and they especially recalled how in the early days "the stuff would get all over our hands and we'd have to throw the sacks in the dam to clean them out."[39] The price of the fertilizer, usually called "super" for short, was the key factor. Farmers are always thinking about their inputs with respect to their yield and costs. Regular use of fertilizer is one of those inputs, and an agricultural scientist from the Commonwealth Scientific and Industrial Research Organization, Richard Simpson, emphasized to me that this was an economic and lifestyle choice for farmers.[40] Not everyone is keen to have farms running at maximum output because that requires extra labor and hours that some farming families cannot sustain. Some smaller farms run on other principles, such as biodynamics and organic farming, which are increasingly popular models today, and these farms would never use industrially processed superphosphate, though they might use guano.

The stories of the phosphate flyers, the Better Farming Train, and rural development concerns in twentieth-century New Zealand and Australia are little windows into the developmentalist manner in which nation-states come into being. At some point farming was the norm, but now the majority of Antipodeans purchase their food from supermarkets, where an endless chain of commodities seems to magically appear. New Zealand was one of the first countries to mainstream economic neoliberalism and is widely seen, outside of New Zealand, to be a beautiful, peaceful, and uncontroversial nation. Australia is today one of the most politically and financially successful and stable countries in the world, with one of its claims to fame being how well it not just survived but thrived during the global financial crisis of 2008. And still, while electricity did eventually reach

Phosphate House on Collins Street, Melbourne, 1940.
Courtesy of the National Archives of Australia

most parts of inhabited Australia, there is now the same concern about national-izing the broadband network and, particularly, getting the rural regions onto the internet grid. Years from now, some other idea, some other must-have mineral, fertilizer, or technology will capture the imagination of politicians, scientists, and businessmen (or women) and become an all-consuming enterprise. More than likely, there will be losers in the scramble for these things.

Kainga Tahi, Kainga Rua (First Home, Second Home)

Banaba is now fragmented across time and space with the accumulation of most of its fragments, at least in the short term as far as geological time goes, in the lands and waterways of Australia and New Zealand. This pushed me to consider what this history would mean to indigenous Māori or Aboriginal Australian communities. With some important variations across tribes and clans, indigenous epistemologies in both countries outline deep spiritual connections to either Papatuanuku (Earth Mother) in New Zealand or "the Dreaming" in Australia.[41] Both Papatuanuku and the Dreaming are not just fixed places or spaces but dynamic complexes that include people, animals, spiritual beings, ancestors, landscapes, and the relationships between all these things in deep time. So I wondered what knowledge of other indigenous lands, similarly imbued with complex relations, would mean in twenty-first-century Oceania.

In 2003 the renowned Māori sculptor Brett Graham created a multimedia installation based on my research exploring Banaba's connection to Aotearoa/New Zealand. Kainga Tahi, Kainga Rua, or "First Home, Second Home," commented on three central aspects of the Banaba experience: the loss of land through mass industrial extraction, the dominance of the island landscape by Western technology, and the political, economic, and organic relationships between New Zealand and Banaba, since a good portion of the island has been scattered across New Zealand farms. Graham created ten stark white vessels covered in phosphate; each symbolized two million tons of shipped phosphate. Above these he suspended three rusted steel cylindrical forms representing the mining technology that carved up the island and now remains in a decayed and decrepit state. Projected onto the steel were two sets of images from the visual portion of my work, one depicting a metal grab excavating the side of a rock face and the other showing the Banaban Dancing Group on Rabi retelling their history through song and dance.[42] The third image was a loop of a crop-dusting plane taking off and soaring over the New Zealand hill country.

In addition to engaging various phosphate histories, what was important about this exhibition was that it highlighted the many groups, cultures, lands, and nations that were transformed by the existence of Banaba and the activities of the mining company. Banaba was central, not peripheral, to the development of one of the most powerful settler colonies in the South Pacific, and the New Zealand landscape today is a "second home" to Banaban land and, by association, Banaban bodies. Graham's artwork captured both the political and poetic resonances between the past and present and the very material and organic forms in which such resonances are embedded.[43]

While historical, social, economic, and cultural issues in New Zealand today are regularly framed by the politics of biculturalism between Māori and pakeha, the Banaban phosphate history temporarily disrupts this binary and provokes questions about the connections between people and land as the basis for indigeneity. Who belongs to the Banaban soil that was dispersed across the New Zealand landscape? Could Banabans come to New Zealand or Australia and feel "at home"? Is indigeneity simply an imagined connection to land located in a specific place, space, and environment, or is there an inherent "organic" relationship between peoples and their ancestral homelands? Such questions have specific consequences for any Banabans who might seek resident status in New Zealand, where indigenous systems of land tenure and social organization are occasionally honored on the basis of an alternative ontological interpretation of the law.

The celebrated Guyanian author Wilson Harris has written convincingly about "fossil identities" for which memory exists within all people of their ancestral forebears.[44] Such memories are triggered by specific events in which all things appear to "magically" connect to a deeply inhabited past. Such ideas similarly permeate the work of African American writer Toni Morrison for whom memory is not just what one remembers today but the potentially visible and audible trace of something that actually happened in the past, in a specific place.[45]

While indigenous epistemology usually asserts the integral connections between bodies, lands, practices, identities, and spiritual beliefs, further exploring this possibility becomes problematic in an age in which indigeneity is also defined with respect to an unchanging sense of "tradition" or "the past," to political relations with a dominant and often alienating state, or to separatist nationalisms that assert difference based on essentialist notions of belonging or identity.[46] Some aspects of Banaban and other indigenous nationalisms take on these forms. It behooves us to pay close attention to the material and symbolic nature of imperial formations and resistances that destroy or sustain indigenous connections to both people and place.

An approach to indigeneity that is conscious of the historically contingent construction of physical, cultural, ethnic, or national boundaries allows us to better articulate and strategize for political and economic struggles in the present or future. But in what forms should temporally and spatially extended indigenous relationships take place? A Banaban may no longer be consciously connected to the bits of phosphate from Banaba that now so effectively fertilize the algae that clog and choke New Zealand rivers and streams. Or is she? Do we as indigenous peoples, whether of New Zealand, Australia, Banaba, or Rabi, just imagine we are connected to land, or are we connected in a corporeal sense? Do the journeys of phosphate rock parallel those of the Banaban people in their struggle to make meaning in new homes? Do Banabans and Nauruans have specific relationships with Aboriginal Australian and Māori populations, or for that matter, to Australians and New Zealanders in general, because of the agricultural integration of their islands into those landscapes? Or does the sheer weight of contemporary indigenous struggles and ongoing injustices in both countries dwarf the relevance of such lines of inquiry?

Kainga Tahi, Kainga Rua by Brett Graham. Courtesy of the Adam Art Gallery

The struggle for Banaban rights has primarily been rooted in Banaba, the homeland that still exists in the middle of the Pacific Ocean, but not always in the Banaba that disappeared into the lands and rivers of Australia and New Zealand.[47] If what James Clifford writes is true and "diaspora exists in practical, and at times, principled tension with nativist identity formations,"[48] it is the diaspora of the displaced people *and* the scattered lands that provides this tension. Clifford has further explored this in "Indigenous Articulations," where he suggests a rethinking of indigeneity and the indigenous *longue durée,* "the precolonial space and time that tends to be lost in postcolonial projections," together with transformation, movement, and diasporism.[49] I believe that understanding such transformation and movement needs to go beyond anthropocentric approaches and, in our studies of the global, be highlighted with respect to peoples, commodities, and landscapes with multiscalar, relational, and temporal depth.

The land *is* the people, *is* the money, *is* the superphosphate, *is* the farm, *is* the grain, *is* the cattle, *is* the development, enrichment, and pollution or destruction of lands, seas, and the numerous forms of life dependent upon them. As exciting or seemingly disorderly as global connection or complexity might be in theory, the never-ending connections take us along a spiraling, not linear, journey where the present eternally devours the past.[50]

6 Interlude
Another Visit to Ocean Island

THE FIRST TIME I visited Kiribati, in 1997, I stayed at the Otintaai (Rising Sun) Hotel in Tarawa for five days before my father, John Teaiwa, and I made a trip to Banaba. Our vessel was small and so laden with food, people, chickens, puppies, ducks, and motorbikes that the predicted one-and-a-half-day journey took two nights and three days. The ocean on the equatorial belt is relatively calm, and most of the time I lay with my feet above my head on a pile of mats with my ear to the back of a mother nursing her newborn baby. I survived stubbornly on a cup of water, three biscuits, and a mandarin orange a day. Finally, the rock of Banaba appeared on the horizon. It looked like the gentle hump of a great turtle floating on the ocean, and I was indescribably thankful to see it. Most important, from a distance it appeared green and not like the lunarscape that I'd imagined.

The two main political factions—Banaban caretaker families from Rabi on one side, and Gilbertese government workers on the other—were not speaking to each other. There were effectively two kinds of authority dividing the three hundred or so residents, so we had an official welcome from each one. Each expressed bitter sentiments rooted in the political clashes between Banabans and Gilbertese on the island that had turned violent decades earlier when the BPC was still working the mines. One meeting was conducted in the main mwaneaba near the Homebay Harbor and the other at the Catholic mwaneaba in Fatima. Teaiwa, the newly elected Banaban Council chairman, was there to help negotiate the conflict, and he did seem to make some progress over the numerous bowls of Rabi kava consumed every night. I kept to myself most of the time and enjoyed meeting my uncle and his wife and children. I noted in amusement that the nightly ritual consisted of the viewing of Fiji One television programs on VHS cassettes. Back in Suva, the West was streamed into our living rooms via the local pirated-video industry of Australian and New Zealand television shows, and here was Banaba 1,600 miles away, feeding its imagination on Fijian TV programs, replete with advertisements for goods that no one could buy.

We were accommodated upstairs in Albert Ellis's once-comfortable home. It was now a dilapidated colonial-style mansion on the side of a hill above the phosphate processing plant. At first I was in awe of the structure with its picturesque balconies and ceiling-to-floor windows, but it soon took on the quality of something out of a horror movie.

There was a tennis court outside, strangled by weeds, with a huge water tank above it. A tree with a trunk as wide as I was tall lay severed in front of the court. I would sit on the first-floor balcony every morning, writing in my little notebook, with that dead tree in front of me. Usually, one of the three women hosting us would bring a pot of tea, and we would sip it dutifully in the heat. The kitchen was straight out of a Jane Austen novel with a massive fireplace and a large kettle always on the boil. Rare flush toilets with mysterious dark bowls, and no water or seats, featured in each of the four bathrooms throughout the house. A winding wooden staircase extended from the first to second floors, rotting and groaning in many places. The house was free of furniture, save for our beds and a few mats. There were numerous ceiling fans, countless electrical outlets, and not a drop of power.

Every night one benzene and two kerosene lamps were lit for ten very large rooms. I never appreciated modern technology more than in those five nights in Ellis's old house. I was terrified of the place, was certain I could hear voices in the dark, and longed to stay with my uncle and his family in the workers' quarters down by the harbor. Dad got rather irritated with me as I stayed awake every night, waving a flashlight and jumping at every cockroach and rat, and there were many, that dared to peep. I cheered myself up in those sleepless hours by laughing at how staunch I was on indigenous ways of knowing when I was at university. Dad said that I should not be afraid because the rats were my ancestors coming to visit. He wasn't joking, but in my sleep-deprived state I didn't fully appreciate this interpretation of events.

Banaba was, on the surface, a rather depressing place. The Company had stopped work in 1981 and left an entire mining town behind. Huge processing and storage sheds housed piles of broken glass, wire, iron, steel, and wood that residents casually strolled through. Wrecked trucks, tractors, bulldozers, and graders littered the roads, which were lined with electricity-free power lines and poles. There were no windows or doors in most of the old rows of laborers' quarters, and the outdoor movie projectors so fondly remembered by Banaban elders lay rusted and dilapidated in the sun. The atmosphere of the place was almost thoughtful, in that people did not often laugh or smile, but did not exactly look sad either. According to BPC and British projections, Banaba would have been barren and unlivable by now, but there was an abundance of fruits, vegetables, and root crops available, and I was impressed with every meal we were given. Things were growing in whatever was left of the phosphate-rich soil.

On the fourth day of our visit my uncle Eritai, accompanied by three men from the boat, came to collect me. We were going to visit a bwangabwanga, an underground freshwater cave. Being mildly claustrophobic I was excited but nervous and almost talked him out of it. We hired the only passenger vehicle available and drove as far as possible into the center of the island. We then walked through the bush, around or across massive jagged pinnacles of limestone, passing lumps of phosphate rock, and through some rather dangerous plant life. Finally we reached a deep hole in the ground. The men lit a benzene lamp, and we made our way down a rusted ladder into the darkness.

We emerged at the mouth of an immense cave with stalactites twinkling in the light of the lamp. The rock was a deep golden brown with streaks of amber, copper, and iron gray. We walked across the cave and made our way farther down into a water-filled passage where we waded, swam, crawled, and slithered for three hours, sometimes through openings that couldn't have been more than eighteen inches wide. I saw lines of pipes, said to have been laid by the occupying Japanese forces in the 1940s, and words like "Takei was hia 1993" marked on the walls. The water was refreshing, very cold, but I did not shiver. I knew I was in a special place with so much significance, a realm that had once been exclusively for women and the only source of fresh water for countless generations of Banabans. It was exhilarating. I slept much better that night, after giving my uncle the fishhook necklace that I'd worn throughout college. All the original Banaban fishhooks, long admired by Europeans, had been made from bwangabwanga stalactites.

On Friday night it was time to leave, and we made our way down to the harbor where our boat was supposed to be waiting. But the vessel was just a flashing light far out in the ocean because the captain was finding it difficult to sail into the harbor. They decided we should take smaller boats to reach the ship, so we sat on the dock while people scrambled around soliciting outboard motors, hose pipes, fuel, containers for bailing water, spark plugs, and other essential items. I passed the time with my cousins by flashing signals to the vessel with our little flashlights. It would sail in as close as possible to the harbor, shut off the engine, and promptly get dragged back out to sea by the current, over and over again. We watched this back-and-forth ballet for four hours until the boats were ready. Later, thinking about this experience, I understood better the vast amount of correspondence by the Company over how best to transport the rock and to moor and secure hundreds of cargo ships within adequate reach of the Banaba shore. With no nearby land mass to break the force of the waves that crash upon the fringing reef, there is nothing simple about any attempted arrival or departure on this island.

When the logistics were finally sorted, we were transported out of the harbor by some local navigators, who seemed to know their way quite well through the pitch black. I half-scrambled, half-crawled aboard the waiting vessel after balancing precariously on the bobbing motorboat and holding on for dear life to any projecting piece of the ship. We were traveling much lighter, so the journey back to Tarawa took only a day and a half. For me, the "homeland" had been slightly demystified.

Three years later, after completing archival research and getting a much better sense of the phosphate industry itself, I prepared to return to the island on a catamaran named *Martha*, chartered from the Bahai community on Tarawa. To

Bwangabwanga (water caves) on Banaba, showing stalactites, April 2000.
Photo by Katerina Martina Teaiwa

subsidize my costs I put out a radio announcement for potential passengers and cargo for Banaba. I was surprised at how many had been waiting for weeks for an opportunity to return home. It seemed ironic that in the twenty-first century, transport to Banaba was rare given the immense amount of shipping activity between 1900 and 1980. At the wharf an I-Kiribati man inquired if it was my first trip. He warned me to be careful: "There are many angry spirits on the island, so don't try any magic. . . . Oh, you're Banaban? You'll be okay."

7 *E Kawa Te Aba*
The Trials of the Ocean Islanders

> When suffering knocks at your door and you say there is no seat for him, he
> tells you not to worry because he has brought his own stool.
>
> —Chinua Achebe, *Things Fall Apart*

Pity the Land, Pity the People

The motto of the Banaban Council of Leaders is *Atuara Buokira*, or Our God Help
Us. In this chapter I explore the historical context in which the motto of a community of five thousand or so Banabans became not *Nano Matoa* (Stand Strong), or
some such inspiring phrase, but rather a plea for God's help. I discuss the broader
conditions under which the Banabans' attempt to maintain a sense of independence and efficacy was systematically eroded by the agendas and interests of far
more powerful actors and decision makers in the British Empire.

During fieldwork I heard two expressions repeated regularly throughout the
course of a typical day on Rabi Island. If a child tripped and fell, someone would
say "e kawa te aba." If we were discussing the dramas of a family that had just
lost a beloved member, someone would say "e kawa ke?" And if we were discussing any aspect of Banaban history, throughout the conversation people would
repeat "e kawa te aba, kawa te aba" (the land and people are to be pitied). Elfriede
Hermann, in her exploration of the role of Banaban emotions in the context of
displacement from Ocean Island and self-placement on Rabi, describes the predominant theme of pity as a process of "eliciting pity for oneself as part of Banaba
(or as a member of the Banaban community) and thus for one's collective self . . .
divested of the fixation on individuality as conceived in western cultures."[1]

The phrase in practice means "pity the land and pity the people" conjointly,
and the ways in which it was relevant to almost every misfortune, from the mundane to the severe, including the contemporary and the historical, were at times
overwhelming. It would often be combined with another phrase: "ti rawata iroum"
(because of you, we are burdened). *Rawata* can refer to a burden, heaviness, or

intensity, or can mean "it's too much!" as yelled to us by a woman when our boat nudged hers in the middle of Tabiang Harbor.

Every December 15, and throughout the year for tourists from the South Pacific's premier luxury-adventure ship, *Tui Tai,* the Banabans of Rabi Island present a historical dance drama and sing the following song about pity, codeswitching between English and Gilbertese to punctuate the "pity" in the chorus.

I.

During the year 1900
there came there came on Ocean Island
Te Kambana ae te BPC
Ao an tanimai ao kareke matam
   te universe.
Ba te kun ae mainaina
te tia rabakau, ni kaminoa
   boon te phosphate
nakoia ake ngkoa!

During the year 1900
there came on Ocean Island
the company, the BPC.
Face and look this way universe.

At these clever white skins
confusing us with the price of
   phosphate,
and our ancestors of long ago!

II.

It gave its price the BPC
One pound note or 24 pennies?
They said, they said, they said
Ti tangira 24 pennies ba e plenty
   riki kanoana.
Ao an tanimai ao kare matam
tei Buritan o!
You really gave a bad result
nakoia students of Ocean Island.

It gave its price, the BPC.
One pound note or 24 pennies?
They said, they said, they said:
We want the 24 pennies it must
   have more value.
Face us and look this
way oh British!
You really gave a bad result for the
students of Ocean Island.

Chorus

How pity . . . how pity . . . Oh!
They misunderstood the value of
   money!
Our ancestors! *Ake ngkoa ngkoa.*

How pity . . . how pity . . . Oh!
They misunderstood the value of
   money!
Our ancestors! Of long, long ago.

III.

Oh gentlemen and Ten Tebuke
May God bless you till the end.
E matoatoa te case, be brave ni
   karokoa rekena.
Ao an tanimai ao kareke matam
   iaon abam.
Ba tia reimaurua ibuakon te iango
   e kakaoti

Oh gentlemen and Ten Tebuke
May God bless you till the end.
Your case is strong, be brave till
   you reach the goal.
Face this way to our homeland.

We are struggling with the ideas
and

ibuakon te nang ae almost dull.	emerging through the almost dull clouds.
Ao an oki mai ao kareke matam iaon abam	Come back and face our homeland.
Ba tia reimaurua i buakon te iango e kakaoti	We are struggling with the ideas and
ibuakon te nang ae almost dull.	emerging through the almost dull clouds.[2]

This song and the carefully choreographed drama that accompanies it reflect how the Banabans on Rabi, looking back to the late nineteenth century and the beginnings of mining in 1900, reconstructed and codified their history during a critical period of resistance and revitalization in the late 1960s.

The trials and tribulations of the Ocean Islanders are seen as commencing in 1900 with the confusing negotiations with Albert Ellis and his colleagues. When the two "chiefs," Temati and Kariatabewa, each placed his "X" on Ellis's contract, they would have had no idea what kind of agreement they were entering into, and certainly the actual landowners did not either. The island was divided up meticulously into individual land plots that were circulated among the population and passed to the next generation according to very specific transactions. Sometimes the plots were subdivided and other times they were amalgamated, but each Banaban adult knew exactly where the boundary lines were and the nature of the trees and shrubs on these plots. In his research on the Banaban struggle, August Ibrum Kumaniari Kituai cites a section of a report by a deputy commissioner of the Western Pacific, Arthur Mahaffy, on the matter of Banaban lands:

> I fear I may be considered as guilty of exaggeration when I state what is a well known fact and one which has been proved over and over again, namely, that the natives not only know the complicated limits of their lands thus perfectly, but also that, in the case where the land bears cocoanuts, they are able to identify the nuts from the trees growing on that land. I have seen this done on more than one occasion, the owner having picked out his own from a heap at a trader's station, and the native who had stolen them having confessed of the theft, because he knew that the owner was perfectly correct in his recognition of the stolen property.[3]

While the colonial administrators recognized that Islanders held intimate knowledge of their landscapes, they were not always convinced that the natives' intense attachment to place was justified. Thus when it came to matters of imposed British law and the agricultural needs of the Empire, native land tenure often became irrelevant. In March 1900, however, there was no drama over land as yet, and the Banabans assisted with the process by carrying and piling the valuable rocks for the prospectors. Seventy-eight tons of phosphate rock were shipped in November 1900, and by December 1,550 tons had left. In 1901, the engineer

"Elderly Native," Banaba, 1901. Courtesy of the National Archives of Australia

Moral economy (handwritten annotation)

Danvers Power had estimated about 12 million tons were available on Ocean Island and possibly more; he gave a slightly inaccurate estimate of the size of the island as 1,389 acres of which he claimed 99 acres were occupied by villages and food gardens, leaving 1,290 available for mining.[4] The Banabans could have had no idea the Company was mentally carving up their island, with little thought to what that actually meant for the indigenous population and their way of life.

Eroding Banaban Efficacy and Independence

The colonial and Company sanctions, restrictions, and ordinances placed on the Banabans between 1900 and 1942, when World War II reached the Pacific, allowed for the kind of order required to strategically acquire land as needed by the Company. They also helped to transform Banaban practices so that the people were increasingly reliant on the colonial administration, the Church, and the Company for their basic needs, including a new moral economy through which to interpret their rapidly changing world. They viewed the resident commissioner (RC), the representative of the British government in the colony, as someone whose primary role was their welfare, particularly when it came to phosphate mining matters. The Banabans became very close to many of the RCs and, as is customary with friends, had utter faith in their loyalty, believing it was impossible that such men would not act in the Banabans' best interests.

Harry Maude and Arthur Grimble in the 1920s and 1930s were able to gather knowledge of Gilbertese and Banaban customs and history because they were in the contrary position of being both government representative and "friend," if not "father." There were five main periods during which agreements between the Banabans and the Company, brokered usually by the British RC, were entered. There was first the very questionable agreement of May 1900, which did eventually raise alarm bells in the British Parliament. Agreements were then renegotiated under varying circumstances in 1909, 1913, 1931 (by force beginning in 1927), and 1947 after the Banabans had been removed to Rabi.

Ocean Island fell to the east and thus to the British side of a geopolitical line drawn in the middle of the ocean as dictated by the "Anglo-German" agreement of 1886. While the island was not formally included in any protectorate or colony, it was vaguely in the British sphere of influence—unbeknown, most likely, to every Pacific Islander on the ground. The Anglo-German line passed directly between Nauru and Ocean Island, with the former on the German side. When phosphate was discovered on Nauru, the Company had to include several Germans on the board and had a mix of German and British personnel on the ground.

Ocean Island had a rather different situation, and the first task of the chairman of the board of directors of the Pacific Islands Company, Lord Stanmore (Sir Arthur Gordon), who was also the former governor of Trinidad, Fiji, and New Zealand and thus very influential, was to secure a mining permit from the right authority. Stanmore managed some political gymnastics and got a license, but only after mining had already commenced by Ellis and his colleagues. This made for a sticky situation that the Company and its board of directors regularly attempted to hide from public scrutiny. How was it that the British government had the right to grant a license for mining on an island not formally and definitely not technically administered by the Western Pacific High Commission? Subsequent resident commissioners of the Gilbert and Ellice Islands, to which Banaba was hurriedly incorporated, including Captain John Quayle Dickson (1909–1913) and Edward Carlyon Eliot (1913–1920), challenged the British government and the Company on what they saw as a very raw deal for the Banabans. Dickson was demoted and Eliot brokered a new lease agreement but then later published a book called *Broken Atoms* where he outlined in detail the machinations of key business and political figures apropos Banaba. According to Eliot, by 1909 many questions about Ocean Island were being asked in the British Parliament.[5]

In addition to arguing for a trust fund to be established for the Banabans, Eliot regularly challenged the Company on the "two-price" system it had for Europeans and natives, including the Gilbert and Ellice Islander laborers. All had no choice but to purchase items from the one Company-run store, but the management would double and sometimes triple the price of goods for non-Europeans. Eliot saw this as scandalous and attempted several times to put in a strict one-price policy. He soon discovered that the real authority on the island was the Company and that certain folks in London had placed him there to work in support of the mining enterprise, rather than for the natives. For many in the colonial service this was viewed as a breach of their duty to generally work for the welfare of the colonial subjects.

While trying to intervene with their own form of justice and fairness, Eliot and Dickson, like Maude, Ellis, and most others, still viewed the Islanders as primitive and backward and therefore better off with, rather than without, "civilization." In addition to reorganizing kainga into villages and establishing a native council, or kaubure, the colonial authorities introduced "native ordinances" that placed certain restrictions on most aspects of Banaban social and spiritual life. Some of these were in accordance with missionary principles and ideas about sexuality, gender, and health. Most of the ordinances took a particularly restrictive approach to music, dance, and other kinds of performance, which would have drastically reduced the Banaban capacity to maintain aspects of their oral and embodied knowledge that were maintained and transmitted in those genres. Below is an example of some of these restrictions. To the right of the ordinances was a column listing the "penalty for non-observances," usually a fine between one and ten shillings.

Ocean Island

Island Regulations
Made Under Section 15(1) of Part I of the Schedule to the Native Laws Ordinance 1917
Approved English Version [1939]

No. 2
BURIALS
The dead shall be buried only in those cemeteries provided for the purpose.

No. 3
CRUELTY AND NEGLECT
1. Parents or guardians shall feed, clothe, and otherwise look after their children or adopted children in a proper manner.
2. All natives shall supply food, clothing, and all reasonable comforts to their aged parents or adoptive parents.
3. All cruelty to bird or beast is prohibited. Parents or guardians who condone such cruelty in their children will be punished.

No. 4
DANCING
1. No native shall be forced to dance.
2. Dancing shall take place only in village maneabas or on the Government station, or in such places as may be sanctioned by the Administrative Officer.
3. No native shall dance on Sundays or Public Holidays of a religious character.
4. Dancing is prohibited before 6 PM and after 10 PM except with the prior knowledge and consent of [a] European Government Officer or the Native Magistrate of the island.
5. No dancing shall take place in darkness.
6. It is forbidden to perform the Kabungiro and Kaeke [incantations] in the maneaba.
7. Words in dancing chants which directly or indirectly refer to sexual intercourse, and also all gestures and movements of the body which imitate the sexual act, are prohibited.
8. Words in dancing chants which bring any native or particular section of the community into public derision are prohibited.
9. Dancing rehearsals shall be allowed during daylight hours provided that the numbers of native participating therein does not exceed eight.

No. 6.
FEASTS
1. No feast shall last longer than one day without the prior knowledge and consent of a Kaubure [member of the island council].
2. Competitive feasts and the raising of competitive subscriptions of food or other gifts to strangers are forbidden.

No. 9

LAND AND TREES

1. Interference with boundaries is strictly prohibited.
2. All natives owning coconut trees which overlean the public road or any house shall pull down dried leaves or maturing nuts therefrom as a precaution against accident.
3. The Native Court shall have power to require an owner to remove any tree which, in its opinion, is a source of danger to the public.
4. Fallen trees in the road shall be removed by their owners.

No. 15

RELIGION

2. It is forbidden to hold prayer meetings or perform magic rites in village maneabas, but customary native ceremonies may be performed therein with the prior knowledge and consent of the Native Magistrate.

No. 16

SCHOOLS

Parents or guardians must see their children attend school regularly between the ages of seven and sixteen.

No. 17

TRAVELLING

No native shall land on Ocean Island, other than a full or half-Banaban, a native missionary or school teacher, or a native who owns land or has assured employment on the island, unless he is in possession of a permit signed by the Native Magistrate of Ocean Island.

No. 18

VEHICLES

1. Lights shall be carried on a bicycle and other vehicles between sunset and sunrise.
2. No native shall ride a bicycle or drive a vehicle at a speed or in a manner dangerous to the public.

No. 19

VILLAGES

No native shall live outside a village area without the prior permission of the Administrative Officer and the Native Government.

The Banabans did not ask to become part of a British protectorate or colony. They were acquired as such because of the phosphate deposits: the Company, incorporated at various stages as the Pacific Islands Company, the Pacific Phosphate Company, and the British Phosphate Commissioners, wanted to work within a clear British jurisdiction. It needed the law not to protect the Banabans but to prevent other companies or foreign powers from bidding for and working the valuable phosphate. The social, cultural, political, and economic consequences of this hegemonic state of affairs was nothing short of devastating for the Banabans and to this day, in addition to the great suffering during World War II, has left them in a state of social and political ambiguity and disorientation.

Since the Company dominated the island, the colonial administration was often in the awkward position of having to support the various wants and needs of the Islanders. Banabans did not put up any resistance until it became clear that the newcomers were not going to take just a few rocks but rather the ground beneath their feet. Their existing customs were being eroded along with the disappearing land, and this was not just natural erosion, but motivated suppression. It became increasingly difficult to "look after their children" or their "aged or adoptive parents" without the food-bearing trees, the circulation of plots of land, and the practice of te kauti and other sacred rituals associated with rites of passage. It was difficult for Banabans to raise their children well, according to their own customs, since the boys had to be in school, giving them less time to spend with the men on the terraces, learning how to become men. It was difficult to achieve all these things, including intergenerational respect, while Banaban, Gilbertese, and Ellice Islander adult men and women on the island were being treated as children and often called "girls" and "boys" by the British.

Mining proceeded despite protests from the Banabans until things came to a head in 1909. In 1905 the Company's manager, Harold Gaze, had made a trip to Ocean Island and found Ellis engaged in "lengthy and very troublesome negotiations with the natives as to land leases." Extraordinarily, no one in the Company in Australia, England, or elsewhere had foreseen such problems persisting and prejudicing the obtaining of more land for mining. Gaze's report said, "This matter will I fear still continue to be a source of annoyance. Even during my stay on the island, the new house being put up for Mr. G. I. Ellis, Bertie's brother, had to be placed in a different position to that originally intended because an obstinate old woman refused to grant a lease."[6] Clearly the house of Mr. George Ellis, "Bertie's brother," was more important than this old Banaban woman's "obstinate" connection to her plot of land.

Technical Challenges

The technical side of the operation was also under major scrutiny, and in those years they faced the problem of "wet phosphate," rock that was not sufficiently dried out for superphosphate processing and thus the cause of a variety of costly mechanical problems for the industry. A French "expert," M. Nicaise, who had a great reputation for his work in the phosphate fields in Algeria, was sent to Ocean Island to look at the matter. According to Williams and Macdonald, Albert Ellis and the rest of the Australian crew on the island were not particularly keen on having their work inspected by various technical experts and likely resented the Frenchman. Ellis had started the enterprise with pick and shovel and was comfortable with his slowly improving methods, but the demands of manufacturers and farmers were rapidly increasing and it was more cost effective for the Company to ship larger volumes of dried rock. The operations had to be mechanized and streamlined for maximum and high-quality output. Quoting Gaze's report again, Williams and Macdonald give an amusing account of the Frenchman's reception by an aggravated Australian workforce:

> The fact that he could not speak English was a preliminary difficulty compounded by the general feeling on the island—now staffed almost totally by colonials—that everyone from Ellis down to the junior carpenter was heartily sick of the procession of visiting experts who walked around making supercilious faces and obviously critical notes; a procedure that everyone found exceedingly irritating. As Gaze said in his letter to the directors: "The 'Australia for Australians' spirit is very strong and includes in the Australian view the islands of the Pacific. . . . the arrival of any 'expert' is looked upon as a misfortune to be endured. . . . it is not the slightest use for any foreigner to get an Australian workman to change the customary method."[7]

As an example of the sort of conversational exchange between the French gentleman and members of the island staff, Gaze offered the following:

MONS. NICAISE (TAPPING HIMSELF ON THE CHEST): "Me expert."
MR STAMP (ENGINEER): "Expert humbug no doubt."[8]

As a result of this cross-cultural impasse, a new engineering firm, the Australian Coane Brothers, was employed, and its representatives fit in very well with the rest of the workforce. They installed cableways and improved the phosphate drying equipment, which resulted in more effective mining and shipping. Williams and Macdonald write that the Company's dividends for shareholders were the envy of less adventurous British investors with the visions of the early pioneers, such as John Arundel, becoming "extravagantly tangible."[9]

This momentum was under threat in 1909 when the Banabans refused to lease more land. In that year there were between four and five hundred Banabans, a thousand Pacific Islander laborers, about four hundred Japanese, and eighty or so Europeans with a contingent of Fijian police on the island. The European families had comfortable lives, and there were many social and recreational events similar to those discussed in chapter 4. An enthusiastic employee, for example, established a brass band, which the Banabans have maintained to this day on Rabi.

The seat of the resident commissioner of the Gilbert and Ellice Islands was moved in 1908 from Tarawa to Ocean Island, several hundred miles from the center of activity in the Gilbert Islands. This move was good for the Company because there would be an office to assist with settling disputes, but on the other hand there was now an authority in place to question the Company on Banaban matters and on the conditions of the island laborers. Resident commissioner Mahaffy in 1909, for example, challenged the Company regarding the health and living quarters of its Islander workers. Mahaffy, who had visited the island in 1896, was struck by the effects of the mining and quickly realized the industry was rendering it uninhabitable. He argued to the Western Pacific High Commission that a program of land rehabilitation must be put in place. Albert Ellis, on behalf of the Company, said that was fine, they could plant thousands of coconut trees away from the mining area, and added: "not that I think they will ever do much good, unless some magic wand is waved, which will transform the Banabans into an industrious population."[10]

The subsequent RC, John Quayle Dickson, who had just come from a posting in Africa and was nearing retirement, found his position balancing the Company's needs and Banaban welfare challenging. He suggested the establishment of the Banaban trust fund with a view to the purchase of a future home, given the devastation of the mining. If the Company's activities appeared devastating in 1909, one can only imagine what had happened to the landscape by 1979 when the operations ceased. Dickson suggested the Company donate £250 a year to the trust fund, but the chairman of the board, Lord Stanmore, did not think much of this idea. William Lever of Lever Brothers sat on the PPC board and suggested this would not be costly and would be an excellent solution to the ongoing problem of having to secure leases for further mining. The Company directors believed the scale at which it had to negotiate the use of land with each individual landowner was fiddly and inefficient. In 1904, for example, "phosphate and trees" leases created by the Gilbert and Ellice Islands RC, R. H. Cogswell, involved thirty-seven leases worth sums of between £5 and £15 per lease and per Banaban landowner.[11]

Dickson, the new RC in 1909, had a clear idea of how agreements and mining should be adjusted. He suggested the island might be mined more systematically in one section at a time and, even better, progressively restored in other areas. Each block of land should be worked to its limits, the mining blocks should be contiguous and not dotted all over the landscape, and food-bearing trees should not be destroyed at such a rate. He also thought that because the Company dividends to shareholders were rather high, the Company should pay more for the leased land. Williams and Macdonald write that Dickson, however, in his zeal to create more just terms on the island, did not contend with the fact that some of the most powerful men in the British Empire were on the receiving end of the dividends, including Lord Stanmore, William Lever, and Lord Balfour, one of the biggest investors, who "dined from time to time at Buckingham Palace with King Edward and his Ministers."[12]

In 1909 the Company did not have the most reliable technical information regarding the available deposits. Danvers Power's study in 1901 was preliminary. It was not until Owen's study in the 1920s that the knowledge that the most valuable deposits were in the center and north of the island began to direct the industry's mining strategy. The estimates of the depths of the deposits and the number of tons this would yield were also fairly sketchy. All this was relevant to the shareholders, who were receiving dividends based on the sale price of tonnage with a particular phosphoric acid (P_2O_5) yield. They needed to know where on Nauru and Ocean Island the yield was highest and potentially stop going for random land leases in areas for which they had thin technical information.

The board directed the senior administration to take an integrated approach to mining at both islands, to hold a conference once a year, and to focus on ways of unifying procedures and reducing labor costs and expenses generally.[13] Certain senior staff members, including Ellis, were of the opinion that mining the highest-grade phosphate was not necessary and that they should develop the fields systematically while maintaining average-grade shipments, and save the richest deposits for when needed. The grade of phosphate at both islands was the highest in the world at the time and therefore their average far exceeded that of other global supplies. Dickson wanted mining confined to the eastern side of the island, but the Company had started mining in the western and central areas where the phosphate was richest. Dickson's efforts were starting to hamper the Company's goals.

According to Williams and Macdonald, "everyone was sick of Dickson" by 1911.[14] But they were civil throughout the Ocean Island celebrations of the crowning of George V, which involved flag raising, a marching drill, a royal salute, segregated picnics and sporting events, and a performance by the Banaban brass band that included "Eileen Alannah" and "The Old Folks at Home." Lord Stanmore passed away that year and Lord Balfour of Burleigh, an in-law of the Stanmore family, took over as chairman of the board of the Pacific Phosphate Company while William Lever became Lord Leverhume, the most influential member of the board. In London, the efforts of the industry were lauded, and after seeing the Company's annual report, a reporter for the *London Times* wrote:

> The turning of these vast accumulations into dividends; the exploration of these two little spots in the wild waste of water; the civilization of the native inhabitants by the agency of the man of science and the merchant—these constitute the romance of the Company and invest with a piquant interest the cold figures of its balance sheet and the material satisfaction of its profits. . . . The natives were in a primeval condition; now the island possesses electric power for driving machinery and supplying light and ice, a good telephone service, recreation and billiard rooms and libraries; in fact in a small way all the bustling activities of civilization.[15]

In 1913, R. C. Eliot drew up a new agreement allowing the Company to lease additional land at the rate of between £40 and £60 an acre in defined areas. The price was to be fixed by the resident commissioner. This was double the amount proposed by the Company, and Eliot also suggested an increase of the royalty of six pence a ton paid to the government and an additional six pence to be paid to the Banaban trust fund. The interest of the fund was to be used for the benefit of the Banaban community, and upon the signing of the agreement, £4,734 was to be paid immediately into the fund. Landholders could use the plots until they were required for mining, and after the phosphate was removed, the plan was that the Company would return the land and attempt to replant it with food-bearing trees where possible. Eliot also attempted to institute his one-price-for-all system and also required the Company to sell the Banabans fresh water at the rate of one gallon a day for three farthings.[16] The new agreement was signed on November 28, 1913 by 257 Banabans, including 72 children, in the presence of Eliot and Ellis. Eliot became disillusioned about whether the terms of the agreement would ever be honored, but in 1914 a cadet of the Colonial Service joined his team. Trained at Cambridge, Arthur Grimble learned to speak Gilbertese quickly and had a particular interest in native languages and customs.

Three Countries Take Over

World War I drastically altered the political and economic landscape on which the Pacific Phosphate Company operated. Nauru became an Australian territory and, given the strategic value of the phosphate to Australia, New Zealand, and Britain, the PPC eventually sold its interests to the newly established British Phosphate Commissioners for £3.5 million with the United Kingdom providing 42 percent of the funds, Australia 42 percent, and New Zealand 16 percent.[17] Prime ministers William (Billy) Hughes of Australia and William Massey of New Zealand were key to the establishment of this deal. It was especially important to New Zealand, which in the past had been dependent "for its supplies of high grade fertilizers upon the phosphate mined by British and French companies in the Pacific and processed in Australian and Japanese factories, with all the heavy costs that this entailed."[18] This was a grassroots New Zealand issue, and the country's leadership wished to build their own fertilizer works and provide ample supplies for farmers.

The Nauru agreement was drawn up in 1919, with little thought given to the nature of the industries in each of the three countries or their capacities to make use of phosphate shipments; it was stipulated in Article 14 that the countries would receive percentages of the rock from Nauru and Ocean Island based on the 42:42:16 ratio. Any surplus not used by one country could be taken up by one of the other two and then be made available for foreign sale, but in the first instance all phosphate was to be consumed by the three countries. Article 13 stated that none of the governments were to interfere with the direction, management, or control of the business of working, shipping, or selling the phosphate. The BPC was to be an entity unto itself, in charge of its affairs under the supervision of three commissioners, each representing one of the countries. Increased income from the industry would continue to fund the governing of the Gilbert and Ellice Islands colony, thus saving British taxpayers the cost. Albert Ellis became the first New Zealand commissioner and thus maintained much of the spirit and corporate knowledge established under the PIC and the PPC along with the general manager, Harold Gaze.

In the first meeting of the three acting commissioners, it was recommended that the headquarters of the Gilbert and Ellice Islands colony be moved to another island and that Arthur Grimble remain on the island as a colonial officer. In the wrangling over how the benefits and costs of the industry should be administered under this new nationalized scheme, it became clear that the United Kingdom and Australia would always be on opposite ends of the table. There was an inherent suspicion and disdain on the part of British personnel toward the Australians and a reciprocal dislike on the part of the Australians for British business and politics. New Zealand was often caught in the middle with the United Kingdom regularly expecting New Zealand to take its side. The history of Australia as a British penal colony had much to do with the mutual lack of respect between the nationals, and in my reading of the Company and relevant government archives, the problems between the commissioners, especially in the first two decades of the BPC's existence, played out like an intense family feud with Australia representing the bad seed and New Zealand being the favored son of a British father.[19]

Australia instigated and eventually won a mighty push to move the center of gravity of the whole enterprise from the United Kingdom to Australia, where the general manager, Harold Gaze, was located. But the respective governments were constantly concerned about the "personal differences and mutual recriminations that went on" and how "the sole responsibility for the . . . working of this very valuable asset rests on the shoulders of three men. Yet they attempt to transact their business from three separate points thousands of miles apart."[20]

The Banabans, in the meantime, had no idea of the changes playing out on the political and business side of the mining operation, and many people became very close to Arthur Grimble. Grimble, later of radio and publishing fame, who wrote *A Pattern of Islands* and *We Chose the Islands,* was described in a 1997 article in *Pacific Magazine* as one of the "nicest colonial administrators" in history.[21] He had risen from a cadetship in the colonial office on Ocean Island in 1914 to district officer on Tarawa, Abemama, and Beru, to become the first native lands commissioner and, finally, resident commissioner (1929–1932). He was drawn to the islands by his studies in anthropology at Cambridge University under W. H. R. Rivers and later became acclaimed as both an excellent scholar and a storyteller.

Banabans, on the other hand, today joke about how some people name their dogs after "Kurimbo" (Grimble).

By the end of 1924, 1.5 million tons of superphosphate had been shipped from Ocean Island, with 950,000 tons going to Australia, 160,000 to New Zealand, 39,000 to the United Kingdom, and 360,000 to Japan and other countries. By 1925 BPC sales were around £1 million and the operations were running smoothly and efficiently on both islands. But the Banabans were again refusing to lease more land. That year, another drama erupted, which caused the acting resident commissioner, Grimble, to request a British warship be sent to Ocean Island. There had been a violent outbreak between Chinese and Gilbertese laborers that apparently ensued after an argument and scuffle between two men—one from each group—who were working side by side making phosphate-loading baskets. The problem ended after a struggle between police and fighters on both sides; eventually, ten Chinese workers were arrested and several Gilbertese workers were sent back to their home islands.

Banabans Push Back and Receive a Threat

People with larger and more numerous plots of land also gained considerable status, the most notable of all being Rotan Tito of Buakonikai. Tito was the first leader of the Banaban council and came from a family of early converts to Christianity. He had received religious education in the Gilbert Islands, was literate, and became increasingly savvy regarding the manner in which both the Company and the colonial office were trying to acquire land at the cheapest price. As land became commercialized, the Banabans' approach to land shifted. In the 1920s, after a series of negotiations for the Company to acquire more land at £150 per acre with a royalty of ten and a half pence per ton, Tito demanded more. The Banabans were refusing to lease more land under the Company's terms. In 1903 their land had been acquired under the Phosphate and Trees Purchases Act, and in 1923 their surface and mineral rights were ensured by the secretary of state for the colonies, albeit at paltry sums. But when they refused to lease more land in 1927, things became very tense. Williams and Macdonald describe an exchange between Grimble and Tito: "When Grimble said that the rest of the Empire was 'holding out its hands to them, asking to be fed' . . . Tito answered: 'if the Empire wants our phosphate so badly, let the Empire pay £5 a car [ton] for it.'"[22]

A brief but revealing passage in Barrie Macdonald's history of the Gilbert and Ellice Islands colony describes the particularly gendered nature of concerns over leases and protests involving the destruction of trees:

> As early as 1923 McClure had observed, "it is the young men who appear to express the opinions of the majority. But behind them and most formidable of all

is the feminine influence on which everything depends a[...]
reactionary." Grimble found this to be only too true and at B[...]
where their influence was greatest, opposition was "massive a[...]
reported: "Women, especially owners within the proposed new [...]
bitrarily and blindly opposed at present to transfer of land under [...]
tions whatever." Later, when the BPC tried to take possession of its co[...]
rily acquired lands, it was the women who clung to the trees in an atte[...]
prevent them being destroyed.[23]

The following is one of the few passages that explicitly states the attitude o[...]
women toward the mining, in Macdonald's opinion:

> Largely as a consequence of mission influence, there were women's social groups
> in all villages and these, as recognised entities, met Grimble and BPC officials
> to discuss the land issue. It may have been thought by the Banaban commu-
> nity at large that to run counter to government wishes was a hazardous course
> of action and that women might be less vulnerable to coercion or reprisal. Or,
> and more probably, women represented the conservative element within the
> community; they had not, in most cases, worked in the phosphate mining in-
> dustry as many of their menfolk had done, few had any formal education, but
> all were landowners with clear and recognised rights to speak and act on their
> own behalf in any matters affecting their property.[24]

One way in which Banabans described their home island was "Banaba, te aba
n aine" (Banaba, the women's land). This has two meanings: the first characterizes
the island as a peaceful land, free of war, and the second points to the active participation of women in politics before the arrival of Christianity and the advent
of mining.[25] One major difference between the Banaban and Gilbertese political
systems is that Banaban women were allowed to speak in the mwaneaba and were
always active in decision making and social organization. Nei Anginimaeao, a key
figure and migrant from Beru some eleven generations before the 1930s, was the
woman who carved up the Banaba landscape into new divisions that remained
unchanged till the advent of mining.[26] Nei Tituabine, a female embodied by the
stingray and lightning, is today the main surviving ancestral deity. Female elders Nei Tearia and Nei Beteua were two main sources of oral history as recorded
by Maude.[27] And Nei Teienemakin, a powerful figure, was described by many a
miner and visitor in the early 1900s as the "old queen" of Banaba. Furthermore,
an acceptable marriage custom on Banaba in the past was for husbands to leave
their kainga for their wife's (in anthropological parlance, uxorilocality). Today,
on Rabi, either may live in the other's village or kainga, and women's leadership
roles are less visible publicly.

Maude describes how women would inherit important roles, but the duties
associated with them were almost always carried out by a male representative.[28]

nd which is entirely
uakonikai village,
nd abiding." He
area, [are] ar-
any condi-
mpulso-
f

rights but since 1900, at least, men have
; positions in the community. On Rabi,
f Leaders was not elected until 1996, and
tatives for the various families and the

r of £150 an acre for an additional 150
n improved trust fund, and a royalty
£5 a ton. Grimble was in poor health
he Banabans' unwillingness to lease
by many for decades later as a most
ondon when the Banabans sued the

...ent:

10 the people of Buakonikai, Greetings,

You understand that the Resident Commissioner cannot again discuss with you at present as you have shamed his Important Chief [the British king], the Chief of the empire, when he was fully aware of your views and your strong request to him and he granted your request and restrained his anger and restored the old rate to you—yet you threw away and trampled on his kindness. The Chief has given up and so has his servant the Resident Commissioner but I will put my views as from your longstanding friend Mr. Grimble who is truly your father, who has aggrieved you during this frightening day which is pressing upon you when you must choose LIFE or DEATH. I will explain my above statement:

POINTS FOR LIFE. If you sign the agreement:—(1) Your offence in shaming the Important Chief will be forgiven and you will not be punished; (2) The area of the land to be taken will be well known, that is only 150 acres, that will be part of the agreement; (3) The amount of money will be properly understood and the company will be bound to pay you, that will be part of the agreement.

POINTS FOR DEATH. If you do not sign the agreement:—(1) Do you think your lands will not go? Do not be blind. Your land will be compulsorily acquired for the Empire. If there is no agreement who then will know the area of the lands to be taken? If there is no agreement where will the mining stop? If there is no agreement what lands will remain unmined? I tell you the truth—if there is no agreement the limits of the compulsorily acquired lands on Ocean Island will not be known. (2) And your land will be compulsorily acquired at any old price. How many pence per ton? I do not know. It will not be 10½ d. Far from it. How many pounds per acre? I do not know. It will not be £150. Far from it. What price will be paid for coconut trees cut down outside the area? I know well that it will remain at only £1. Mining will be indiscriminate on your lands and the money you receive will be also indiscriminate. And what will happen to your children and your grandchildren if your lands are chopped up by mining and you have no money in the bank? Therefore because of my sympathy for you I ask you to consider what I have said now that the day has come when you must choose LIFE or DEATH. There is nothing more to say. If you choose suicide then I am very sorry for you but what more can I do for you as I have done all I can. I am your loving friend and father,

Arthur Grimble

P.S. You will be called to the signing of the agreement by the Resident Commissioner on Tuesday next, August 7, and if everyone signs the agreement, the Banabans will not be punished for shaming the important Chief and their serious misconduct will be forgiven. If the agreement is not signed consideration will be given to punishing the Banabans. And the destruction of Buakonikai village also [will be] considered to make room for mining if there is no agreement.[29]

The period after receiving this letter was traumatic for Banabans. Far more than the work of the Company, which they had started to loathe years earlier, the betrayal of one they had related to as "kin" was devastating. The threats especially frightened the elders, the adult men and women who were accorded great respect for their knowledge and skills in providing for their clans. This letter had the kind of impact of the order outlined by Chinua Achebe in his now-classic novel: "He has put a knife on the things that held us together and we have fallen apart."[30]

The gloves were off and the Company and colonial administration were now enforcing the principle that the phosphate rock was "for the good of mankind," and this seemingly universalist and yet quite specific imperialist and capitalist intent was to now guide their attitude toward the Banabans. In 1928 the British government put into place an ordinance that required the compulsory acquisition of land for mining, the removal of Banaban rights to minerals beneath the surface, a fixing of the royalty price for mined land, and holding such royalties in trust for the natives. The royalties would now be paid directly to the resident commissioner to be held "on behalf of the former owners or owners."[31] The Company would no longer make direct transactions with Banaban landowners but rather would acquire individual plots of land and pay all funds to the British official on the island. At this point, the manner in which money (or trade in kind) heretofore had provided some kind of substitution or compensation for the loss of land access and food shifted dramatically. Any Banaban sense of individual efficacy and independence with respect to individual plots of land was removed, and the community was amalgamated into a homogeneous whole for which the resident commissioner of the Gilbert and Ellice Islands colony and the Western Pacific High Commission based in Fiji, more generally, were responsible. The Banabans were infantilized and no longer treated as people with their own agency, social and economic interests, and rights. Under this ordinance any Banabans residing on acquired land were required to move, and there would be no negotiation over the mineral rights. These now lay with the Crown. The surface rights, however, could be discussed, and in this case the colonial office attempted to bedazzle the Banabans with some inflexible interpretations of the legal and economic factors.

The Banaban sense of confusion is lucidly illustrated by the minutes of a meeting held on January 24, 1931. The British government sent an arbitrator named J. S. Neill, the consul for Tonga, to explain to the Banabans how things would now proceed under the authority of the RC, Grimble. The minutes of the meeting were constructed so that the European officials appear rational and reasonable and the Banabans seem whiny, evasive, and irrational. From 1931, on both Ocean Island and Rabi, all minutes taken by a colonial representative of any meeting between the Banabans, the Company, and colonial officials maintained this bias. From then on, a very specific picture of Banabans as greedy, selfish, and lazy was disseminated so that in the late 1960s and 1970s, even the Gilbertese government could not view them in any other light. It is well worth it to include a good portion of this unpublished transcript:

NOTES TAKEN AT MEETING WITH BANABANS
24th January, 1931.
The Resident Commissioner introduced Mr. Neill to the meeting and then withdrew.
Mr. Neill addressed Banabans.
PEOPLE OF BANABA
You have been informed by the Resident Commissioner that I have been appointed to arbitrate on your behalf in assessing the amount of compensation payable to you for the lands which were acquired this month and which have now been leased to the British Phosphate Commissioners for the mining of phosphates and other purposes connected with the work of the Commission. It is not my intention today to deliver to you a [lengthy] speech. I want, as your arbitrator, to hear your views and I shall listen carefully and sympathetically to any representations you may wish to make. . . . Though a stranger to you I have served for many years among the Fijians and Tongans and the ideas and thoughts of the Pacific Islands are known to me. . . . You have discussed, time and again, the value of the surface rights and the amount of royalties. Finality was once almost attained and an agreed settlement was reached but the negotiations broke down. This month possession was taken of the land after you had declined the terms offered.

I want to inform you definitely that we are now concerned only with the compensation for the land which has been acquired. Let us therefore dismiss from our minds the question of royalties. . . . With the amount of royalty I, as arbitrator, have nothing whatsoever to do. In assessing the compensation the Arbitrators have to take into account the following factors—

1. The market value of the land excluding any increase in that value by reason of the fact that there are phosphates on it.
2. The improvements of the land.

3. Damage caused by severance.
4. The amount due to any land-owner who resides on the land and who is compelled to vacate his holding by reason of the acquisition of the land. . . .

There remains . . . the question of market value and of improvements. . . . I
would ask you to remember that the right to work the phosphate deposits cannot be granted to any other person than the British Phosphate Commissioners.
The Commission holds an exclusive licence. . . . Now in the Colony law, market
value of land is not increased because there are phosphates or minerals under
the land. The law says so. . . . You will see therefore that no other Company can
come in and offer you a price for the phosphates. I ask you to remember this
point and keep your minds free from confusion. . . . You can reasonably raise
the question of the value of the trees on your land and its possible use for copra and food production. . . . The nuts on your trees differ greatly from the nuts
on native areas in Fiji, Tonga and Samoa. Your trees are not heavy bearers. . . .

I trust that I shall be able to report to His Excellency the High Commissioner
and His Honour the Resident Commissioner that our conversation today has
been guided by a spirit of reasonableness and that you will realize, whatever
the decision which will be reached next week may be, that your interests have
been carefully and sympathetically considered. . . . you know that it is impossible in life for every person to obtain everything which he or she may desire
and that it is for this reason that the settlement of differences is referred to the
judgement of others.[32]

After this meeting, the Banabans were told, a notice fixing the date for arbitration would be served to them. The Banabans asked that the notice not be served.
The scribe then proceeded to summarize and not fully transcribe the Banabans'
questions, which were put forth by the emerging leader Rotan Tito, whose family
owned much land, and another leader, Iete.

ROTAN: Why did you come here? Would you listen to what we have to say
about the land?

NEILL: Certainly.

ROTAN: We know nothing about the royalties. Who prescribed them?

NEILL: The Resident Commissioner in accordance with the law.

IETE: Who leased the 150 acres to the British Phosphate Commissioners?

NEILL: The land was acquired as prescribed by law. . . .

IETE: We were surprised lease was issued unknown to us.

NEILL: You all received Notices.

IETE: Yes, that is true, but we do not like it. We do not agree with the Notices.

IETE: [He referred to the days when the Company first came to Ocean Island
and, according to his statement, obtained areas of land in return for sewing
machines. He went on to say that in the time of Mr. Eliot leases were issued

and that Mr. Eliot stated that no more land would be leased until the leased area was worked out. The people could then lease further lands if they wished. They wished to adhere to this. The old area was not worked out.] . . .

What is your personal opinion? Have we enough land left? Why was the British Government so strict?

NEILL: I am here as your Arbitrator. . . .

ROTAN: Is everything the Resident Commissioner does to us known to the High Commissioner?

NEILL: As a matter of official procedure all important actions are reported. . . .

ROTAN: Did the High Commissioner know about the Notice?

NEILL: Under law the form of the Notice is prescribed by the High Commissioner. . . .

ROTAN: We do not agree with the 150 an acre and the 10.5 d. royalty.

NEILL: The question of royalty is finished. . . .

ROTAN: We know the question of royalty is finished with. We just do not agree. We want to let you know that we will not agree to 150 compensation. We want 180 per acre and the following payment for trees:

Coconut (large)	£ 2-0-0
(small)	1-10-0
Pandanus (bearing)	1-10-0
(small)	0-10-0
Almond	1-0-0
Mango	1-0-0
Kaitu	0-10-0
All other trees	0-5-0

The scribe added at the end of this summary: "Questioned as to how many trees they had on their own land Rotan and Iete gave evasive replies and finally remained silent."[33]

The meeting continued with Iete and Rotan putting forward alternative methods for calculating payment. Iete suggested by the square foot but could not give an example of rental on that scale. Rotan asked that money be paid half-yearly, not yearly, and that a truck of phosphate be treated as weighing one ton with the royalty paid when it left the phosphate fields. The arbitrator said that the issue of when payments are made was not included in the topics for the meeting. The Banabans repeated that they did not want any notice about arbitration served and were told this would not be granted. In another meeting a week later, Neill presented the new price to the Banabans, highlighted that some of the old men were not in agreement with Rotan and Iete, and reminded them all: "Do not listen to foolish remarks if made to you."[34]

In August 1932, obviously not dissuaded by Neill's remarks, the Banabans wrote to a higher authority, the secretary of state for the colonies in London, asking for help and intervention. In addition to taking 150 acres for mining, the BPC was taking an additional 27.75 acres for buildings at a rental of £3 per acre and £2 per coconut tree to be cut down. The letter stated, "They forced us in a frightful way so that we will give away our land and to agree with satisfaction to the above prices privately judged by them but we were unsatisfied."[35] They outlined the agreement of 1913 made by R. C. Eliot, saying they would prefer that those terms be honored and future leases held off till the area was worked out. They believed they had been offered a bad price for the compulsorily acquired land, and they pointed out that those 150 acres were on some of Banaba's most fertile and productive lands. They wrote that neither the high commissioner nor the resident commissioner were supporting them and signed the letter: "Your Lordship's most pitiable people, The Banaban Community."

War Arrives and the Banabans Are Moved

There were countless occasions in which the Banabans attempted to stand up to the Company and colonial officers, mostly to no avail. The regular dismissal of their hopes and expectations built up over forty years until it exploded on the international scene in 1968 with petitions for independence to the United Nations, a battle with the local government of the Gilbert Islands, and an eventual lawsuit in the British High Court.[36]

Grimble left the Gilberts in 1933, moving to a post in St. Vincent before he became governor of the Seychelles, at which point he was knighted. He went on to publish numerous bestselling books and stories on the Gilbert Islands, which were translated into several languages and included a few references to Banaba.[37] He gained fame throughout the Commonwealth and the United States for his radio programs, which carried titles such as *Priest & Pagan, The Obliging Lunatic, The Stinking Ghost of Utiroa,* and *Thin Man in the Moonlight.*[38] In 1956 a British film based on his life, *Pacific Destiny* starring Denholm Elliott (of *Indiana Jones* fame), Susan Stephen (of less fame), and the prolific Sir Michael Horden, was released. *Māori* opera singer and artist Inia Wiata played one of the Islander characters. The film was not a huge success.

After World War I, the agricultural landscape in both Australia and New Zealand shifted dramatically with a drop in fertilizer prices and a postwar boom in food production. There was significant migration of Eastern Europeans to Australia, and returning servicemen were encouraged to go into farming. A variety of credit, subsidy, and other schemes were introduced along with research and educational services, such as the Better Farming Train. But in 1930 the Depression swept through the Antipodes, drastically affecting farmers who relied heavily on exports of their wool, lamb, and dairy products. There were massive job losses and farmers went into debt. By contrast the BPC was erecting new jetties and cantilevers at Ocean Island to speed up loading and shipping. It was amassing hundreds of thousands of tons of phosphate that in 1930 few could buy. The Company had frightened the Banabans into leasing more land to mine more phosphate, not to be consumed immediately, but to reduce costs and amass stockpiles. While the global market was depressed, the BPC was still in the black and in 1931 commissioned a second ship to be built, the *Triona*. The *Triaster, Trienza,* and *Triadic* were added to the group in rapid succession with the capacity to transport thousands of tons of phosphate, and with luxury accommodations for senior Company and other official staff.

In the late 1930s an annuities scheme was running whereby interest from the consolidated trust funds administered by the colonial office was distributed to the whole community at the rate of £8 per adult and £4 per child. This, the Company assumed, would placate the Banabans and entice them to lease more land. By comparison, due to increased sales and low costs, £6,000 was divided among the Company's European employees in 1942 with additional payments to senior staff. The annuities system did not recognize individual landholdings: it was irrelevant whether one had more or less land, everyone received an equal share, and this system continued, for the most part, into the 1990s when the annuities system ceased.

The *Triona* was sunk by a German raider in December 1940, followed by the *Triadic* and the *Triaster* not long after. Everyone was nervous about Japan entering the war but continued to ensure that they shipped Japan the required supplies of phosphate, hoping this would prevent the country from moving into "the enemy camp."[39] Japan entered World War II on December 7, 1941, and the Company and the colonial office on Ocean Island made preparations to leave. They had already evacuated European women and children and sent home several hundred Chinese workers with compensation. It was clear that both phosphate islands would be targeted due to their developed facilities and valuable phosphate. At midnight on December 10, 1941, a demolition gang wrecked the key mining installations. With the assumption that the Gilbertese and Ellice Islander workers and the Banabans would be treated reasonably by the Japanese, due to the fact that they were neither European nor Chinese, the Company departed, leaving behind all the Islanders and a small group of Europeans, including the acting resident commissioner, two labor supervisors, and a Catholic priest and Brother. There were 2,413 people on the island when 550 Japanese took possession in 1942. Phosphate production ceased, and during the war the Company obtained Australian supplies from Quseir and Safaga on the Egyptian coast. New Zealand turned to a French mine in Makatea, French Polynesia, for its needs. Throughout the war the BPC worked consistently to maintain its phosphate supplies from sources in the Middle East, Makatea, and Florida and drew up plans for the reconstruction of mining facilities on Ocean Island the minute the war ended.[40]

All the British and many Islanders died during the Japanese occupation, including several Banabans who were beheaded and others who were electrocuted in a perimeter fence test. Shennan and Tekenimatang include several accounts of this harrowing period on the island: many also died from disease and starvation, and over a hundred young Gilbert and Ellice Islands men were executed when it was declared that Japan had lost.[41] Makin Corrie Tekenimatang was nine years old in 1942 and witnessed her father's beheading. She forever enshrined that incident in a Banaban Dance Theater first produced in the late 1960s that to this day features the reenactment of the executions on the island. The rest of the community was removed to camps in Kosrae, Tarawa, and Nauru. My great-grandfather Tenamo was included in this group, and in the Kosraean camps he developed farming skills since most of the Islanders were tasked with growing and supplying food for the Japanese troops. In addition to their physical hardships, they were most troubled that they were forced to fertilize the gardens with human waste.

In May 1942 Rabi Island was purchased for £25,000 from Lever Brothers and in the months following a thousand Banabans and three hundred or so Gilbertese who had joined the community were gathered from various war camps, assembled in Tarawa, persuaded to head for Fiji rather than Ocean Island, and thus boarded the *Triaster* en route to Rabi. They landed on the very large, green, wet northern Fiji island on December 15.

In 1946 a memo from H. E. Maude, then lands commissioner of the Gilbert and Ellice Islands, made several key points to the British administration:

28. As long ago as 1914 the Authorities were worried about the fate of the Banabans when the phosphate industry on Ocean Island should end, and in 1927 the creation of a Provident fund was proposed, which should be used for the purchase of a future home for the community. The Resident Commissioner pointed out that if the phosphate industry were to fail, "the race would literally be blotted out of existence: five hundred and fifty denaturalised natives could not possibly live on the interest yielded by the Banabans fund."

34. It will take some time for the Banaban community to recover from their treatment during the Japanese occupation: they were only a shadow of their former selves when discovered by the allied occupation forces. It appears, furthermore, that their attitude towards the Government, and Europeans in general, may have undergone a change. While for years they have distrusted the Government's good faith, they are now said to be more openly critical than before, which is ascribed to their having seen the European[s] beaten, if only for a time, by a brown-skinned race such as themselves.

48. I may state here that I have known the Banabans for seventeen years ... and since then contact has been renewed periodically until the war. It seems to me that during this period the community has progressively degenerated morally and physically, and that urgent messages are now indicated if they are not to sink into a state of indolence and apathy.[42]

The language in Maude's document suggests that the Company and the co-lonial administration saw themselves, at the outset, as saving the Banabans by bringing the mining industry to the island. The phosphate industry was seen as rescuing them from extinction even though there is clear evidence to show that they had survived a devastating drought three decades earlier and successfully re-turned to their home island. There is also the concern, typical of that period, for the "denaturalised" natives, who have been transformed not just by mining but by their shocking experience of Europeans being momentarily defeated by an-other "brown-skinned race"—the Japanese—during World War II. What is not discussed is that the Banabans and many Gilbertese and Ellice Islander workers were left behind on the island because there was an assumption within the Com-pany and the colonial office that they would be treated reasonably because they were not European. There was some oblique element of racialized kinship in that assumption. Company representatives were mistaken on most counts; the period of occupation was devastating for those who were left behind, and many were killed.[43]

Our God Help Us

In 1945 the Banabans, devastated from the war, irritated at being treated like chil-dren by both the Company and the colonial office, and alarmed that they were now far away from their home island, proceeded to make a number of key choices on Rabi. In 1947, by a majority decision, they voted to remain on Rabi after a re-turn trip to Ocean Island during which land boundaries were marked and further leases were granted. According to one story, a man on this trip met Nei Tituabine, that powerful female ancestral spirit, who proclaimed "So you Banabans are not dead!" and proceeded to follow them back to Rabi.

By 1968 Banaban leaders were making submissions to the United Nations call-ing for their independence from the Gilbert and Ellice colony, and by 1971 they had mounted a full-blown lawsuit against the BPC and the Crown. They had consoli-dated their sense of outrage considerably, built up their courage significantly, re-constructed their culture creatively and politically, and materialized everything in the form of new emblematic songs, dances, theater, and motto. Their sense of faith in the justice of their outrage was rock solid, as was their faith that they should push to the limits of extremity. From 1968 onward newspapers across the Pacific, the Commonwealth, and beyond were filled with headlines such as these:

Freedom Sought for Pacific Isle:
Absentee Population Hopes to Repair Mining Ravages

New York Times, November 25, 1968

Micronesia Irked by Strip Mining

New York Times, October 10, 1972

Pacific Islanders Ask Britain for 53-Million and Repairs

St. Petersburg Times, April 1975

2500 Want Pacific Isle Back

New York Times, September 21, 1975

The Struggles of a Ravaged Island

The Age (Melbourne), December 16, 1975

Islanders Start War for Independence

Toledo Blade, February 19, 1979

Excerpts from a *Foreign Correspondent* program in the 1990s, which included footage from the 1970s, and the transcript of Jenny Barraclough's critically acclaimed documentary film *Go Tell It to the Judge* give a poetic and vivid depiction of the Banaban struggle between 1945 and 1977. In the film, narrator James Cameron announces:

> So the remaining Banabans, 1003 of them were rounded up on Tarawa and shipped to the island of [Rambey] in Fiji 1600 miles away. They were ill, demoralized and in no shape to argue. . . . On December 15, 1945, the Banabans first saw Rambey in the rain. It was a daunting change from home. It was nine times bigger than Ocean Island, five times wetter, overgrown with jungle; it had been bought for 25,000 pounds of their own trust fund, their own money. Only now did the British Government realize that they were dumping the Banabans on Rambey in the middle of the hurricane season.
>
> Voiceover: "Considerations have been given for the disadvantages of canvas housing during the hurricane season. It can be expected that a considerable number of tents would be lost during a strong gale. For this reason the number of tents has been fixed at about 30% more than would actually be erected in the first instance."[44]

Cameron then states that "at this point the Banabans as a people came very near to extinction." He describes how, already weakened by three years under the Japanese during World War II, they slept on stretchers in tents awash with the relentless rain. In the first few months forty of the elders died and with them went a whole system of knowledge, rights, and authority. He remarks, "Two things probably saved them. One was their compulsive and cohesive belief that God was on their side. The other was the presence of Rotan Tito, the man who stood up for them against Grimble and then against the Japanese. He thought that the move to Rabi would be only temporary."[45]

The BPC now wanted virtually all that was left of Ocean Island. Later, the lawyers would ask why the British government, as trustee for the royalty funds, approved an offer so far below the going world rate. During 1947 the British High Commission had actually instructed the Banabans' advisor not to give advice when the BPC was negotiating for the price of the final land leases. By 1950 the Company was exporting 276 million tons of phosphate, and this greatly advantaged the farmers of Australia and New Zealand, who saved about half a million pounds a year by getting this subsidized fertilizer.

> James Cameron: Slowly and clumsily the Banabans tried to build a new life on Rambey Island but it wasn't home and never could be. . . . there's an overwhelming ancestral feeling about land, their own land, their father's land but no longer their children's land. . . . Over 20 years they acquired a bus, a hospital, a school, and a petrol pump, and a race of skilled and crafty fishermen had diminished into a race of tin openers living on Australian canned pilchards.[46]

Almost twenty years after Barraclough's documentary, in 1995, the Australian Broadcasting Commission's *Foreign Correspondent* program ran a story revisiting the Banaban struggles in the 1970s and organized a trip back to Banaba for Tebuke Rotan, son of Rotan Tito, who had led the movement and the lawsuit against the British Crown:

> Narrator: When peace [after the Japanese occupation] was restored, only the miners made it back. All Banabans were shipped to Rabi. . . . By the late 1960s Banabans were feeling thoroughly cheated. Mined land was not replanted as promised, and Banabans' share of the lucrative phosphate cake was still confined to crumbs.[47]

Tebuke Rotan is heard saying, "We are not greedy. But we want fair share." The narrator describes how Rotan, then a young Methodist minister like his father, was dispatched to London by the Banaban elders. There, they believed, Banabans would find justice. But initially the trip did not go so well because they had no legal contacts or even accommodations. Tebuke Rotan apparently spent his first night in Hyde Park, although eventually he did find a flat and an unlikely friend, a despondent, homeless man.

> Tebuke Rotan: He was about to commit suicide at 4 AM at Friar Bridge . . . very low bridge. He could easily jump, finish. So I persuaded him: don't commit sui-

"Native and Canoe in front of canoe house, 1936, from a photograph by Mr. A. F. Ellis." Courtesy of the National Archives of Australia

cide. I've got some money, I'll take you to my flat . . . and from there, he was the one who showed me where to go. "You have to see that lawyer . . ." Very knowledgeable man. [Cut to Banaban brass band][48]

When Rotan returned to Rabi, it was with the barrister John Macdonald, who met with the Banabans and assured them that they would be given a fair trial in London. Macdonald gathered the testimonies that allowed the Banabans to sue not only the phosphate commissioners but the British government. In all, Banabans estimated, they had been shortchanged US$100 million. The documentary then cuts to a group of Banabans in black suits and coats led by a figure in a white suit, Taomati Teai, Rotan Tito's grandson, walking solemnly through the streets of London. We hear the voice of Justice Robert Megarry: "I am powerless to give the plaintiff any relief."

The litigation occupied 206 days of court hearings in addition to a trip to the island for the entire court. Two cases were heard—one against the attorney general on behalf of the Crown, and the other against the commissioners. Ten thousand pages of documents were placed before the court and the judge remarked that these stood well over six feet high. The case against the attorney general was

breach of its fiduciary relationship
ase against the commissioners in-
th their replanting obligations and
l, plant coconut trees, and provide
ce Megarry felt unable to find the
view that the only fiduciary mat-
r there had been a breach of trust
rords, the ethical duty of the co-
e natives, were beyond his juris-
a litigation against the Crown to
k a judge ought to direct attention
nnot right, and leave it to the Crown

, *Tito v. Waddell,* Justice Megarry arrived
...usion that the burden of replanting passed to the BPC from the Pacific
Phosphate Company based on the 1913 agreement. In spite of the same Company
officials, farmers, fertilizer manufacturers, and investors benefiting from all three
iterations of the Company, he deemed that the BPC, however, was not the original
signatory to the agreement and the burden of replanting the island in its current
state would be a tremendous technical endeavor which he believed would not re-
store the island to its former state. He therefore concluded that expectations for
such an enterprise were unreasonable and assessed damages to be paid at AU$75
per acre.

The Banabans' simultaneous quest for independence from the colony of the
Gilbert and Ellice Islands was also squelched by the Gilbertese government, which
produced a report arguing that the Banabans were in fact Gilbertese and were
very selfish in wanting to keep the profits from their island for themselves in comparison to the tens of thousands of Gilbert Islanders struggling to make a living
on small atolls with limited resources.[51] The Banabans said they did not begrudge
the Gilbertese revenue and were willing to work out a compromise, but there was
a singular desire for independence.

According to Martin Silverman, who did fieldwork on the island in this critical
period but published little about the international efforts of the time, the Banabans
on Rabi did not see themselves as developed, well-to-do, independent, or free.
They saw themselves in highly gendered terms, as bound to the British like wife
to husband or child to father.[52] "Pitifully bound," to be more specific. He quotes a
Banaban song about a woman who is constantly deserted by subsequent husbands
(the string of Banaban advisors appointed by the High Commission) and who becomes sick in the process. Her husbands are the servants of a great chief (the British government). After she is deserted by so many husbands the chief stops finding
husbands for her, but "she still wanted to marry as she said she lived more com-

fortably in marriage than in single life."[53] The woman decides to go find her own husband and sails to Britain, lamenting about the chief and the husbands who have lied to her in the past. The song ends with "the husband of Miss Abandoned has now been found: Mr. J. C. Saunders, the lawyer from Britain."[54] Saunders was an attorney with a firm in Suva that the Banabans wished to employ for legal advice. They had just got rid of the previous British advisor because he seemed to act for the government rather than for them. The song describes the Banabans as a "pitiable girl" and invokes numerous gendered, patriarchal, and heteronormative metaphors about their feelings of intense dependency on the Crown.

This theme is also exemplified in a 1979 report by Richard Posnett, a representative of the UK secretary of state, who spent about four days on Rabi and came up with a sympathetic but still infantilizing assessment: "They have become dependent on royalties and when royalties cease they are going to suffer 'withdrawal symptoms.'"[55] Posnett's report resulted in an ex gratia offer of AU$10 million and forever dispelled the idea that Banabans were unique and different, racially or culturally, from the Gilbertese, who were themselves pursuing independence. Ocean Island became a territory of the newly independent nation of Kiribati in 1979 with a sizable phosphate reserve fund, while the Ellice Islands, with far less support and funds for independence from the United Kingdom, became the nation of Tuvalu in 1978. Kiribati's phosphate earnings formed the basis for the "revenue equalization reserve fund," today valued at approximately US$400 million.

For Silverman, the song of pity was a revealing aspect of the Banabans' self-image. For me, it also illustrates the fact that Banabans knew exactly what was happening to them and knew they could not get out of the situation because their values were tied up in their land, which was tied up with money, which was tied up with the British, who controlled the money. In 1945 the Banaban Settlement Act under Fiji law established the regulations of the new community on Rabi and the formation of a Council of Leaders and the Banaban trust fund's board. By a secret ballot, 85 percent of Banabans had agreed to remain on Rabi in 1947. The Banaban advisor was to be an "officer of the Government of Fiji to advise the Banaban community resident on Rabi on all matters connected with its social and economic advancement."[56] It was this office of the advisor that people referred to in the song. In 1947, when further lands were requested for mining, the advisor conveniently stayed away from the negotiations. The Banabans felt betrayed by his absence because they depended on him for good advice and they depended on the royalties from mining for compensation for their land.

This dependency on outside advice and support for something that already belongs to people (like land) is fast waning on Rabi. The younger generations don't like to depend on anyone for their welfare and sometimes resent their elders for their colonial outlook. This has created an atmosphere of intergenerational disrespect and serves as background to younger people's interpretations of the dominant theme of pity. The imagery of Banabans as wife of their advisor or child of the English father, a relationship exemplified by Grimble and other resident commissioners, contrasts with the motherly or nurturing role of the island of Banaba with respect to the hungry Australian and New Zealand farmers. There was an umbilical relationship between Banaba and the BPC countries, and I don't believe you can stretch this metaphor too far. Ironically, while Banabans were imagining themselves as children or dependent women, with respect to the white advisors or husbands, their island, in a maternal sense, was nurturing the Australian and New Zealand children of the British Empire, indeed, feeding them. These children had healthy appetites, were growing up fast, and were always asking for more. They eventually sucked Ocean Island dry and then packed up in 1980, leaving their mother in a devastated mess.

After World War II, while decolonization was generally encouraged, the United Nations was unwilling to interfere in a British territory. Ellice Islanders chose and were granted their own independent nation of Tuvalu through a referendum but received zero seed or development funds for their new state. By contrast, the Republic of Kiribati was launched with significant trust funds from the phosphate revenues. The Banabans lost their case against the BPC and the British government but received in 1980 the ex gratia settlement, which they left untouched for four years until poverty on Rabi forced them to accept. By then, the fund had grown slightly with interest and was worth close to AU$15 million. During this critical period, in 1979, Banabans sent a "war party" to Ocean Island, which bombed mining facilities and had an all-out brawl with Gilbertese police during which one Banaban was killed. Gilbertese and Banaban relations came to an all-time low, and mutual suspicion and political tension have remained for decades after.

From *Foreign Correspondent*:

Narrator: After years of legal wrangling Banabans walked away with just AU$15 million and even then, they had to promise they'd take no further action. . . .

[Back on Banaba, the female narrator climbs between coral pinnacles]

Before the mining started it was a leisurely stroll from across the island to Buakonikai, Tebuke's ancestral home and once the most fertile part of the island. . . . Today there is no trace of the village; it, like most of the island, was sacrificed for the cheap phosphate which helped New Zealand and Australian agriculture to flourish.

We didn't just ride on the sheep's back. We rode on the back of the Banabans.

* * *

In an interview with anthropologist Wolfgang Kempf in 2005, Taomati Teai, a grandson of Rotan Tito, who had held various positions of Banaban leadership

including a period as the Banaban secretary, relates how the Rabi C[...]
ers came up with their motto:

> When the first Council was established their logo was simply, "Our God[...]
> Help." And then we got into the time of fighting. We started the struggle for o[...]
> rights in London in the late 1960s, and it lasted into the 1970s. That was when we
> changed our motto to: "Banabans' Extremity is God's Opportunity." . . . It's a
> religious idea. "Extremity" here means tapping at the very end of your struggle
> into your very last power, your very last endeavour. "Extremity," you know, is
> the point you've reached when you've given it all you have, when you cannot
> go any further. Well, when the Banabans cannot go any further, that is what
> we call "God's Opportunity" to come in. So the idea was for the Banabans to
> take all the steps they can take by themselves, to fight all the battles they can
> fight on their own. To do all that they can by themselves, until they can do no
> more. At that point they can expect God to come to their help. . . .
>
> Later on we changed the letterhead again, this time to "Atuara Buokira"—
> which is actually people crying out. People in extreme plight. They've given
> their best, as they firmly believe, but still they don't have anything to show for
> it. So now they are crying out to God: "Please help us." . . . after that we have
> never changed the motto again. We are still crying out for help—that's why
> we've got that letterhead now.[57]

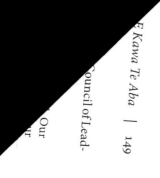
ɪosphate

" there but there is a "there" here and plenty of "here" there.

, quoted in *Thoughts on Screen by Dave Sag*

Sometime in the mid-1880s, on a typically overcast day in the Taotaoroa Hills between Cambridge and Matamata, a pair of brothers mounted their horses and went exploring the New Zealand hill country. They followed a track through the ti tree and fern scrub and discovered a deserted homestead some distance from the road. Farther down the path they came upon a rough signpost on which was scrawled "The road to ruin."

The younger brother later lamented that a promising farm was now a scene of desolation and that the owner had given up the obvious struggle. Recalling their father's recent success in applying fertilizer from Sydney Island to their own farm, the brothers Ellis were inspired to devote their lives to prospecting for phosphate.[1]

Those Ocean Islanders are hard cases. You take your rifle and revolver with you, and as soon as you get on the beach show the natives you can use them.[2]

* * *

Rotan: Why did you come here? Would you listen to what we have to say about the land?

Neill: Certainly.[3]

* * *

The soil is hungry for phosphate—use super phosphate, says the sign. There can be no doubting the magic of it.[4]

* * *

Now I would like to tell the Council a little about the phosphate. The white man goes to Nauru and Banaba and takes away plenty of phosphate. What does he do with it? He puts it in a machine and then puts a very strong acid on it and that

Taotaoroa, Waikato, New Zealand, 1993. Photograph by Michael Jeans

"Ocean Island 1900s, Native Missionary and Followers."
Courtesy of the National Archives of Australia

"Ocean Island—Very good phosphate country—No coral pinnacles in picture except the mass at back of Mr. A. F. Ellis and the corner one at right of picture, half way up—Lower levels untouched—Ooma—September 1910." Courtesy of the National Archives of Australia

Table 8.1. A Sample of Ocean Island Shipments, 1903–1904

Vessel	Arr.	Dep.	Ooma (Uma)	Tapiwa (Tabwewa)	Tons	Consigned to
Mintaro 2	Jan. 29, 1903	Mar. 5, 1903	2223	827	3050	William Crosby and Co., Melbourne
Ariake Maru	Feb. 27, 1903	Apr. 3, 1903	1728	1772	3500	Mitsui Bussan Kaisha, Tokyo
Rapallo	July 21, 1903	Aug. 18, 1903	1125	5175	6300	PIC, London
Isleworth 4	Sept. 7, 1903	Sept. 17, 1903	1533	967	2500	Theo Davies & Co., Honolulu
Windsor 1	Jan. 21, 1904	Feb. 20, 1904	3950	0	3950	PIC, Sydney
Croyden	Sept. 28, 1904	Sept. 30, 1904	0	5000	5000	Maemdray & Co., San Francisco
Oceana	Nov. 30, 1904	Dec. 8, 1904	650	0	650	MBK, Osaka

Source: BPC Archives, CA244, MP1174/1/1050, reproduced in Teaiwa, "Our Sea of Phosphate."

makes it good to put on the ground. When that is done everything grows very well, the sugar cane and the wheat and the grass for the cattle—every kind of food. That is good for the white man but it is also good for all the other people too. The rice, sugar, tinned beef and flour and other kinds of food which have been grown with the phosphate come back, come to Rambi [sic]. To work the phosphate is good for the white man and good for the Banabans. I am an old man but I am very glad to be doing useful work with the phosphate because it is good work for the white man and good work for the native too.[5]

* * *

Phosphate production was clearing the jungle off with the bulldozer usually, grabbing the soil out with a grab, into trucks. . . . Bringing the trucks up to the crusher up there. Crushing it. Putting it into storage bins. From the storage bins onto conveyor belts into . . . this particular drive behind us . . . dropped out the other end, along conveyor belts into the storage bin . . . from the storage bins to the ships—and then ships to Melbourne.[6]

* * *

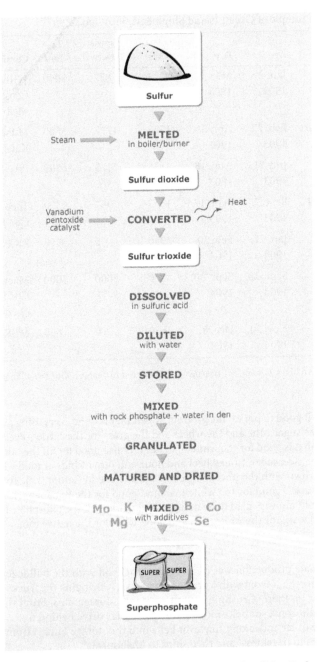

Superphosphate manufacturing diagram. *Te Ara: The Encyclopedia of New Zealand*
© Crown Copyright 2005–2012, Ministry for Culture and Heritage, New Zealand

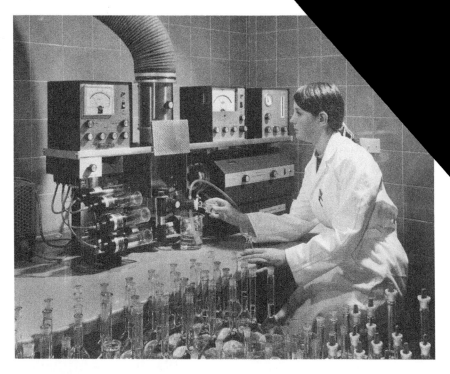

Lab worker, Phosphate Co-operative Company of Australia, Geelong, 1969.
Photo by Wolfgang Sievers. Courtesy of the State Library of Victoria

"Why do the smoke-stacks have those things like balconies around them?" inquired Lenina.

"Phosphorous recovery," exclaimed Henry telegraphically. "On their way up the chimney the gases go through four separate treatments. P_2O_5 used to go right out of circulation every time they cremated someone. Now they recover over ninety-eight percent of it. More than a kilo and a half per adult corpse. Which makes the best part of four hundred tons of phosphorous every year from England alone." Henry spoke with a happy pride, rejoicing wholeheartedly in the achievement, as if it had been his own. "Fine to think we can go on being socially useful even after we're dead. Making plants grow."[7]

* * *

the whole reason for banaban displacement is colonial agriculture. i like to say "agriculture is not in our blood, but our blood is in agriculture." . . . banabans equated blood and land and . . . kinship was constructed not simply on blood or biological relations, but on the exchange of land which signified adoption. these social relations then were no less meaningful and sometimes more mean-

Detail of phosphate factory, Phosphate Co-operative Company of Australia, Geelong, 1969. Photo by Wolfgang Sievers. Courtesy of the State Library of Victoria

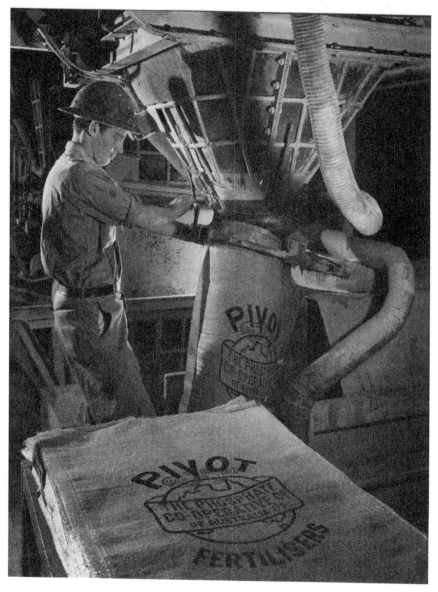

Bagging Pivot Fertilisers, Phosphate Co-operative Company of Australia, Geelong, 1969.
Photo by Wolfgang Sievers. Courtesy of the State Library of Victoria

Cape Hawke, Lyle Shipping, Lithgows, Port Glasgow, 1941. The *Cape Hawke* sailed from Ocean Island for Australia on November 25, 1981, with the last shipment of phosphate. Photo courtesy of R. A. Price

ingful than biological kinship. if banabans think of blood and land as one and the same, it follows then that in losing their land, they lost their blood. in losing their phosphate to agriculture, they have spilled their blood in different lands. their essential roots on ocean island are now essentially routes to other places. places like new zealand, australia, and fiji.[8]

* * *

P.S. You will be called to the signing of the agreement by the Resident Commissioner on Tuesday next, August 7, and if everyone signs the agreement, the Banabans will not be punished for shaming the important Chief [the British king] and their serious misconduct will be forgiven. If the agreement is not signed consideration will be given to punishing the Banabans. And the destruction of Buakonikai village also [will be] considered to make room for mining if there is no agreement.[9]

How pity . . . how pity . . . Oh!
They misunderstood the value of money!
Our ancestors!
Ake ngkoa ngkoa.[10]

PART III
BETWEEN OUR ISLANDS

We do not have frigate birds . . . on Rabi. It would take a great deal of time to catch the fish needed to feed them—and we have to catch fish to feed ourselves instead. But the movements in our dancing were originally inspired by frigate birds flying, so in a sense they are with us still.

—Karoro Tekenimatang, "Catching a Frigate Bird"

9 Interlude

Coming Home to Fiji?

We have been dancing
Yes, our anklets and
Amulets now are
Yes, grinding into our skin
No longer are they a décor
Yes, they are our chains

We have been dancing
Yes, but the euphoria has died
It is now the dull drumming
Yes, of the flat drums
Thud dada thud da thud dada thud
Yes, it is signaling, not the bliss
But the impending crisis.

—Vincent Warakai, "Dancing Yet to the Dim Dim's Beat"

ONE OF THE clearest memories I have after returning to Suva, Fiji, from research on Tabiteuea, Tarawa, and Banaba in Kiribati is of people sitting in a bus waiting for the traffic lights to turn green at the junction of Princes Road, Waimanu Road, Ratu Mara Road, and Edinburgh Drive. I was looking up from the window of our Toyota station wagon to the large Tacirua Transport bus stopped just next to the car. The family of a dear childhood friend, now resident in Sydney, owns this company and it has long been a regular pink and yellow feature on the landscape I call "home." That day, all the passengers were sitting stiffly in a row, facing forward in total silence. It suddenly struck me that I'd never seen such a quiet bus in the streets of Suva in all my life. Usually people would chat away, laugh, look outside, look at each other, or look down and giggle at the cars next to them. Usually the radio was blasting the eclectic and sometimes annoying sounds of FM 96, and people were nodding or tapping the window frames to the music. On this day there was something both steely and fearful about the passengers on the bus.

I had arrived back in Fiji on May 3, 2000, and on May 19 a group of armed men led by the now-infamous, self-proclaimed Fijian nationalist leader George Speight took over the government at the Parliament complex in Suva. Their main target was Fiji's first Indo-Fijian prime minister, Mahendra Chaudhry, who was in the process of initiating major pro-labor changes and land reform.[1] Chaudhry had won the 1999 elections and incensed Fijian nationalist groups as well as a few businessmen who were not in favor of his hard-line approach to economic transparency.

On the day of the coup I was in town to buy black leggings for a performance I was directing at the Oceania Centre for Arts and Culture at the University of the South Pacific. Our dance group, including Letava Tafuna'i and the now-renowned Samoan choreographer and artistic director Allan Alo, were due to dance in Canberra for the Pacific History Association conference in June. Since I'd returned from Kiribati I'd spent most of my time rehearsing for this performance, which was about celebrating the cultural diversity of Oceania. I had not read a Fiji newspaper or watched television news in months and did not know that earlier that day a crowd had marched through the streets demanding the protection of Fijian rights.

As I headed toward the Suva market I thought it unusual that most of the shops around me were closing down in the middle of the day. The sounds of doors, bars, and grills slamming shut rang in my ears, but at first I was oblivious to the rising wave of panic. Then, people began to run, and I instinctively did the same, reversing my direction and heading to my father's office at Banaba House near the Suva Cathedral.[2]

Within minutes we both discovered that after thirteen years another coup had taken place in Fiji.[3] I was stunned to find that the central Suva police station just outside my father's office had also pulled its shutters down, and there were no police officers in sight. My father refused to leave the office, fearing it would be vandalized. In more than a little panic I got into our 1984 Toyota Corolla and drove straight to the Tamavua service station, where I filled the tank with petrol and the trunk with noodle soup, milk, rice, cans of tuna, corned beef, sugar, and tea. When I was done I saw that at least thirty cars had lined up behind me.

This was the context in which I viewed the passengers in the bus at the four-way junction in Samabula. The coup had created an air of uncertainty and fear not just because the government had been violently toppled but because people in general, and particularly Fijians, no longer trusted their own friends and neighbors.[4] Many people became suspicious of each other as a matter of course, and many Indo-Fijians stopped driving alone. Rumor-mongering reached an all-time high as people searched for a way to explain what had happened and imagine its consequences. The international media in particular provided sensational coverage, which catapulted the smartly dressed Speight into temporary stardom. A friend of mine from the eastern islands of Lau kept telling me over the phone that President Ratu Mara had to give up his office or face the consequences. Since the president was the high chief of Lau, I realized that factions in the Fijian provinces cut right through normal allegiances.

Since I had never written about politics in Fiji, rather than thinking through what had happened in terms of academic and media discourses about Fiji history, I observed the impact of the coup in the looks and sounds of the city and how people's words and movements changed. During the first six months after May 19 people rode around in groups, did not look each other in the eye, and seemed to be sad, lost, or nervous. The air was always filled with tension, which seemed at the very point of yielding to outright chaos.

I remember watching one of Fiji's most prominent lawyers, an Indo-Fijian woman, run nervously with shopping bags from a supermarket to her large four-wheel-drive vehicle. Her movements were periodically interrupted by a jerk of the head and a quick scan of the eyes. Because there was a curfew, public transportation stopped running early and people would walk miles to get home on time. There was a running joke about how people who did have cars and who worked in Suva and didn't want to drastically alter their weekly drinking habits, would finish work at 3:00 PM, go to the pub at 3:15, and be home by 5:45 in time for the 6:00 PM curfew. When it shifted to 8:00 PM they finished work by 5:00, went to the pub at 5:15, and were home by 7:45.

Temporarily, the things I had learned and seen during my intense trip to Kiribati and my studies of Banaban history melted away. The celebratory dance show we were rehearsing at the Oceania Centre, headed by the late Epeli Hau'ofa, no longer seemed appropriate and was duly retitled *The Boiling Ocean*. When we weren't rehearsing I stayed at home watching the news, feeling depressed about the future of Fiji. The footage from one event in particular astounded me. An Australian journalist had been filming near one of the military posts outside the Parliament complex, and a whole group of people stormed the barricades.[5] Fijians fought Fijians with guns and fists, their actions made more bizarre by the crazy angles captured by the running cameraman. The sounds of firing weapons emitted from the TV screen. Few weapons had been fired during the 1987 coups because for the most part the military achieved total and peaceful control of the nation.[6] In the 2000 coup, those with guns were civilians or ex-servicemen rather than members of the army.

On the first day of the coup crowds of people rampaged through Suva looting shops. Men, women, and children all participated. In the weeks after May 19, houses near the Parliament complex were temporarily evacuated by their owners. A friend of our family had his home ransacked. When he finally returned, he found feces smeared on the walls and floor. Deuba Primary School (a Fijian school), just across from the complex, was similarly vandalized. For the first time I started to contemplate the reality that Fiji no longer felt like home.

Indigenous nationalism took on a whole new meaning for me during this particular coup and influenced my interpretations of some aspects of Banaban history. In this period I did no research and, not knowing what else to do with the Australian National University Anthropology Department's brand-new AU$3,000 digital video camera, I focused it on the television.

10   Between Rabi and Banaba

Between our islands the sea lurks like a monstrous storm wrapped in mystery.
On it we conquered mountains and dared valleys in our puny wooden
boats. Just visiting relatives.

—Ruperake Petaia, *Patches of the Rainbow*

Unraveling Kinship

The inhabitants of Rabi Island today speak of those places on the island where the Banaban spirits live, and those where the Fijian ones might get you. Banabans, who are now also known as "Rabi Islanders," became Fiji citizens when the country gained independence from Britain in 1970. Their rights were enshrined in the Banaban Settlement Act and the Banaban Lands Act.[1] Governance and law in Fiji have always been heavily racialized; politics and voting, for example, for decades were organized by both race and geography. Before Fiji's first coup in 1987, the Banabans had legal rights of the same order as other legally defined natives of Fiji, including the indigenous Fijians, who are now called I-Taukei, and the Rotumans.[2] This allowed them access to affirmative action and other programs designed for those deemed native to Fiji. After the establishment of the new Fiji Constitution in 1990, Banabans' status was changed and they were classed as general citizens, or "others," along with groups such as Chinese and Europeans.[3]

Banabans are also recognized as still belonging to Banaba and therefore are "residents" of Kiribati. They have representation in the Kiribati Parliament, and the Rabi Council of Leaders is responsible for affairs on Banaba along with the Kiribati government. However, tensions between Banabans and I-Kiribati still exist as a result of the Banaban quest for independence from the Gilbert and Ellice Islands colony. Earlier, a profoundly damaging sense of ethnic and class difference had resulted from the hierarchy set up by the Company on Ocean Island between the indigenous Banabans and the predominantly Gilbertese workers. Martin Silverman, for example, quotes the charismatic leader Rotan Tito as saying, "We did not come to Fiji to be workers on the land, but to get our money."[4] So, while speaking the same language by the end of the twentieth century, Banabans and I-Kiribati are seen to be culturally and historically distinct.

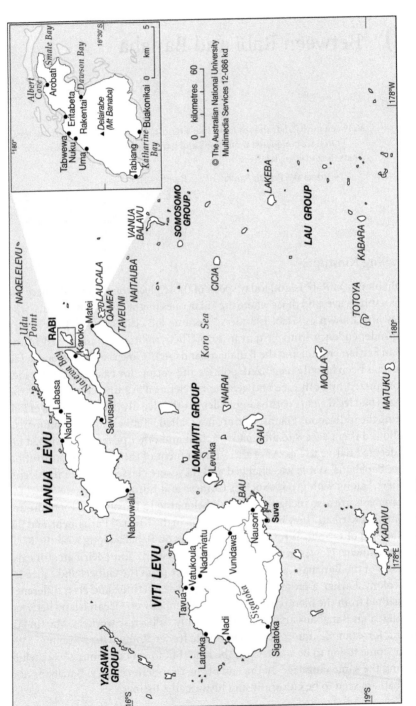

Map of Fiji with Rabi inset. ANU CAP CartoGIS

There were centuries of sporadic contact and intermarriage between Banabans and the people of various islands in the Gilbert chain, the most well known being the fifteenth-century arrival of the Beru ancestress Nei Anginimaeao, who created new land boundaries and new kainga, and who promulgated the reconfiguration of certain rights and privileges on Banaba.[5] The conversion of land into mining rents and phosphate royalties, and the recording and fixing of the once-fluid land tenure system, resulted in Banabans becoming socially and economically distanced from other Islanders as "landowners." They began to articulate their identification with a perceived wealthy, white other. Under colonial rule and as a matter of political necessity to challenge exploitative colonial policies, groups previously differentiated by kainga or district became the homogenized "Banabans"; "Gilbertese," meanwhile, became not distant kin, but "others."[6]

The following extract from a 1976 letter to the editor of the *Fiji Times* from Thomas Teai, the secretary to the Rabi Council of Leaders, lucidly illustrates this tension.

Reply to the Gilberts

We would not mind if the Gilbertese were to refer to us as "Our Banaban cousins" in the same way as the British refer to their "American cousins," a relationship that is not to be taken too literally. But the kinship that the Gilbertese are so anxious to claim goes no deeper than that.

Intermarriage between Banabans and Gilbertese does not change the racial origin of the participants. A Gilbertese marrying a Banaban remains a Gilbertese just as a Fijian marrying a Tongan remains a Fijian.

The Gilbert Islands statement mentions, rather puzzlingly that when we Banabans came to live in Fiji after the war we brought 152 Gilbertese men with us. So what?

They had been with us in Japanese captivity and we had shared many hardships. They asked us to take them to Rabi. That established sympathy and friendship. Nothing more. They remain Gilbertese. They own no land on Rabi, as they would if they were Banabans.[7]

Teai's British/American–Gilbertese/Banaban analogy is fraught but reflects a very charged political context. From the late 1960s till the early 1980s, the Banabans had been fighting for two things: independence from the colony of the Gilbert and Ellice Islands, and compensation from the British government and the BPC for the damage caused by the mining industry. These two aims were powerfully connected. Mining taxes paid to the colony since 1947 had been divided so that the Banabans received 15 percent and the colony 85 percent.[8] Thus, one of the major strategies toward independence from the Gilberts was for Banabans to establish themselves as culturally and racially different from Gilbertese. This incensed Gilbertese politicians in the 1970s, who were themselves working toward a more amicable separation from Britain and were relying on a reserve fund, based on income from phosphate shipments, to seed and sustain their economic future.[9] Many in the general Gilbertese population, however, thought Banabans should have a larger right to the monetary benefits from their own land and did not share the views of the Gilbertese government.[10]

The characterization of kinship that Teai responded to above was created by the Gilbert Islands government in order to refute Banaban claims that they had not been consulted when Banaba was annexed into the colony in 1901, ostensibly to secure phosphate for the British Empire. The government issued a bulletin called *Ocean Island: Some Facts the Banabans Ignore*, in which it was stated that Banaban claims for independence could apply just as well to all sixteen islands in the group.[11] The bulletin argued that all the islands had previously been autonomous but were then united under one British colonial rule. It further suggested that the administration of all the islands as one colony had been advantageous for the Banabans, in that the colonial government secured better deals for them with the mining company than they would have had if left to the exploitative terms of the original agreement signed by the so-called king. The bulletin then cited the numbers of Gilbertese who had moved to Rabi with the Banabans and concluded, "Even today of the 2,000 people living in Rabi over 250 have both parents born in the Gilbert Islands other than Banaba. It is indeed doubtful whether there is a single Banaban family which does not have relatives in the other Gilbert Islands."[12]

Of the 1,003 people brought to Rabi on December 15, 1945, 300 were indeed Gilbertese.[13] During the Japanese occupation, families of the Gilbert and Ellice Island laborers who were left behind by the Company were invited into Banaban families in a relationship called *te bo*.[14] This was partly because the material benefits of the mining industry had eclipsed certain Banaban survival skills and they sometimes had to rely on the knowledge of fishing and healing of other Islanders. Silverman describes the predicament faced when this mixed group arrived on Rabi: "a new problem had to be handled, and that problem was one of the definition of the community itself."[15]

Initially, people adopted into Banaban families who received Banaban lands were considered Banaban. Adoption had always been as binding as direct descent. In Fiji this became problematic as the Rabi community started to redefine a Banaban identity in relation to the Company, the former colonial administration, the nearby Fijian and Ellice Islander communities, and other Gilbertese. The Banaban nationalist movement in the 1970s then shaped the way in which this process of differentiation played out.

The letter to the editor of the *Fiji Times* by Teai was one of a slew of carefully worded insults and accusations between Banabans and Gilbertese in Fiji newspapers, particularly between 1976 and 1979. These exchanges, along with articles and commentary about the Banaban court case in London from both supporters

and critics, were so frequent for so long tha
balavu, wrote to the newspaper in 1979: "S
cerned about the Banaban case which has b
wants to know about their business with th
settle this matter, why don't they all take-o
there since they're both fighting over it."[16]

At the time the Fiji Trade Unions Cour
misese Mara, were playing major roles in the
in solidarity with the Banabans, and Ratu I
behalf with the Gilbertese, Australian, and I
had achieved its own independence, suppor

In the *Fiji Times* a lot was said about "facts and lies, and the Gilbertese and Banaban "facts" were almost always different. Teburoro Tito, who would later become president of Kiribati, was then a student at the University of the South Pacific. After Teai's letter responding to the Gilbert Islands government's *Ocean Island: Some Facts the Banabans Ignore,* Tito and another student at the University of the South Pacific wrote:

> What cannot be tolerated is the fact that for too long the Banabans have been publicising their motherland (Banaba) as a place where they shall live and die when in reality they have demonstrated beyond any reasonable doubt that they would rather remain on Rabi. . . . For obvious reasons, including that of Fiji being naturally more fertile than the rocky, waterless Banaba, they chose NOT to go home.
>
> Is Mr. Teai not clear that his grandmother came from the Gilberts, his lands are still waiting for him at Arorae . . . and that according to a Banaban custom one must inherit the identity and birthrights of the mother. Furthermore as a descendant of a Gilbertese woman, he should be more versed with the legendary and historical background of the Gilbertese . . . people than what he has so far demonstrated.[17]

The authors also insinuated that the Banabans had not wisely spent the royalties they had earned through the mining and were heavily dependent on foreign advisors. They also stressed that there were fifty thousand people in the Gilberts and only twenty-five hundred Banabans, further implying that the financial distribution had really been to the advantage of the Banabans.

Another letter to the editor, from a T. Kata, took a humorous approach to the whole thing. He wrote, "Ideally speaking, the most feasible sounding solution is to physically drag Banaba out of Kiribati and tie it next to Rabi island. With the help of some sophisticated technology yet to be invented I am sure this will not be a very distant solution."[18] Ironically, by that point over twenty million tons of the island had already been "dragged" elsewhere. It was not such a humorous fantasy that the island might have the capacity to be moved.

ere further exacerbated by a particular incident on Banaba
as forever been a sore point for both Banabans and Gilbertese.
d the island over twenty years later, the wife of the Banaban mana-
luan woman, recounted this event to me as if it had just happened yes-
She said that Gilbertese policemen were particularly harsh toward the
abans when they returned to "occupy" their island in February 1979, hav-
ng lost the court case in Britain. In one skirmish a Banaban man was killed. In
March 1979 fifty-five Banabans were charged with firebombing BPC mining installations, and they were held in Tarawa.[19] Apparently, Ellice Islander workers
refused to act against the Banabans, and so the lines were clearly drawn with the
Gilbertese on one side and the Banabans on the other.

The Banaban story became a well-publicized Pacific drama, and some across
the region thought that the lawsuits and activism were motivated by greed rather
than genuine grievance. For example, the Papua New Guinean scholar August
Kituai's master's research in 1982, also published in *Bikmaus*, sought to clarify just
what lay behind Banaban nationalism. By talking directly to Banabans he found:

> The Banabans' struggle for complete independence was . . . frustrated by the
> BPC but, more seriously, by the inconsistencies of the British colonial policies.
> The Tuvaluans were allowed to gain their own independence separately from
> the Gilbertese without any fuss. There was, of course, nothing to lose by their
> separation. But when the Banabans tried to gain the same privilege, the way
> was obstructed, obviously for fear of losing the handsome source of revenue
> from the phosphate. The myth of Ocean Island being traditionally an integral
> part of the Gilbertese group was unashamedly created as an excuse for block-
> ing the way of these poor people towards gaining their legitimate and inalien-
> able rights for complete political independence.[20]

While it might have seemed like the Ellice Islands had been allowed to gain
independence as the new country of Tuvalu without a fuss, this is not quite accurate. According to a former prime minister, Tomasi Puapua, Britain considered
them too small and had only granted freedom on the condition that there would
be no financial support.[21] All the phosphate reserve funds and any colony assets
went to the new country of Kiribati. Today, Tuvalu is one of the smallest nation-
states with a population of around ten thousand citizens.

After the Banabans lost their lawsuits against the Company and the British
government along with their quest for independence, they realized they would
have to carve out a meaningful citizenship in Fiji, learn to live off the land of Rabi,
and explore other economic opportunities. Compared with their life on Banaba,
where the Company and the colonial office provided infrastructure, health and
municipal services, commodities, and entertainment, the material life on Rabi
was very different. The ex gratia payment of AU$10 million was established as

the Banaban trust fund with a clear policy about protecting the principal of the fund and using the interest for the benefit of the community as a whole. However, a string of council chairmen violated these policies and either overspent the interest or used funds from the principal. Corruption in the council became rampant, and a slew of con men presenting themselves as financial advisors targeted the Banabans, often making off with thousands of the community's dollars.[22]

Furthermore, if before the mining industry the notion of who could claim to be a Banaban was more fluid, the definition became particularly rigid on Rabi. In the early 1990s the council chairman, Rongorongo, a man not Banaban by blood but by adoption, was thrown out of office for corruption, and a new definition of "Banaban" was formally established. According to my father, John Teaiwa, who was the next elected chairman after Rongorongo, these definitions were initiated by the Banaban Council of Elders, an advisory body established to maintain cultural continuity between Rabi and Banaba, during the period of interim administration between 1991 and 1996. Rongorongo's behavior had caused such discord that the Fiji government had to step in and appoint three administrators who were neither Banaban nor Gilbertese. Today, only a Banaban by blood can run for Rabi Council elections and only Banabans by blood can vote in those elections.

On Rabi, assertions of identity at public gatherings often take a Banaban essence to be the most important measure of identity and "rights."[23] If a Gilbertese or other non-Banaban, even one who is married to a Banaban, wishes to speak in a public meeting, he or she will most likely be silenced. Silverman recounts one particular example where a meeting was held to sort out a Banaban genealogy, and a Gilbertese married to a Banaban woman tried to present his wife's lineage. He was told, "You have nothing to do with this matter; leave the meeting house!"[24]

Gilbertese on Rabi are usually barred from actively participating in any position of responsibility or leadership even if they contribute their labor to the village or the larger Rabi community. This is one of the things Teaiwa tried to change during his four-year chairmanship of the council from 1996 to 2000. He would always start a public meeting by inviting everyone to speak, and all people understood that this was regardless of blood. Gilbertese began to take an active role in village committees but as soon as his term ended, they were once again barred from participation.[25]

If the mining industry precipitated identity as a rigid formation reduced to "blood," it also facilitated the incorporation of a vast array of cultural practices that now pervade both I-Kiribati and Rabi life. These fluid, more open connections manifest in everyday activities and the cross-cultural exchange of oral, embodied, and material traditions.[26] While Banabans have intermarried with Fijians, Tuvaluans, and Indo-Fijians, there is still a higher rate of intermarriage with I-Kiribati.

An example of continuing Banaban resentment over the Gilbertese government's position was demonstrated at the University of the South Pacific in Suva after I presented a video edited from archival film footage, photographs of Banaba, and contemporary images of Rabi.[27] The main questions I received from Banabans were not about the new visual archival material that I had uncovered but about whether I had discovered any evidence to reinforce the racial and cultural differences between "our people" and I-Kiribati. I replied that I had no problem being of both Gilbertese and Banaban heritage, though I recognized that Banaban anger over the events of the 1970s and indeed of the whole century was still salient and quite justified.

Ambivalence on Rabi

Raobeia Ken Sigrah and Stacey King list the following kinds of knowledge as central to Banaban identity: knowledge of genealogy, knowledge of the family role within the kainga and district, knowledge of the land, and especially knowledge of the kainga.[28] This is true but from 1945 the intergenerational glue became unraveled so that on the new island, and especially after many elders passed away in rapid succession, younger people constantly challenged the unimwane and unaine on norms that favored elderly wisdom. As seen in the Fiji map with Rabi detail, while all four villages were replicated on Rabi, the new landscape allowed young people to discount emplaced knowledge and the practices ensuing from them. So it is now members of the Rabi Council, made up of a chairman and elected representatives from the four villages, or kawa, and their kawa-level counterparts—along with church organizations, schools, youth groups, women's groups, and so forth—that provide some of the functions of decision making, municipal services, greeting and hosting visitors, calling the sports competitions or performances, and apportioning resources.[29] The Council of Elders is still there but with diminished authority.

The context of the meeting from which the following discussion is taken is the period after the May 19, 2000, civilian coup in Fiji and a century after mining commenced on Ocean Island. Although Banabans live some distance from the capital city and operate with considerable autonomy, as citizens of Fiji they are always affected by the political climate in the rest of the country.[30] When they first arrived, the Banabans had no knowledge of Fijian culture or language, and when they were invited to visit the villages across the bay they did not know what protocols to follow. According to research on the Methodist Church on Rabi by Temaka Benaia

> the people were not informed of the kinds of physical, social, and cultural changes they could expect on arrival in Rabi. As a result, readjustment to the new environment involved both minor and serious mistakes which even cost the lives of some men and women. In the late 1940s a group of Banabans went to Taveuni

island (12 miles south of Rabi) to attend a special function, and were welcomed with a full Fijian traditional ceremony. When the first cup of grog [kava] was served to each of them, one of the men, Beniamina, refused to take it. In the Fijian customs, this is very rude and unacceptable. After a while Beniamina went out of the house and he was never seen again.[31]

In the decades before Fiji's first coup in 1987, relationships became more amiable, and today there are many shared events and exchanges centered on both the Catholic and Methodist churches. The Banabans on Rabi have also tried to maintain a good relationship with the former indigenous owners of Rabi (or Rabe) Island, who now live in Lovonivonu on the island of Taveuni. The title "Tui Rabe," or chief of Rabe, continues to exist even though Fijians no longer have legal rights on this freehold island. While not wanting to officially recognize the indigenous claim to their island, in 2000 Banabans decided to include the Rabean descendants to represent Rabi at national rugby matches. While having already proved their mettle in this Fijian-dominated game, the Banabans felt that by including members of the original Rabe people, they would win the island zone competition; victory had eluded them thus far. Thus in 2000 the Rabi team consisted of mostly Fijians from Lovonivonu and a handful of Banabans. They played under the Rabi flag and they indeed won the island zone. The team won again in 2001, and in August the *Daily Post* online ran a story titled "Rabi Proves Too Strong."[32] This time none of the players were Banaban, so at least in rugby the original Fijian descendants of the island have reclaimed their title. In comparison with the "Our God Help Us" motto of the Rabi Council, the motto of one of the regularly strongest rugby teams on the island, from Tabwewa village, is Nano Matoa, meaning "strong" or "persevering."

There have, however, been marked tensions with Fijian villages in Buca Bay over fishing rights. The Tui Tunuloa, who lives in Koroivonu, "keeps an eye" on the Banabans to make sure that they do not fish for commercial purposes without a license. Legally, Banabans are only allowed to fish on the reef for subsistence. They have an agreement with the Tui Cakau, who is head of all the chiefs of Cakaudrove.[33] The restrictions on Banaban economic practices have remained a sore point for some people on Rabi, especially as they are used as political leverage during national elections. When the chiefs of Cakaudrove need Banabans to vote for their political candidates, they always remind them of their generosity in granting them rights to fish on their reefs.

When there was political trouble in the rest of the country and especially when it became known that Fijian nationalism was gaining momentum (despite the differences between factions of the Fijian nationalist movement), some Banabans began to feel uneasy about their status in Fiji. They started to look back to Banaba as their true home. In 2000, the coup prompted another such bout of insecurity. The Banaban elders immediately wrote to the Rabi Council to call a meeting, which convened on November 11 in Nuku. The sixteen elders raised three points with chairman Teaiwa over the course of the two-hour-long meeting, which I was allowed to videotape with the elders' permission. The meeting was conducted in the Gilbertese language and so all quotes are translations.

Originally, the elders on Banaba had the traditional authority along with the various clans that comprised the genealogical hierarchy from the village of Tabwewa through to Uma, Buakonikai, and Tabiang. In 1947, however, the Council of Leaders was set up by the British colonial administration. Since then the old men and women, te unimwane ao unaine, have maintained symbolic leadership, and have periodically raised the issue of their desire to return to their ancestral lands. They represent a generation that remembers both the prosperity on the island and its demise during the Japanese occupation in 1942.

The first point raised at the meeting was regarding a review of the Kiribati Constitution that had occurred in early 2000, which Teaiwa and three other councilors had attended on Tarawa. The elders especially raised an issue with chapter 9, which dealt with the protection of Banabans and Banaban lands. During that conference, the Rabi Council had presented its views on both chapter 9 and chapter 3, which dealt with Banaban constitutional rights and citizenship in Kiribati. Teaiwa explained that the council had expressed its desire to have both chapters strengthened in order to reflect the friendly relations they were trying to foster between the Banabans and the Kiribati government. In his thinking, the Banabans had a unique opportunity to create economic and cultural exchanges with Kiribati, given their dual citizenship.

The second point raised by the elders was their continuing desire for secession from Kiribati. They still wanted independence, and many were rattled by the 2000 coup. Karawa from Uma said: "There is insecurity in Fiji and a desire to resettle on Banaba. There is no doubt that Banabans own Rabi under the law, but they can return to Banaba, which they own too. Recent events and rumors about Fijians wanting their land back are a real worry and a cause for concern about Banaban safety. The Banaban history of destruction and exploitation could repeat itself."[34]

The suggested economic benefits of life on Banaba in 2000 were rather hard to prove, but a man named Karoro Corrie reiterated a popular rumor that Banaba actually contained mineral oil as well as phosphate. This possibility was seen to be sufficient grounds for independence from Kiribati. My father, however, resisted this idea. As a former Fiji civil servant, he firmly believed that the Banaban status in Fiji was not threatened and that the people of Rabi could maintain good relations with both the Fiji government and the Kiribati government. As chairman, however, he supported the third matter that was raised, the desire to resettle Banaba, but only after the Kiribati government put into action a rehabilitation plan with the assistance of the former phosphate company governments.

The Tui Rabe's desire for recognition on the island combined with the events of the coup made the elders feel that the Banaban people were not welcome in Fiji. They worried that they would be displaced again and the island repossessed. While some might argue that their status is relatively secure since Rabi is a free-hold island alienated from its indigenous owners long before the Banabans arrived, events in Fiji in 2000 and again in 2006, when the fourth coup ensued and the law changed again, seemed to suggest otherwise.[35] In 2000 the elders worried that if Fijians could "kick Indians out of the country," maybe they would do the same with the Banabans. My father replied that while Indians were perceived by some as a threat to Fijian authority, Banabans were not.

After the 2000 coup, an interim government led by Laisenia Qarase was appointed. This was an almost completely Fijian government of which Teaiwa was temporarily a member, until he resigned and a second group was appointed by the interim president of Fiji, Ratu Josefa Iloilo. One goal of the Qarase government was to return to indigenous ownership the reefs and shorelines up to high-water marks, which were previously owned by the state rather than the Fijian provinces. This would mean the I-Taukei of each area would have more rights over fishing waters than groups like the Banabans, the resettled Tuvaluan Kioans, and the general public, including the tourism industry. Teaiwa expressed his immediate concern regarding this move and the government representatives said they would take it into consideration. This, however, did not help the Banaban elders feel any better about their situation in Fiji.

The November meeting went on, and Teaiwa, at the time well versed in the technical language of the civil service but less in the cultural and spiritual needs of Banaban elders, made a statement:

> The council supports resettlement of Banaba but for reasons different from the elders. [The] council has liaised closely with Kiribati on Banaba rehabilitation, including potential remining, upgrading roads and other public works, investigating underground water, and possible commercialization of pinnacles. It is important to pursue these issues in conjunction with resettlement because [the] council needs to know whether it is feasible. Therefore, we should proceed slowly, carefully, and patiently.[36]

Teaiwa said that much had to be done on Banaba before resettlement was possible. This included a new survey of land boundaries since the last one had been done in 1947. The meeting ended after several people repeated what others said about wanting to return and their worries about Fijian pressure. Are Moote of Uma said: "It has always been our prayer and hope to return to live in our spiritual homeland. Living away from Banaba makes us feel homesick, and recent events have strengthened our desire to return to Banaba to live. Even if we have to face hardship there, at least we will live peacefully."[37]

Banaban Council of Elders, including the Rabi Council chairman, John Teaiwa (*back row, far right*), and Councilor Makin Corrie Tekenimatang (*seated, second from right*), 2000. Photo by Katerina Martina Teaiwa

The meeting then ended, we had a generous morning tea provided by Nei Makin Corrie Tekenimatang and her family, and I took a photograph of everyone outside.

Dancing History

Of his studies on Rabi, Silverman writes, "I mentioned that when the Banabans look at certain magazines, they look for themselves inside. This is a special case of a more inclusive phenomenon: they are looking for themselves in general. They are trying to clarify who they are, how they got where they are, what they are doing and what they should do, where they are going and where they should go."[38] The "two-island" theme was viewed as one of the most difficult aspects of Banaban identity and history and of Silverman's own anthropological project. The discipline was traditionally geared toward dealing with people and culture "in place" so that environment, language, material culture, and behavior can be comprehended within one system. In Silverman's view, the deep exploration of one symbol, like land, for example, should illuminate the entire culture. The Banaban displacement from their indigenous land complicated this assumption.

In the 1990s, Wolfgang Kempf's and Elfriede Hermann's work on Rabi focused on the ways in which Banabans were "placing" themselves in the Fiji environment and national context while continuing to invoke Banaba as a key source of historicity and identity through story, song, and dance theater.[39] Kempf theorizes Banaban resistance on Rabi in terms of the choreographed space of the stage, where versions of history are performed and multiple sites invoked, using the concept of Michel Foucault's heterotopia and extending this "thirdspace" as developed by Edward W. Soja.[40] For Kempf and Hermann, a heterotopic Banaba on Rabi is created, lived out, and regularly reinforced with creative political and, in Hermann's analysis, "emotional" tools and tactics. Banabans' history is thus reinforced and reenacted on every occasion they perform the now-iconic historical dance theater in Fiji and beyond.

Originally composed to solidify an alternative identity and culture for Banabans against Gilbertese claims of ethnic homogeneity, the dance theater gained momentum in the lead-up to the 1972 Festival of Pacific Arts held in Suva. The festival is a quadrennial event for the whole Pacific region and an important opportunity for national contingents to show off their vibrant and resilient cultures. Until the coups of 1987, Fiji would regularly include the Banabans, but they were then left out until 2012, when a contingent from Rabi High School was added to the Fiji group at the last hour. The festival has developed in a way that reinforces notions of what is "traditional" and what is "contemporary" with respect to Pacific dance, music, visual, and culinary arts, along with navigation and sailing.[41] Guam, for example, while initially bringing its Spanish-influenced dances to the festival stage, transformed its entire repertoire, costuming, and music to better fall in line with "Pacific" perceptions of Pacific dance.[42]

From the arrival of missionaries in the 1880s, Banaban dance was in a constant state of transformation, resulting in the loss of some performance genres. Christian and colonial policies directed when and where people were allowed to dance. When the Banabans refused to lease more land, Arthur Grimble, while wildly passionate about defending the rights of Gilbert Islanders in the rest of the colony to perform and maintain their dances, banned Banaban dancing temporarily as a punitive measure for not agreeing to sign more leases.[43] By the time Banabans were settled on Rabi, it was Gilbertese dance and music that dominated the cultural landscape. But as tensions mounted between the Banabans and the Gilbert Islands government, Banabans turned to their oral and performing arts traditions in order to articulate a radical alterity. They established the professional Banaban Dancing Group, and began to reconstruct and express their ethnic difference via music and dance.[44] With the urging and direction of festival organizers Beth Dean and Victor Carrell, the Banabans also revived ancient costumes in muted, earthy colors and quickly dispensed with the red, pink, green, and yellow crepe paper and raffia that now featured prominently on Rabi.[45]

The focal point of their efforts was a thematic dance theater that, in Hermann's words, divides history into key "chapters," each of which serves a specific political and cultural purpose: "Pre-Colonial Times on Banaba," "Phosphate Mining, Relocation of Banabans," and "Struggle for Independence." Within each theatrical chapter, significant aspects of identity and history are identified and choreographed to reinforce the Banabans' political goals. In the precolonial chapter, the arrival of missionaries bringing the Bible and "the light," and the collecting of water by women in the bwangabwanga, "Te Itiran," are highlighted. This special role of women is absolutely critical as a distinction from the Gilbertese, who live on atolls without water caves. The performance is a combination of pantomime and rhythmic movement with the lyrics of the accompanying song, composed by Nei Tebwebwe, signaling key figures. For example, the lyrics challenge a chief minister of the Gilbert Islands, Naboua, who asserted that Banabans and Gilbertese are the same:

> You, how come you are doing the talking, N.B.U.A.?
> Change your inner attitude, because they're not the same [as yours]
> Our customs and culture aren't!
> Because we ourselves, the Banabans,
> We fetch the water from the cave.[46]

The next section of the performance features the "How Pity" song in which the Banabans are confused by the price and appearance of money. Twenty-four pennies appear to have far more value than a flimsy piece of paper, a one pound note. This is a way of Banabans saying they had no clue about the monetary value of the land, or even about the value of money itself. They are kept in the dark on the "use value" and the "exchange value" of things in the colonial and industrial context. All this leads to the ultimate state of pity, which Hermann calls the ever-present *nanoanga*, which specifically refers to a heavy or sad heart.

The reenactment of their relocation to Rabi is often performed with a combination of humor and more pity. With promises of good houses and an abundant island, the Banabans board the ship at Tarawa and cross the ocean. They are confused that there are no houses waiting for them. They erect what they call "awnings" in the rain and huddle underneath. In the middle of the night, cows, which they believe are ghosts, stumble through their camps making extraordinary sounds. At the end of this section the Banabans gather and pray and ask God to watch over them on Rabi. The performers usually then present a range of contemporary and traditional Banaban dances, including *te karanga*, a dance involving both men and women beating long sticks while chanting and known as the only non-Gilbertese traditional dance remaining in the Banaban repertoire.[47]

As this historical dance theater was choreographed before the Banabans took up and lost their case in London, the court cases, the attempts to reoccupy Banaba, and subsequent problems with the council are not performed as chapters but are implied throughout the performance. The efforts of the Banaban men and women who constructed this creative expression of history, a theater that has become iconic of all Banaban performance, received global attention when they accompanied a group of plaintiffs to London in the 1970s. Jennifer Shennan lucidly captures this moment: "In London, during the protracted court case involving Banaban compensation claims for the destruction of their Ocean Island homeland by phosphate mining, a daily newspaper posed the question: 'Who are these Banaban people anyway?' A group of Banaban dancers were in London at the time and they responded to the question. They announced a performance of music and dance with the simple and powerful statement: 'We, the Banabans, are the people who dance like this.'"[48]

(Re)placing Culture

Invoking James Clifford's work, the Banaban dance theater is described by Kempf as a dramatic rendering of Banaba's "routes and roots." However, Kempf does not engage as much with the world of the youth, the next generation of Banabans whose ties to the homeland are thinning. While the dance theater was for many years a professional enterprise with strict rules about who could join and who could perform, and the emphasis was usually on the young adults—the *rorobuaka,* or warrior cohort—it has shifted dramatically so that in 2007 primary school children were performing the theater for tourists on the *Tui Tai* ship. The Rabi High School students who traveled to the Solomon Islands for the 2012 Festival of Pacific Arts presented no political or historical performances but those of their own liking and choreography: the Banaban choreography was remixed with MTV-inspired moves à la pop stars such as Beyoncé, Rihanna, and Usher.[49]

The departure of key members of professional dancing groups—there were, at one time, three on the island—has provoked a shift serving a number of cultural and economic purposes. Tourists like to see children smiling and dancing; the salience of the dance theater constructed in the late 1960s is waning and needs youthful rejuvenation; and the next generation of Banabans needs to be reminded about their painful history and to embody this in their performance. Several of the key figures of the dance theater now live in Kiribati, where Banaban choreographic innovations have transformed I-Kiribati dance genres.

While the two-island theme dominated Silverman's approach, and both Hermann and Kempf engaged with the complexities of dance, place, and history, my own research attempts to articulate Banaba and the Banabans with several islands, cities, and nation-states, all linked by the phosphate industry chain. In many ways while Silverman, Hermann, and Kempf are following the people, I attempt to follow the land, which in a Banaban ontology *is* the people. But it is important not to reproduce the Company's myopic and at times fanatical desire to keep its eyes firmly on phosphate, come rain, shine, war, or native resistance. It is important to engage with anthropological observations: Banabans belong now to two islands,

Banaban dancers, Ocean Island, 1901. Courtesy of the National Archives of Australia

Banaban dancers on Rabi, 2007. Photo by Nicholas Mortimer

and the ways the phosphate industry disrupted relations with land and kinship are critical to understanding cultural processes on Rabi.

Silverman describes Banaban values and their institutionalization in a hierarchy where you "maximize your options" or "keep your options open." He says, "A 'have your cake and eat it too' outlook dominates the manner in which Banaban alternatives are confronted; there is an attempt to get the best (or at least something) of all worlds."[50] While his focus is on the people and on individual and community dynamics, the dual aspects of te aba and kainga hold true if the focus is switched to land. If the very ground of one's identity is mined, shipped, and dispersed across foreign landscapes, then "all worlds" truly do become available for Banabans to route, root, articulate, and seek.

A set of ideals and the potential to realize them is open to individual Banabans. On Rabi, this is also possible due to overlapping loyalties and memberships. Each Banaban has a large number of kinship-based, religious, and social connections on Rabi and elsewhere to other families, clans, villages, church communities, sports groups, dance groups, work groups, school groups, kava circles, and so forth. Furthermore, members of the same nuclear family could have very different loyalties because of decisions made within and beyond the family, especially in the past. If someone's great-grandmother helped heal or care for someone's niece thirty years ago, a baby born today named after the niece or healer may have to participate in whatever obligations were formed from that action.

A detailed study of Banaban kinship was beyond my phosphate research but in trying to understand the impact of mining on Rabi, I found it difficult to keep track of all the loyalties and, indeed, bodies. Banaba was a communal but also highly individuated social field because of the correlation between individuals and their parcels of land, regularly in a state of exchange. Land tenure on Rabi is fixed, however, so the fluidity has transferred to the realm of sociality. Today one "household" will have eight members. Tomorrow there will be four, and next week there will be eighteen. Banabans can draw on multiple layers and complex networks of relationships to develop personhood within the expanding social and geographical contexts. Even children will take this into their own hands and temporarily move to reside with aunties, uncles, or cousins across or beyond Rabi in order to gain some sense of individual agency and independence.

Within a family, if someone has a calamitous argument with someone else and needs to relocate, he or she will have several different options for whom to discuss the problem with, where to live, and where to get support in the meantime. In a way, this mode of life also preserves a major part of the past because it is that knowledge of relationships that is essential for survival. For example, some years ago in Nuku my father encountered a man who asked him for some money. Teaiwa immediately gave it to him because he remembered going with his mother as a child on Tabiteuea, fifty years earlier, to this man's father for a similar request.

Because his mother received help from the man's father five decades ago, he had an obligation to him in the present. They both retained knowledge of the past exchange, even though they had not spoken for many years.

Sometimes people "remember" things on Rabi because of the intervention of ancient spirits, Nei Tituabine in particular. She is supposed to have traveled to Rabi with Banabans on their return from the 1947 *te tautia* (boundary-marking) trip to Ocean Island. Silverman's version says: "The young man's story was that when the people returned to Ocean Island, Nei Tituabine appeared to members of that hamlet and said: 'So you Banabans are not all dead. I have been looking for you.' She came back with the people on their ship. After the return, the health of the community improved; before, there had been many deaths. The improvement was Nei Tituabine's work. Ocean Island had come to Rabi."[51]

Other gods and ancestors have also followed certain individuals from their homes on Ocean Island or in the Gilberts. These spirits can be vehicles for the preservation of relationships and obligations because they will appear when necessary to remind those who stray from their duties. For example, a request put forward to the Rabi Council of Leaders by the Te Aka clan regarding the return of an ancestral skull stolen from Banaba by a visiting American physician, a Dr. Gould, during the early mining period reflects this dialogue between past and present.[52] The clan members said that their ancestor had come to Rabi in dreams to remind them to bring him back home from the basement of the U.S. museum in which he rests.[53]

The tautia trip also marked a growing uneasiness among younger Banabans on the importance of genealogical information. It was apparent that they had to rely on their elders for knowledge of the land, and many disputes arose over the accuracy of "memory," among other things. Silverman illustrates this through the reproduction of a song composed by Kawate Maibintebure for the trip:

> The boundary marking on Banaba.
> Where is the boundary?
> This is the boundary.
> I really don't know
> The boundary
> But I hear that
> Miss What's-her-name and Mr. So-and-so
> Are next to me.[54]

As Silverman suggests, Banabans face a continuing problem with the speed of the social and institutional transformations since Albert Ellis's arrival in 1900: "in a period of five years, the phosphate operation began, with its people, work, money . . . ; Ocean Island was drawn into the protectorate and a native government was set up; the children were in school."[55] Then, forty-five years later, they

were faced not just with new institutions but with an enti~~
new provincial and national context: the politically unstable ~~

All Banabans are connected through genealogy and history to~~
of individuals and families; they can seek to harness the benefits~~
nections depending on the context. Membership in family, church, ~~
ployment, and sports groups allows a person to exercise a certain amou~~
tonomy in terms of where his or her actions or energies might be focused. ~~
the political and material conditions on Rabi may have changed over time, t~~
dynamic aspect of Banaban personhood perdures. Silverman writes, "With the
possibilities for creativity and elaboration increased, with differentiation between
cultural and social spheres, objectification and the growing systematisation of the
culture . . . become correlates at the individual level."[56]

Aspects of Silverman's analysis are dependent, however, on Maude and Maude's
1932 original descriptions of "traditional" Banaban culture, which, he theorizes,
"change" on the basis of this seemingly a priori stable system. The fluidity of Banaban culture appears to him to be a consequence of Rabi displacement rather than
a feature of the culture in general. But even Maude and Maude acknowledge that
as many as fifteen hundred Banabans dispersed during severe droughts in the
1870s, returning to Banaba after years of living in Tahiti, Hawai'i, and other islands.[57] Many more perished from lack of food and water on the island. The division of Banaba by Nei Anginimaeao more than a century before these droughts
also highlights another important example.[58] Anginimaeao and her relatives seem
to have drastically transformed the social structure of groups on the island, and
it would be hard to imagine that Banabans ever lived in an unchanging world.
What was always constant, however, were the connections to the land and to kin,
broadly or narrowly defined depending on the political and economic context.

As well as fluidity and multiple connections in political, interpersonal, or
group relations, as illustrated by both Hermann and Kempf, embodied dance and
musical practices similarly evince confluences and multiple sources. The impulse
for creativity, fluidity, and permeability does not just come from metropolitan centers or transnational media but reflects aspects of intra-Pacific and other cross-
cultural exchanges and connections. Moreover, far from being politically disinter-
ested, this fluidity is about creative survival. Silverman cites the small population,
the small area of interaction (the island), and the egalitarian ethic as reasons that
an individual Banaban could actually make a difference at the island level.[59] This
may be more true for certain Banaban men than women, but he was correct in
describing the nature of the social field. It is a relatively level terrain, or it appears
so, compared to traditionally hierarchical Pacific societies in, for example, Fiji,
Samoa, or Tonga.

Though most Banabans have been displaced and no longer live on their indigenous lands, they also exist on the margins of the "diasporic" as it is theo-

not migrate by choice but were moved en
litan center in the West; and in Fiji they
and. James Clifford defines the contours
suppose longer distances and a separa-
on return, or its postponement to a re-

emselves as being "in exile," and this
d prevalently in both media coverage
ray from Kiribati as India is from the
say the Indian or Samoan diaspora,
aban Rabi Association, have moved

colonial powers. A cultural studies focus on diaspo-
former colonies to imperial centers inadvertently elides the experiences of indigenous groups like the Banabans and Tuvaluans in Fiji.[62] In her research theorizing diaspora and "the Native," Teresia Teaiwa writes: "The term 'diaspora' traces its origins to the Jewish experience of displacement from a homeland and dispersal in phases over hundreds of years throughout the Middle East, Africa, Europe, and America. The diasporic experience engenders a diasporic imagination and identity which keeps in tension the memory of the homeland and the exigencies of making a home in a new location."[63]

Most Banaban leaders have been Methodist ministers, including Rotan Tito, his son Tebuke Rotan, and Terubea Rongorongo, and many likened their experience to that of the Israelites. In the preface to his thesis on the history of the Methodist Church on Rabi, Temaka Benaia writes:

> Biblically, the Banabans are like the Israelites who were called from Egypt, the land of bondage and hardships. The Banabans left and traveled to Rabi under very difficult conditions. They journeyed by sea but upon reaching Rabi, they realized that, like Canaan, the land was overflowing with "milk" and "honey," in the abundance of water and fertile soil to plant food crops. . . . Like the Israelites, the Banabans had put their trust in God and they believed that God could help them too.[64]

There is thus a salient discourse on exile from "the homeland" that is kept alive by particular actors—many members of the older generations and a few younger people. Banabans, like many Pacific Islanders, have plural and situational identifications that are not played out in a metropolitan center or in close proximity to a dominant white other, at least not since 1941. But, following Clifford's further discussion on diaspora cultures, the community on Rabi "articulates or bends together, both roots and routes to construct what Gilroy . . . describes as alternate public spheres, forms of community consciousness and solidarity that maintain identifications outside the national time/space in order to live inside, with a difference."[65]

Kempf emphasizes this in his discussion of the politics of emplacement on Rabi.[66] Banaban cultural politics, as they have developed in Fiji, reveal how their strategies and tactics resonate with both diasporic and indigenous ontologies. At one level Banabans consider Rabi to be Banaban land because it was bought with phosphate money—money from Banaban land. But throughout the decade in which the people approached the United Nations, the British government, and the Gilbert and Ellice Islands colony for Banaban independence, they never once approached Fiji for Rabi independence. Rabi, after all, was originally indigenous Fijian land.

The removal of the Banaban community as a whole is probably what most distinguishes them from diasporic communities or individuals who articulate their identities against a still-present "home" culture. The current population of about four hundred on Banaba is not the home culture but rather consists of "caretakers" from Rabi. The objectification of culture plays out uniquely on Rabi because most Banabans are committed to cultural change, and they debate it in the new environment. There is enough of a sense of autonomy on Rabi for them to "test out" possible ways of organizing the community as a whole and in its various parts—villages, church groups, and so on.[67] The way Silverman views all this in relation to the past is worth mentioning: "Kinship and descent, politics, economics and religion are implicated in the testing-out process. Through this process Banaban culture evolves, and individuals try to give sense to and make sense from their experience. Their experience is neither personally nor historically static. It is calamitous; and the experience of their parents and grandparents, transformed, is alive within them. Again, they are in history and history is in them."[68]

Developing Roots

Despite the continuing talk of going back to the homeland, Banabans have created an increasingly self-sufficient life on Rabi, which is necessary since people no longer receive annuities from phosphate royalties.[69] In her analysis of the Rabi Island community's political position with respect to the national arena, Teresia Teaiwa describes "two major 'peripheralities'": the way Rabi exists for the most part in the peripheral vision of the nation, and the way the nation occupies the periphery of Rabi Islanders' imagination.[70] She carried out thirty-three formal interviews on Rabi, which revealed some interesting features of Banaban historical and national consciousness. Her interviews were done in the context of voting practices and education during a period of elections. The first issue she faced was the reference to the "government" in her questionnaire. Invariably she was asked "which government"? The Rabi Council of Leaders is seen as the govern-

ment for the Banabans, but there is also the Fiji government, the Kiribati government, and previously the British government.

A most revealing aspect of her survey was the strengthening of relations between Banabans and Fijians, despite the perceived peripherality. Thirty of the
thirty-three Banabans spoke Fijian fluently, and nineteen ranked Fijians as the
group they felt closest to above Tuvaluans, Gilbertese, Rotumans, Indo-Fijians,
Chinese, and part-Europeans. Ten ranked the Gilbertese as the group they felt closest to. While not being completely sure how Banabans contribute to the national
welfare of Fiji (in fact their trust fund has brought in important foreign exchange
for decades), many responded by describing how Banabans interact with Fijian communities across the bay through church groups or with the chief of Cakaudrove
through *soli,* monetary contributions for village, community, or church functions.[71]

A distinctive Fiji-based Banaban identity had been slowly unfolding in the
decades since their arrival. A song transcribed by Teaiwa illustrates how Rabi is
increasingly replacing Ocean Island as the source of Banaban identity:

Roron Rabi (an anthem)	"Youths of Rabi"
Roron Rabi teirake	Youths of Rabi rise
Nora tamaroan otin taai	See the beauty of the morning sun
Antai ae wene man aoria	Who would lie wastefully
e na reke te kabaia n tera	when there is prosperity to be earned?

Chorus	
Baina te nano n aba ae riai	Be patriotic and truthful
Tabeka rake aran Rabi	Proclaim the name of Rabi
Tangiria kain abara	Love all your people
Ni waaki nakon te raoiroi	March towards peace
Ko taku ba tei Rabi ngkoe	You claim you are from Rabi
Kabonganako ibukina	Be of value to it
E boni kanganga te makuri	This is not an easy task
Tai toki e na tai bara nanom	Be strong of heart
Ti na tei iaon ara berita	Be faithful and loyal
N toro iroun te atua ma te queen	To God and the Queen
Ni buokia aomata nako	For the sake of all the people
Ni kawakin taian tua nako.	And preservation of law and order.[72]

While I have only heard this anthem sung twice, both times in Suva during
the December 15 arrival celebrations, it is said to have been composed in the late
1970s when Banaban nationalism was at an all-time high. This, however, is puz-
zling given the absence of any reference to Banaba. The song clearly privileges a

"Rabi" identity rather than a Banaban one, highlights loyalty to the British queen, and focuses on youth. These are the generations born and raised in Fiji who have grown up with kava, netball, rugby, and subsistence farming rather than phosphate royalties.

The line "Who would lie wastefully when there is prosperity to be earned?" seems to encourage Banabans to make use of the fertility of Rabi rather than sit "wastefully," perhaps dreaming of the prosperity long gone from the home island. The word "earned" is particularly illustrative in the context of an economy that was basically sustained on phosphate funds. The anthem clearly locates loyalty and identity with Rabi Island quite differently from the preoccupations of the Banaban elders with the homeland.

In April 2002 four children and two adults were tragically killed in Buakonikai village. Several months later Cyclone Ami caused widespread damage that left the island in a very challenging economic and material state for almost two years. Roads were impassable, transport was scarce, and houses and farms were destroyed. The anniversary of the Banabans' sixtieth year on Rabi was approaching, and it was then that Nei Makin Corrie Tekenimatang and Jennifer Shennan devised the plan to compile a "people's history" of the Banabans—told from the perspectives of children, adults, elders, leaders, and non-Banabans. This important and moving collection of stories outlines the pains and triumphs of our people, who now number about seven thousand and are living on Rabi, across Vanua Levu and Taveuni, in Suva and elsewhere on Viti Levu, on Tarawa and other islands of Kiribati, and in Auckland, Wellington, Brisbane, and beyond.[73] It has been a reminder for the community to not forget Banaba in spite of the challenges and successes of life on Rabi and elsewhere.

Banabans are a resilient people but as one Banaban woman, reflecting on the annual December 15 celebrations and education on the island put it: "On the special day, the elders, both men and women, have time to talk about the first arrival here, and tell the new generations our history so that we know that we have been cheated. I am so glad that we have schools on the island . . . to educate our younger generations so that they cannot be cheated any more."[74]

Teaiwa's Kainga

What does Banaban life, at the family level, look like a hundred years after mining? The politics of identity and of the homeland are usually articulated beyond people's everyday concerns and activities. Politics in general do not mean much for people under the age of thirty, who are primarily occupied with school, gardening, fishing, participating in sports or dance groups, church activities, and raising children. A small number of students have had opportunities to go to technical schools on Viti Levu and to the University of the South Pacific in Suva. I

Aerial view of Teaiwa's kainga at Tabona, Rabi
(along coast north of old airstrip). Google Earth

will explore some aspects of my own extended family's experiences to illustrate; I do this because Banaban custom dictates that you represent yourself and your own family and not try to talk with authority about someone else's experiences.

The reason our family lives as part of Tabiang village today has to do with a significant favor one of my ancestors gave on Banaba. He shared key knowledge of fishing with other families during the great droughts of the 1870s. Specialized knowledge related to everyday survival is usually carefully guarded by Banabans, and even close family members will not always share skills with each other. It is because of the preserved memory of this favor by my grandfather Teaiwa's first cousin that we now have a kainga in Tabiang even though we also have roots in Tabwewa village. Within our family group there are members who are not cognate, who do not belong to the same church, and who live in the kainga only some months of the year.

Most of Teaiwa's descendants and their children live just outside the village of Tabiang at a place called Tabona. The layout of Banaba was mapped onto Rabi with the establishment of the four villages, including the placing of Buakonikai at a fair remove from the others, signaling its historical geographic, social, and political "distance" from the others. Banaban village and place names now exist alongside older, Fijian, and other names assigned to the island. Our settlement is one of the few on Rabi that resembles an actual kainga as it existed on Banaba and in the Gilberts before the system was transformed under colonialism. In many ways our settlement operates as a kainga with my father as head, and we are based on a plot of land given to us for agricultural purposes.[75] While this is not our ancestral land, and therefore not kainga in the traditional sense of the word, a hundred years from now it will be ancestral land to our descendants. Spatially, this group of houses on Rabi is a kainga in the way that Clifford, paraphrasing Michel de Certeau, describes space as "discursively mapped and corporeally practiced."[76]

The diagrams are spatial and genealogical snapshots of the kainga at Tabona in 2000, a century after mining began, with genealogical relationships between the members going back to Teaiwa and Takeua on Tabiteuea, and to Teaiwa's Banaban grandmother Kieuea, Toariki, and their parents on Banaba. The nine boxes below Teaiwa and Takeua include their children, spouses, and grandchildren with the numbers of their children in 2001 in parentheses. Teruamwi and Terianako, for example, were both married before their current spouses; I have included all their children's names from both marriages and put an asterisk next to those from previous marriages.[77] Terianako's husband Takabobwe was from Tabiteuea and passed away there about thirty years ago. Teruamwi's first wife, Ramane, is still on Rabi. Many people on the island have had more than one partner.[78] Of the nine children, Tabakitoa, Terianako, Rakomwa, and Tebarutu married non-Banabans or non-Gilbertese. Tabakitoa's wife, my mother, is African American; Terianako's late husband was Fijian; Rakomwa's husband was Rotuman; and Tebarutu's husband is Muslim Indo-Fijian. There are definite class, educational, and status issues that play out in the family, but such distinctions are only tolerated to a certain point. Banabans are, at their core, highly egalitarian; other cultures sometimes find Banaban ways excessively lacking in protocol and deference.

At the beginning of the twenty-first century, the kainga on Rabi consisted of six houses belonging, from left to right, to Terianako, Temanarara, Teruamwi, Tabakitoa, Teangatoa, and Takaia.[79] Temanarara is Teruamwi's son and Teangatoa is Takaia's, and both lived with their wives and children in the kainga at the time. These six houses primarily belong to the people listed above, but others in the family visit or stay with them from time to time.

During major events like a bootaki, or celebration, Teaiwa's and Takeua's eldest children, Tabakitoa, Takaia, Teruamwi, and Terianako, make the major decisions on when and how it should happen with input from Veronica and Teburenga.

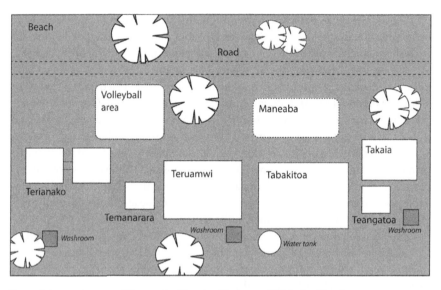

Teaiwa's kainga in 2000. Diagram by Katerina Teaiwa and Nicholas Mortimer

If Rakomwa or Tekarika are available, they also participate. Rakomwa usually lives in Tenamo's old house in Tabwewa village, and Tekarika lives in Teaiwa's house in Tabiang. Teaiwa's grandchildren will visit or sleep over at either of these houses depending on sports, school, or church functions. People's lives are distributed across at least eight different households in three different locations, excluding several households in Suva and elsewhere. While Teruamwi's and Takaia's sons are supposed to follow along with their parents' households, both often try to act independently of them. For example, when it's time to divide up food between the major households and my father directs me to make three basins of food, my cousins will say, "Look, we are separate from our father's houses so you should make one each for our families." These sorts of issues regarding the distribution of food and responsibilities—matters of course at one time on Banaba—are points of debate on Rabi on a daily basis.

Almost all the children's names come from ancestral names from either side of their parents' genealogies, but something new emerged on Rabi. In the same way that Banaban culture on Rabi has become a combination of other cultural influences, like many young Banabans two of my cousins have named their children by combining other people's names. Temanarara's daughter is named Alitalos, from the names (Ali)tia, (Ta)raruru, and Sai(los)i, who are all relatives of the child's mother. The first and third names are not Banaban or Gilbertese. It is also unusual that her family, rather than Temanarara's, named the child. Teangatoa's daughter is Asinta, a name formed from those of the paternal grandmother's son from a previous marriage and his wife: (Asi)singa and Ma(ta). The choices of these

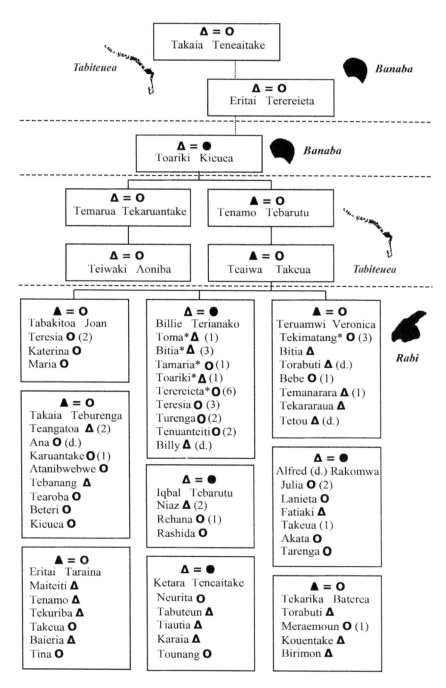

Teaiwa Banaba/Ocean Island/Tabiteuea family tree in 2001. Compiled by Katerina Teaiwa, layout by Nicholas Mortimer

names are very specific to relationships that both Teangatoa and Temanarara are trying to acknowledge. The older people in the kainga, however, see this change from the traditions of giving the names of ancestors and of according the choice to the father's family for the first child, in the case of Temanarara's child, as reflecting a lack of knowledge of genealogy. In 2009 I followed my cousins' lead and called my first child Tearia, to honor my sisters (Te)resia and M(aria), noting that the name was Banaban: Nei Tearia told Harry and Honour Maude her version of our origin stories.

As you can see, our family is rather large and every year a new child is born in the kainga. While women are supposed to give birth in the health clinic at Nuku, many still do so at home. I distinctly remember when my cousin Terereieta was pregnant a few years ago. One day she was pregnant, and the next day there was a new baby in the house. I had apparently slept through the whole thing. In naming the new boy, our *Ten Kaka* (grandfather) Teaiwa had two ancestral names to choose from, and while I was sitting in one of the back rooms he called out to me, "Shall it be this name [I forget] or Kiritama?"[80] Without hesitation I called back "Kiritama," and the boy was named.

Over the course of a year all Teaiwa's children and grandchildren will move between various households on Rabi and in Suva, visiting their other relatives. To see people hanging out on the front steps of someone's house, though, you would never imagine just how much traveling people do or how extensively they articulate their own lives with a much wider world beyond the kainga or Rabi Island. As an example of this I discuss a short film I made in 2001.[81] In one part, my cousins are making a type of music called *karebwerebwe* by tapping their fingers against the side of their mouth.

> Scene 1: *Karebwerebwe performed by Asena and Tearoba.*
>
> Scene 2: *Asena and Tearoba playing hand-game and singing.*
>
> Scene 3: *Women on front steps of Teruamwi's house in front of volleyball field, brushing each other's hair.*

While cut together in the film, the sequence with my cousins making "mouth music" through karebwerebwe was shot on a different day from the scene with the women outside Teruamwi's house. I asked the children to perform karebwerebwe for the camera because the sound was so unique, but the clapping game was spontaneous. We shot it behind my father's house, which I later juxtaposed with the front of my uncle's house. Both spaces are extremely different though part of the same kainga. While all kinds of people are always hanging out in front of (and also behind) Teruamwi's house, few attempt that in front of or behind Tabakitoa's house unless invited to. My father is a very private and usually quiet person, and when he is on the island this respect is accorded by everyone in the kainga. As

head of the family and one-time chairman of the c⟨...⟩
different way from other members.

In my film the children sing:

Be tuai n roko ngkai	It hasn't come yet
Ma raweia Jackie Chan	Catch it Jackie Chan
Taua te baei James Bond	Hold this James Bond
Ururinga Munroe	Don't forget Munroe
Taratara moan waem bwa ko	Watch where you're going
kawa n onakoa Rambo Rambo!	lest you run into Rambo, Rambo!
Tiam ni biribiri	After your running around
Why take away China Brain [O'Brien]	
I'm James Bond, Good Morning Cowboy	
Ti toka n te Yaubula	We're on the *Yaubula*
E moana n Taveuni	It calls at Taveuni
Ti moi n te Fiji Beer	We drink Fiji Beer
E rau nanora	We're satisfied.

The children's song illustrates how they, and Banabans in general, have no problem decontextualizing specific characters and making new meaning for them in a creative and fragmented way. The main logic holding the song together is that it involves action-film heroes, but those heroes are here, in Fiji![82] Besides being part of my own childhood landscape, Jackie Chan, Rambo, James Bond, "Cowboy," and China O'Brien are all characters from the numerous videos watched by Banaban children on Friday and Saturday nights in the village.[83] The song imagines what would happen if the heroes took a boat ride to Taveuni, one of four islands near Rabi, and consumed lots of the deadly Fiji Bitter Beer. Fiji Bitter is not actually permitted for sale on Rabi; alcohol sales are illegal, but it is still available for the imagination.

On the last day of my fieldwork I filmed my auntie and cousins sitting on the steps of my uncle Teruamwi's house. The three women were sitting in a line brushing and braiding each other's hair, laughing and teasing me behind the camera. Auntie Veronica called out: "one, two, three monkey!" A line in the Ocean Island diary of Lillian Arundel, daughter of the Pacific Islands Company founder John T. Arundel, flashed through my mind: "One day we had a visit from Willie's [Tabukin na Banaba's] young wife and baby, and his sister; we took them through the house, and they were much interested to see themselves in the bedroom looking-glasses. The baby was just like a little monkey."[84]

Both my auntie and cousins were very much aware that my footage might be seen by people far away, and they also have some ideas about how people in places like Australia or the United States view Islanders. Her words "We look like three monkeys" is another way of saying, "We are very much aware that people over-

Tearoba and Asena play a children's clapping game, Rabi, 2000.
Photo from video by Katerina Teaiwa

seas think Banabans (and Islanders in general) are simple or primitive." Another way my elderly aunt demonstrated this awareness later, when the video camera was turned off, was by pulling her shirt up over her head so that her breasts were showing. She said, "Hey Kati! Take a picture of this!"

Several members of our kainga now live in Suva, Savusavu, Tarawa, Brisbane, Auckland, Wellington, Canberra, New York, and elsewhere. But we still move back and forth between islands and cities, visiting relatives. My uncles Teruamwi and Takaia and cousins Billy and Tekimatang have now passed away. They were all relatively young.

* * *

A straightforward, anticolonial history or narrative is but one way to explore the multiple sites and events that constitute Banaban stories, experiences, and identities. I end this book with the children's song and my female relatives' dialogue to signal a number of themes explored throughout this book, and some that are not.

Gil Tabucanon, in anticipation of further displacement in the Pacific in response to climate change, described the Banaban relocation to Fiji as a success story and one of social resilience.[85] While families on Rabi are much bigger than they ever were on the smaller island of Banaba culturally, socially, and politically—contrary to Tabucanon's analysis—things are not fully settled for the Banabans in Fiji. Among other issues, life expectancy is lower than in other parts of Fiji, health care is inadequate, the average age of marriage and start of childbearing is relatively young for women, and many Banaban and Gilbertese rituals have ceased to exist.

In the majority of writing by Ellis, Grimble, Williams and Macdonald, and Silverman, the lives, expectations, and desires of Banaban women and children are marginal and regularly squelched. Shennan and Tekenimatang, Kempf, and Hermann pay very close attention to women's agency and brilliantly illustrate the ways in which dancing bodies and voices become the vehicles for showing the world just who they are. Sigrah and King write of the central place of the Te Aka clan and continue their passionate activism and Banaban advocacy from the Gold Coast of Australia via their book and website.[86]

In this book I've presented a variety of stories, perspectives, and experiences of the island and the imperial phosphate mining industry by tracking the phosphate from Banaba to Australia, New Zealand, and elsewhere, while acknowledging the global stakes of the whole enterprise. In the recorded and documented histories, the Banabans are portrayed as simple and friendly, then as selfish, misguided, and pitiful. As the world consumed Ocean Island, the Banabans went into resistance mode and, fed up with being ignored and exploited, sued the British government and the phosphate company. They lost but they continue, at times with great difficulty, at times with much laughter and good humor, with life on Rabi. The everyday world of Rabi Islanders is both more mundane and more profound compared with many of the events and perspectives I've highlighted in these pages.

We live in an intensely interconnected world, and research on this interconnection abounds. Scholars of globalization map the tremendous forces impinging on people's everyday existence, and we celebrate the agency of people who still manage to have meaningful lives, who localize, indigenize, and subvert hegemonic ideas. I hope the multisited Ocean Island story does not merely add to the existing literature. In my experiences of sharing it with audiences across the world, this story of a dispersed and fragmented landscape, of an island that travels, enhances people's sense of the stakes of globalization, their own roles as consumers, and the material, political, and cultural consequences of intense interconnectivity.

Banaba was really a very, very small island, and twenty-two million tons of phosphate later, it's even smaller. Much bigger landscapes, nations, and populations got quite a lot out of it. The Banabans really did take on the British Empire and had their moment in the global spotlight. Their dance theater is still quite compelling. And they are surviving and struggling creatively on Rabi.

VERONICA: She's getting a picture of three monkeys. One, two, three monkey! It will go out to Australia and America.

TURENGA: Serious girl. Eat shit! [Outside frame]

VERONICA: They will see our head lice in America.

VERONICA: [Remember] when Takeua ran and cried *te bareau, te bareau* [like cobwebs] in the house [when Kati was dancing last night], and Nei To ran and went like this. [She gestures] She's not shy!

TIA: Give it to them those kids [making noise]. Who? [from outside frame] Kids—the camera.

ATANIBWEBWE: It's good, she went round [with the camera].

VERONICA: Better for Americans and Australians to see!

TURENGA: Here's Maria! Maria the devil! [Maria is my younger sister, who lives in New York. Turenga means that Tarenga is a hilarious comparison to Maria]

TARENGA: [Looking into the camera and holding up her baby niece] She doesn't speak.

Coda
Phosphate Futures

Whoever holds the phosphate supplies of the world, holds the world's food supplies, and wars in future will not be for lands and riches, but for "our daily bread."

—T. W. Haynes, *Our Daily Bread*

The Last Dig

In August 1968, the same year Banabans were petitioning the United Nations for independence from the Gilbert and Ellice Islands, two Australian women, wives of Company employees, decided to study the remains of Buakonikai village. Three years earlier they had assisted the Australian archaeologist Ronald Lampert with an excavation of the Te Aka kainga of Buakonikai in one of the last fields to be mined on Banaba. Arthur Grimble had threatened the destruction of the village decades earlier, and that moment had come. Recalling that Lampert had run out of time to complete his studies, the women took it upon themselves to make detailed notes and diagrams of the area. A Boy Scout hall had been built on part of the site, but the Company helped remove the concrete and the women proceeded with their dig. They were given six weeks to make notes and collect anything significant before the bulldozers arrived. Using the methods Lampert had taught them, they unearthed several artifacts and a skeleton.

Lorraine Thwaites, the wife of the BPC accountant and part-time editor of the inter-island newsletter, the *Island Nautilus,* was one of the amateur archaeologists and a self-proclaimed "restless" woman who was eager to keep busy: "Being two married women, (myself with 2 children) and obligations of homes, husbands, etc., we could only afford to spend from 8:45 AM to 10:30 AM at work on the site. As neither of us could drive we depended on the bus service to Tabwewa, and then walked about ¼ mile up a steep grade to the site."[1]

The BPC gave them a wheelbarrow and a worker to remove the soil they had scraped from the surface. They uncovered the remains of buildings, shells and fish bones, charcoal, and then a human molar, an intact vertebrae, two shoulder blades, and a skull facing east, the rest of the body facing west. These directions were significant since Banabans were known for two mortuary rituals: one involved burying their dead facing west toward the land of the ancestral spirit, Nakaa, and the other involved the careful cleaning and preserving of ancestral bones in the family house with the conversion of various elements into fishing hooks and necklaces.[2]

The following morning the Banaban representative came to the site and took some notes. The women also asked the resident doctor to advise them since they had now uncovered a pelvis from the same skeleton. They packed up for the night and on their return the next day, found that someone had stepped on and shattered the pelvis. No amount of piecing together, including an attempt to use hairspray, worked. But underneath it they found another skull, this time facing west. They took photographs and then the BPC manager, a Mr. Withers, asked them to put everything in a box and not return to the site. The next day, the machines moved in to level the area for mining.

Lorraine Thwaites sent a detailed and meticulous report of their excavation to Lampert in Canberra but received no reply. On November 20, 1969, as her family was preparing to leave the island on the *Triaster*, she wrote him another letter outlining the political difficulties they faced in continuing their work after discovering Banaban bones:

> At this stage I insisted on knowing what all the fuss was about. After falling out completely with Mr. Withers and having also dragged my husband in to back me up, Mr. Withers stated that there was to be no more excavating on the island. We were led to believe that the Banabans, in seeking independence through the United Nations, were using evidence against B.P.C., such as that the B.P.C. were "Digging up Cemeteries [sic]," and spreading the dust of their ancestors over the ground of the U.K., Australia and New Zealand.[3]

Thwaites's account and the BPC's alarm that the Banabans were portraying to the United Nations that the Company was spreading the dust of their ancestors over the ground of the three countries, while slightly dramatic, is not far from the truth. British manufacturers had a long history of using bones, mostly animal and sometimes human, to produce the valuable fertilizer. Indeed, by any indigenous standards, the Company had dug up, shipped, and spread te aba, the land and body, of the people. What does this mean for Banabans or Nauruans today? They often comment when visiting Australia and New Zealand that they are at home because their land is there. In 2012, for example, a Banaban man, found to have overstayed his visitor's visa, sought refugee status in New Zealand, claiming that the political situation in Fiji created an oppressive context for Banabans and that New Zealand was, in any case, responsible for the Banaban plight to begin with.[4] He was unsuccessful with his claim.

Phosphorus Futures?

In the twenty-first century, while rock phosphate continues to be critical for agricultural endeavors across the globe, dependence on this element is still relatively unacknowledged and undervalued. Phosphorus, perhaps, just cannot evoke the same aura of drama, mystery, urgency, or beauty conjured up by diamonds, gold, coal, and oil, in spite of attempts by various scientists, journalists, politicians, and prospectors over the last three centuries to arouse the public's interest in the mineral. In the twenty-first century a secret cache of British Foreign Office documents was discovered in London, in a compound shared with both MI5 and MI6, which consisted primarily of classified files on Banaba.[5] Phosphate has and always will be a matter of national security for certain countries.

The search for new ways to unlock phosphorus from nature and to identify new deposits of rock phosphate continues, and the Nauru and Kiribati governments explore plans to mine what little is left on their islands. Over a century after Ellis's historical find on Ocean Island, in 2012 the New Zealand government put out a fact sheet on plans to mine deposits of phosphate rock spread over 380 square kilometers of the Chatham Rise east of the South Island of New Zealand. While the deposit was discovered in 1952 and research was conducted on the site from 1975 to 1981, it took almost thirty years for technological advances in offshore extraction to make it feasible to mine the rock from 400 meters below sea level. The project was estimated to cost NZ$34 million (approximately US$29 million) to mine a much lower grade of rock than Banaban phosphate, with the expectation of greatly reducing New Zealand's reliance on Moroccan phosphate and providing twenty years of supply for New Zealand agriculture. The New Zealand government awarded Chatham Rock Phosphate a contract for prospecting, and it commenced designing an extraction plan with partner Royal Boskalis Westminster.

Compared with our story of twentieth-century superphosphate, today the majority of global agricultural phosphate is consumed not as superphosphate but as diammonium phosphate (DAP), combining nitrogen and phosphorus fertilizer needs. Countries lacking phosphate reserves, such as Australia and New Zealand, however, still apply superphosphate to certain soils. The plan in New Zealand in 2012 was to apply rock phosphate directly to farms to reduce the environmental impacts and runoff frequently experienced with the use of superphosphate.

There is a growing awareness among researchers that dwindling global phosphate reserves represent a future crisis for global agriculture. Concerns are also spreading about the pollution that results from the application of fertilizer to lands, the runoff into waterways, and the ethical complications of genetically modified crops. There is an acknowledged need for innovative thinking for both environmental sustainability and food security. Largely absent from these debates, however, is any discussion of the physical, social, or cultural impacts of mining on the people, seascapes, and landscapes where reserves are held. What does this mean for indigenous peoples? How are we to reconcile competing interests with demands for equity and just treatment? What are our obligations to future generations? Do we have the right to use all our resources now or bypass nature with technological innovation? What of the other species, plant and animal, implicated in this never-ending quest to fuel human consumption?

While reminders of the mining history regularly surface in New Zealand, the story is all but lost in the public memory of other beneficiaries in spite of the passionate activities of activists such as Stacey King and Ken Sigrah, who run the Abara Banaba website. Banaban histories live on in the memories of individuals like those whose stories are explored in this book: an aging group of former Company workers and their families, and many in the current generation of Banabans, Nauruans, Tuvaluans, and I-Kiribati. Their stories are partially sedimented, overlapping, interlocking; they are part of the flows and fragments of Banaban rocks, lives, and histories.

The Guyanian poet and novelist Theodore Wilson Harris believes: "Each living person is a fossil in so far as each man carries within himself remnants of deep-seated antecedents. . . . Floating around in the psyche of each one of us are all the fossil identities. By entering into a fruitful dialogue with the past one becomes able to revive the fossils that are buried within oneself and are part of one's ancestors."[6] The Banaba story still means something to those who had both ancient and fleeting experiences of and connections to the island. But our fossil values have two sides. They can be healing or revelatory, as in Harris's case, a continuous source of meaning and grounding for indigenous identities, or they may become prejudices similar to those expressed by both Banabans and Gilbertese in the 1970s, or they may be invoked for national and racial authority as they have been in Fiji and in all places across the globe rife with conflict and with people destroying each other because of ideas about class, gender, religious, and ethnic difference. Fossil identities do not have to be about superiority or difference; they are about the processes, lives, and events that went before us. We would not exist at all if not for them: we are in history, history is in us.

Harris's writing is about coterminous worlds that integrate the material and the spiritual, the past and the present, and he argues for the possibility of architectonic approaches to fossils in which identities are never static, but always understood and made anew. His orientation is somewhat different from those of Aldous Huxley and Isaac Asimov in their concerns over impending chemical and biological bottlenecks. While all are concerned with ethical relations and responsibilities to humankind, one takes solace and wisdom from engaging with ancestral roots and the others fret for and conjure up marvelous and sometimes apocalyptic visions of the future. Development policy makers, practitioners, and aid agencies, similar to their colonial predecessors, often marvel at or are frus-

Banaba phosphate pendant and necklace belonging to Helen Pilkinton.
Photo by ANU CAP CartoGIS

trated with Pacific Islanders' propensity to prioritize what they perceive as the by-gone past over the need and urgency of the present and future.

But from the world view of the average Islander, time is not linear and the past continuously informs, shapes, and even dictates present ideas, values, and decisions. "We live for the dead" is a widely accepted axiom, and we face the dead—once human, plant, animal, bone, and rock—as we walk (facing backward) into that future.

The Phosphate Pendant

In the 1990s I met a lovely couple, Helen and Garth Pilkinton, who live in Canberra and are today close family friends. Helen is the daughter of a former BPC medical officer, Berwyn Deans, who worked on Ocean Island in 1934. She told me about a small, rough piece of phosphate rock that Berwyn and her mother, Ida

"Myf" Deans, brought home from the island in 1935. Phosphate accessories were popular with BPC employees, many of whom had the rock made into cufflinks, bangles, and necklaces. The polished result is visually compelling with swirling bands of cream, chestnut, and brown. Helen took her piece of rock to primary school for show and tell. Later, as a Melbourne high school teacher in the 1950s, she used it as a teaching aid, telling the students about Ocean Island, the mining, and how the phosphate was brought to Australia and distributed across the country by rail. She emphasized how important it was for Australia but also how the island was denuded and left with a forest of pinnacles.

In the 1970s, Myf Deans transformed the family lump of Ocean Island phosphate into pendants set in silver for her three daughters. Helen has never been to Banaba and her parents were there for just a short time. Nevertheless, the island left an indelible imprint on her family history, as it has on the Australian landscape, and she wears a piece of it around her neck from time to time.

Sometimes on a Sunday, we have afternoon tea, tell Pacific stories, and talk about how one day she will pass on the pendant to me and my daughter, Tearia. During these conversations Tearia is usually outside, waving at us while bouncing high on the Pilkintons' trampoline. Laughing in the warm Canberra sun.

Acknowledgments

Kam na mauri and ni sa bula vinaka. It has been many years since I started for-mally studying Banaban history and culture, and I have to admit that there is still much more to learn. The processes of literature review, archival research, and field-work are similar to mining itself: uncovering layers of sedimented information and the diverse and now scattered lives and industrial activities they represent. Along the way to this book, many people and institutions supported my work.

At the Center for Pacific Islands Studies at the University of Hawaiʻi at Manoa, as both student and, later, staff, I benefited from the generous mentorship of Terence Wesley-Smith, David Hanlon, Haunani-Kay Trask, and Noenoe Silva. After re-ceiving the international PhD and postgraduate research scholarships, my work continued in the Anthropology Department of the Research School of Pacific and Asian Studies at the Australian National University with the guidance and warm care of Margaret Jolly, Greg Dening, and Gary Kildea. In this period the late Epeli Hauʻofa at the Oceania Center for Arts and Culture at the University of the South Pacific became a dear friend and mentor, as did Seiuli Allan Alo. Not long after I commenced my research my best friend, Seona Catherine Mary Taito (née Chung), died in a tragic accident, and I still mourn her absence to this day.

I continued my research and writing at the Macmillan Brown Centre for Pa-cific Islands Studies at the University of Canterbury in Christchurch, New Zea-land, with the aid of a research fellowship and support from the director, Karen Nero. David Gegeo, Moana Matthes, Serge Tcherkezoff, Shane Tuffery, Robert Nicole, Brian and Diane Foley, and many others were dear colleagues and friends in that period, and a special bond was formed with Keith Camacho and Juliann Anesi.

In more recent years, as family life, teaching, administration, and other mat-ters took precedence, I tried to stay connected to this work by speaking regularly to former residents of the island and their families, including Jack and Joan Edwards, Lillian Hardman, Lorraine Thwaites, and dear friends Helen and Garth Pilkinton. Special thanks to the wonderful Andrew, Marion, and Joseph Vile and their family and neighboring farmers for kindly sharing stories with me in Burrumbuttock, New South Wales. Sincere thanks as well to Reece Richards, Dinah Dunavan, and their family for permission to cite Mary Hunt's story; to Ray Dobson, Mary Zaus-mer, and Les Cleveland for generously sharing their words; and to all those who gave permission to reproduce their words and images, including Robin White and the National Gallery of Australia. Thank you also to the Museum of New Zealand Te Papa Tongarewa and the Adam Art Gallery in Wellington for putting up projects based on my research, telling this Banaban story to wider audiences.

I am grateful for the generosity, friendship, and wise counsel of many other friends and colleagues, including Zoe Pearson, Maria Bargh, Greg Rawlings, Sina Emde, Tim Curtis, Peter Kirkup, Michael Pretes, Kalissa Alexeyeff, Jenny Newell, Jo Diamond, Jen Badstuebner, Selai Korovusere, Julia Gray, Archana Singh, Yasmin Khan, Rachael Morris, Kylie Addison, Cheryl Irava, Lavenia Emberson, Helen Narruhn, Neil Foon, Claudia Soto, Lucy and Terence Erasito, Steven Ratuva, Elise Huffer, Teweiariki Teaero, Frances Koya, Tarcisius Kabutaulaka, Minoru Hokari, Daniel Morrison, April Henderson, Michelle Tupou, Hokulani Aikau, Ty Tengan, Monisha Das Gupta, Monica Ghosh, Jon Goss, Letitia Hickson, Jan Rensel, Monica LaBriola, Greg Dvorak, Kim Christen, Hilary Charlesworth, Nicole George, Erin Weston, Konrad Ng, Albert Wendt, Reina Whaitiri, Brett Graham, Shigeyuki Kihara, Sia Figiel, Vince Diaz, Eric Waddell, Mandy Thomas, and Donna Dening.

Jennifer Shenran, Max Quanchi, Grant McCall, Ken Sigrah, and Stacey King all helped with useful historical information; Elfriede Hermann and Wolfgang Kempf regularly sent me copies of their published works. The staff at the National Archives of Australia, especially Stephanie Bailey; Susan Woodburn and Cheryl Hoskin at the Special Collections of the Barr-Smith Library at the University of Adelaide; and Kylie Moloney with the Pacific Manuscripts Bureau were all just brilliant. Special thanks to Mark Willie Chung for so generously rephotographing BPC images, and to Cassandra Pybus for the great speaking opportunities.

In 2011 I spent two invaluable weeks at the University of Rochester at the kind invitation of Robert Foster and the Anthropology Department, reimagining my research for the Tracking Globalization series. I continued work on the book with the support of the Pacific Unit in the School of Culture, History, and Language at ANU, including financial support for publication of this book. I'm grateful for the good cheer of my students, colleagues, and friends at ANU, including Kent Anderson, Robin Jeffrey, the students and staff of Pasifika Australia, Katherine Lepani, Rachel Morgain, Anna-Karina Hermkens, Rebecca Monson, Pyone Thu, Siobhan McDonnell and family, Matt Tomlinson, Chris Ballard, Colin Filer, Matthew Allen, Kirin Narayan, Ken George, McComas Taylor, Kylie Moloney, Areti Metuamate, Rose Whitau, Latu and Lotu Latai, Karen Tu, Salmah Eva-Lina Lawrence, Nikki Mariner, Joseph Vile, Maea Buhre, Mitiana Arbon, Phoebe Smith, Sidha Pandian, Eric Bridgeman, Marata Tamaira, Carl Pao, Bina D'Costa, Paul D'arcy, Deveni Temu, and the late Karina Taylor. Beyond ANU, I currently serve as the president of the Australian Association for Pacific Studies, and I'm thankful for the wonderful AAPS executive team.

Kam bati n rabwa to all those on Tabiteuea, Banaba, and Tarawa who kindly helped me throughout my fieldwork or, rather, "homework." On Tabiteuea, kam rabwa to all my relatives, especially Bwakoua, Rainimone, Rikia, Katioa, Raimon,

Riribwe; to the people of Tanaeang, Eita, Utiroa, Terikiai, Tekabwibwi, and Buota, particularly the unimwane: Temokou, Enere, Booti, Ntongantonga, and Teweia; to Temakau for research assistance; to Buota Junior Secondary School, Teabike College, Te Mwamwang Primary School, and especially Tina Maria, Tina Mangarita, and Nei Aom, who generously hosted me with the support of the Sisters of Sacred Heart. On Tarawa I'd like to thank my uncles Eritai and Tebongiro, auntie Temaotarawa, cousin Aren Teannaki, Teaiwa Teniu, and all their families. Special thanks to John Thurston for the yacht *Martha* and to Linda Uan at the Kiribati Film Resource Unit. On Banaba, kam bati n rabwa to Burenimone, Alofa, and Moanatu. I connected with the New Zealand artist Robin White during my research, and over the years we have continued to talk about Kiribati, Banaba, and her wonderful artistic collaborations across Oceania.

On Rabi I would like to thank the Rabi Council of Leaders, the Banaban Council of Elders, the Women's Interest Group, the Youth Group, the villages of Tabwewa and Tabiang, and my own family—the descendants of Kaka Teaiwa and Nei Kaka Takeua on Rabi and in Suva, Brisbane, Auckland, and Wellington—for all their generous support. Especially helpful were my cousins Turenga, Tamanarara (Lala), Toma, Fatiaki, Akata, Teangatoa, Terereieta, Rashida, and Rehana; my aunties Bwaterea, Rakomwa, Taita, Terianako, Veronica, and Tebarutu; my uncle Tekarika; and my late uncles Takaia and Teruamwi.

I am grateful for the frank and helpful advice from three anonymous readers, and editorial comments from Margaret Jolly and Robert Foster. Margaret's care and support throughout my academic career has been a gift. My deepest thanks to the sponsoring editor, Rebecca Tolen, and the editorial team of Sarah Jacobi, Nancy Lightfoot, and Merryl Sloane for all their work. Thank you to my ANU research assistant, Josh Wodak, and to Richard Simpson of the Commonwealth Scientific and Industrial Research Organisation for generously checking "Stories of P." Much gratitude to our resident editor, Carolyn Brewer, who worked at such a pace on the preliminary formatting and editing. In the last stages of writing my dear friend and colleague Rachel Harvey provided indispensable thematic and structural advice. Rachel, you helped me finish this.

Above all, I have my own family, spread across the globe, to thank. I am of Banaban, Tabiteuean, and African American descent, born and raised in Fiji, now living in Australia, and connected to many different lands, peoples, and histories. This sounds very cosmopolitan, and it is, but it is also the norm for indigenous Pacific Islanders to be grounded in their ancestral lands while having globally dispersed networks. In Canberra I would like to thank Deryck Scarr, the late Marion Scarr, and their beautiful daughter, Miranda; in the United States my late grandparents John Thomas Martin and Hestlene Martin, aunt Theresa, uncle Charles, aunt Jane, Amaya, and their families; my younger sister Maria, and Bret, Kea, Bella, and Bruce; in New Zealand my older sister Teresia, and Sean, Manoa, and Vaitoa; and in Fiji my parents, John and Joan. They humbly sacrificed every-thing for their children's education and kept little in the way of material benefit for themselves. Now their daughters live in different corners of the globe, and I know that many of our opportunities have stemmed from their deep commit-ment to service, their love for knowledge and learning, and my mother's Catholic faith. My father was the person who regularly said, "Oh, this is hard? That's good, it makes you stronger," and he has been an integral part of the research journey. Thank you so much, Mum and Dad.

My husband, Nicholas Mortimer, has been a wonderful and generous part-ner in all ways: giving me the space and time to write, being an amazing father to our daughter, and providing critical research assistance. Thanks as well to my in-laws, Nancy and Geoff, for their support and good cheer, and to our loving daughter, Tearia, who brings joy, high levels of entertainment, and much-needed grounding in the middle of our academic lives.

Any errors in the content of this work are mine alone, and I apologize in ad-vance for them and to anyone I forgot to thank.

Kam bati n rabwa ao e a boo te aba.

Notes

Prelude

1. This story is adapted from two Banaban origin stories by Nei Tearia and Te Itirake, translated by H. C. Maude and H. E. Maude, and published in Maude and Maude, *The Book of Banaba*. Nareau is also known as "Nareau the Spider" and while he is missing from other oral traditions that focus primarily on Auriaria, according to Maude and Maude his presence represents an older version of the origin story. The use of the term "heaven" can be assumed to be the choice of Maude and Maude, but "sky" might be better substituted.

2. *Yaqona*, kava, or "grog" is a drink made from the roots of the *Piper methysticum* plant. It is a ceremonial drink among Fijians and still has ritual uses today. However, its consumption is also the major social preoccupation of many people, men in particular, of all ethnicities in Fiji, not least the Rabi Islanders who grow and sell their kava across the islands. We took many bags of pounded grog to Banaba.

Preface

1. Compare with Colin McFarlane's discussion of translocal assemblage in "Translocal Assemblages: Space, Power and Social Movements."

2. This was well critiqued by Haraway in her studies of "vision" and situated knowledges in both "Situated Knowledges" and *Primate Visions*.

3. Fernandez, *Imagining Literacy*, 82.

1. The Little Rock That Feeds

1. In January 2013, Paul D. Miller (aka DJ Spooky) presented the multimedia performance *The Nauru Elegies* at the Metropolitan Museum of Art in New York. It received mixed reviews. See Perry, "Sad History of Tiny Island."

2. Banaba was sighted in 1801 by Captain Jared Gardner of the *Diana* and named Rodman's Island until Captain John Mertho of the *Ocean* renamed it after his ship in 1804. The names Banaba and Ocean Island are used interchangeably throughout this book, while still signaling the dialectic between its competing economic and social values.

3. The "Company" with a capital "C" is used throughout this book to identify the phosphate mining industry on Ocean Island. The three versions of the Company all represented the same interests, had the same managers and founders, and served the same agricultural stakeholders.

4. "Nauru Country Brief."

5. McLeish, "Nauru: The World's Smallest Republic"; and see Rubinstein and Zimmet, *Phosphate, Wealth and Health in Nauru*.

6. Oliver, *The Pacific Islands*, 216.

7. Ellis, "Phosphates: Why, How and Where? . . . Why Needed? How Used? and Where

Found?" in Maude and Maude Papers, MS 0003. Maslyn Williams and Barrie Macdonald cite the same line as a "textbook aphorism." See Williams and Macdonald, *The Phosphateers,* 7. The original quote by Thomas Green Clemson is cited in Collings, *Commercial Fertilizers,* preface, n.p.

8. See Maude, *Slavers in Paradise.*

9. Skaggs, *The Great Guano Rush;* and Cushman, *Guano and the Opening of the Pacific World.*

10. Williams and Macdonald, *The Phosphateers;* Weeramantry, *Nauru;* and Viviani, *Nauru—Phosphate and Political Progress.* Clive Ponting's *Green History of the World* includes a section on Nauru and Banaba that relies on Williams and Macdonald's research.

11. Sigrah and King, *Te Rii ni Banaba,* 61.

12. See, for example, Chris Ballard's discussion of the persistent ties between people and land in the Papua New Guinean context in "It's the Land, Stupid!"

13. There are two somewhat competing and strategically invoked definitions of indigeneity that shape national and international policy and law. The first imagines indigenous peoples as precolonial minorities in their homelands; and the second imagines them as peoples who may or may not be minorities but who have enduring spiritual, economic, and political attachments to the land. These are usually the "first peoples" of a particular place. See Merlan, "On Indigeneity."

14. See Ward and Kingdom, *Land, Custom and Practice in the South Pacific.*

15. Maude, *The Book of Banaba,* 55.

16. Silverman, *Disconcerting Issue.*

17. The Banabans speak the Gilbertese or I-Kiribati language, but they have several words and phrases that are not found in the Gilberts. Years of migration between the islands and the establishment of Gilbertese as the official language of the Bible and the British colony reinforced this linguistic relationship. See Maude and Maude, "Social Organization"; and Silverman, *Disconcerting Issue.*

18. Diffraction is discussed in Haraway, *How Like a Leaf.* Another apt metaphor is found in the rhizome; see Deleuze, and Guattari, *A Thousand Plateaus,* 6–7.

19. Clifford, *Routes,* 11.

20. Marcus, "Ethnography in/of the World System."

21. Sigrah and King, *Te Rii ni Banaba,* 73; and Maude and Maude, "Social Organization," 288–292.

22. This list is from Maude and Maude, "Social Organization," 289–91.

23. Ibid., 291.

24. For an overview of Banaban society and culture from the 1900s to the present, see Maude and Maude, "Social Organization"; Maude, *The Book of Banaba;* Silverman, *Disconcerting Issue;* Benaia, "The History of the Protestant Church in Banaba and Rabi"; and Sigrah and King, *Te Rii ni Banaba.*

25. Sahlins, "Poor Man, Rich Man, Big Man, Chief."

26. Temaka Benaia briefly discusses the transformation of the Banaban language, particularly after the introduction of Christianity and the Gilbertese Bible from 1885. See Benaia, "The History of the Protestant Church in Banaba and Rabi."

27. Kapu (which means taboo) and another Hawaiian missionary, Nalimu, wreaked much havoc on Tabiteuea, eventually inciting a bloody civil war that saw kin from the northern island slaughter over a thousand of their so-called pagan relatives in southern Tabiteuea; this event shocked the ABCFM. See Talu et al., *Kiribati: Aspects of History,* 50–57.

28. Benaia, "The History of the Protestant Church in Banaba and Rabi," 23.

29. See Williams and Macdonald, *The Phosphateers*.

30. Costin and Williams, "Introduction," xiii.

31. "Ocean Islanders: To Go or Not to Go? Bad Outlook for Natives," *Sydney Morning Herald*, April 31, 1912, 17. The story also ran as "Ocean Island: A Land Problem," *Barrier Miner* [Broken Hill, New South Wales], April 22, 1912, 2, National Library of Australia database TROVE; also see CA244 in the BPC Archives.

32. Macdonald, *Cinderellas*, 99.

33. Fortune, "Lever Brothers," 217–218.

34. See Teaiwa, "Ti Rawata Irouia" and "Visualizing te Kainga, Dancing te Kainga."

35. For example, see Mintz, *Sweetness and Power*; and Kaplan, "Fijian Water in Fiji and New York."

36. Narayan, "How Native Is a Native Anthropologist?" 671.

37. See Haraway, *How Like a Leaf*.

38. Teaiwa, "Visualizing te Kainga, Dancing te Kainga"; Marcus, "The Modernist Sensibility in Recent Ethnographic Writing"; Eisenstein, *The Film Sense*.

39. Kaplan, "Many Paths to Partial Truths," 211; see also Stoler, *Along the Archival Grain*.

40. I discuss and critique the formation of Stacey King's Banaban Heritage Society in Teaiwa, "Body-Shop Banabans and Skin-Deep Samaritans." See also Sigrah and King, "Abara Banaba."

41. See, for example, Teaiwa, "Yaqona/Yagoqu."

42. See, for example, Hereniko and Wesley-Smith, *Back to the Future: Decolonizing Pacific Studies*; and Diaz and Kauanui, "Native Pacific Cultural Studies on the Edge."

43. Escobar, *The Making and Unmaking of the Third World*, 50.

44. See Kirsch, "Environmental Disaster, Culture Loss and the Law"; Rainbird, "Taking the Tapu"; and Hanlon, "Sea of Little Lands."

45. See Tabucanon, "The Banaban Resettlement."

46. I explore this further in Teaiwa, "Choreographing Difference."

47. *Oxford Dictionaries Online*, s.v. consume (2013), http://oxforddictionaries.com/definition /english/consume?q=consume (accessed October 11, 2013).

48. Hau'ofa, "Our Sea of Islands."

49. de Castell, "One Code to Rule Them All."

2. Stories of P

1. Roosevelt, "Message to Congress on Phosphates for Soil Fertility."

2. Lougheed, "Phosphorus Paradox: Scarcity and Overabundance."

3. Asimov, *Asimov on Chemistry*, 146.

4. Cordell, "The Story of Phosphorus," 84; see also Cordell and White, "Peak Phosphorus."

5. "Phosphorus: Micronutrient Information Center."

6. Emsley, *The Shocking History of Phosphorus*, 257.

7. Ibid., 241; Cordell, "The Story of Phosphorus," 85; see also Costin and Williams, *Phosphorus in Australia*.

8. Myers, *The One Hundred Most Important Chemical Compounds*.

9. Emsley, *The Shocking History of Phosphorus*, 243.

10. The most useful picture of the global state of phosphate rock reserves and resources is Van Kauwenbergh, *World Phosphate Rock Reserves and Resources*

11. Emsley, *The Shocking History of Phosphorus*.

12. See, for example, Barak, "Essential Elements for Plant Growth."

13. Emsley, *The Shocking History of Phosphorus*, 244.

14. Ibid., 243–253.

15. Whitten and Whitten, *Manufacturing*, 161.

16. The Fertilizer Industry Federation of Australia (FIFA) website, which originally highlighted its relationship to the BPC, is no longer available. FIFA has been renamed Fertilizer Australia with no reference to its history on the site.

17. Proceedings of the Seventh International Congress of Applied Chemistry, London, May 27–June 2, 1909, sec. VII, BPC Archives, CA244, R138/1, box 1, items 1–25.

18. Ibid.

19. Tyrer, *Nauru and Ocean Islands Story*, 9.

20. Power, "The Phosphate Deposits of Ocean and Pleasant Islands."

21. Power, "'Coral Island Phosphates in the Making': A Paper to Be Discussed at a Meeting of Mining and Metallurgy to Be Held at the Rooms of the Geological Society, Burlington House, Piccadilly W., Thursday, October 16, 1919 at 5.30 PM," in BPC Archives, R138/1, box 1, item 6.

22. Ibid.

23. Owen, "Notes on the Phosphate Deposit of Ocean Island" and "The Phosphate Deposit on Ocean Island."

24. Owen, "Notes on the Phosphate Deposit of Ocean Island," 4.

25. "Report on P Quality from July 16, 1915 in Central Area," sample no. 16, BPC Archives, MP1174/107 and item 110.

26. Pearce, "Phosphorus."

27. Cordell, *The Story of Phosphorus*, 3.

28. Cordell and White, "Peak Phosphorus."

29. Wild, "Peak Soil"; Rosemarin, de Bruijne, and Caldwell, "Peak Phosphorus"; Barley, "Might as Well Face It You're Addicted to Phosphorus"; and Pincock, "Peak Phosphorus."

30. Personal communication with Dr. Richard Simpson, Commonwealth Scientific and Industrial Research Organization, May 2011; Van Kauwenbergh, *World Phosphate Rock Reserves and Resources*.

31. Rockström et al., "A Safe Operating Space for Humanity." Rockström and his colleagues outlined "planetary boundaries" that proposed a safe operating space for nine planetary systems. They argued that the boundaries in three systems—the rate of biodiversity loss, climate change, and the nitrogen cycle (which shares a boundary with the phosphorus cycle)—have already been exceeded. Both the phosphorus and nitrogen cycles pollute land and sea: there is an over-extraction of nitrogen from the air, and a near-critical threshold of phosphorus flows into the sea, creating an anoxic environment detrimental to marine life.

32. Iremonger, *It's a Bigger Life*, 26.

33. Ibid., 26–27.

34. Marcus, "Ethnography in/of the World System."

35. See Appadurai, "Disjuncture and Difference"; and Rockefeller, "Flow."

36. Hereniko, "Representations of Cultural Identities," 407.

37. Ibid.

38. Donna Haraway's work importantly reflects on the borders between nature and culture and on "the join between the figurative and factual" (*How Like a Leaf*, 24). The way she uses the language of biology to reflect on history, politics, and anthropology inspired me to imagine how the language of chemistry could be used to tell the story of Banaba.

39. Tyrer, *Nauru and Ocean Islands Story*, 28; Williams and Macdonald, *The Phosphateers*; and Teaiwa, "Visualizing te Kainga, Dancing te Kainga."

40. Stoler, "Imperial Debris," 194.

3. Land from the Sea

1. Thomas, *In Oceania*, 35.

2. Ibid., 23.

3. B. E. Talboys, quoted in Tyrer, *Nauru and Ocean Islands Story*, 4.

4. Williams and Macdonald, *The Phosphateers*, dedication, n.p.

5. Ellis, *Ocean Island and Nauru*, 52.

6. Ibid., 55.

7. Ellis Diary, folder F2, 1–2, Maude and Maude Papers, emphasis added.

8. See Maude and Maude, "Social Organization"; and Maude, *The Book of Banaba*.

9. For a longer discussion of this contract, which would not have been clearly understood by all Banaban parties, see Teaiwa, "Ti Rawata Irouia."

10. Albert Ellis, Agreement on Behalf of His Employers, the Pacific Islands Company, with the Undersigned King and Natives of Ocean Island, May 3, 1900, Ocean Island, in BPC Archives, CA244, and online at Jane Resture's Oceania website (though there are some mistakes in the transcription): http://www.janesoceania.com/kiribati_banaba_history/index.htm (accessed 21 October 2013).

11. Ellis, May 4, 1900, BPC Archives, CA244, MP1174/1074.

12. Maude and Maude, "Social Organization," 264.

13. Albert Ellis to Alfred Gaze, representative for the Pacific Phosphate Company in Melbourne, November 19, 1909, in BPC Archives, CA244, MP1174/1085

14. Sabatier, *Gilbertese-English Dictionary*, 424–426. Among other things, pandanus is used to make fine textiles and certain ornaments for dance costumes.

15. See, for example, discussions of settler-colonial space-making in Mar and Edmonds, *Making Space*.

16. Ellis, Memorandum, 1909, BPC Archives, CA244, MP1174/1085.

17. Ibid.

18. Ellis to Gaze, July 22, 1909, "'The Lightwoods' Cambridge to Melbourne. Section 6, re. Par7, b," in BPC Archives, CA244, MP1174/1085.

19. Rambi is an old spelling for Rabi. Ellis speech, Rabi Island, September 21, 1948, in Maude and Maude Papers.

20. Sontag, *On Photography*, 54.

21. MacDougall, *Transcultural Cinema*, 68.

22. Haraway, "Situated Knowledges."

23. Foster, *Choreographing History*, 5–6.

24. Thanks to Gary Kildea, Margaret Jolly, Maria Bargh, Zoe Pearson, Jennifer Badstuebner, and Greg Rawlings, who shared their thoughts on this BPC film after a group viewing, and to the Victoria office of the National Archives of Australia for reformatting and copying the films for me.

25. Williams and Macdonald, *The Phosphateers*, 246.

26. Ibid., 273, 525–526.

27. Ibid., 299–300. Trying to confirm the age of the film, I asked another man, Kevin Speer, who worked on the island in the late 1950s, what the name of the Company store was. He also said it was the "trade store," and I now believe that the footage was taken between 1935 and 1940—the very short life of the original *Triaster*.

28. *Lavalava* is "sarong" in Samoan. It is *sulu* in Fijian and *pareu* in Tahitian. The Gilbertese word *riri* was rarely used to refer to cloth skirts.

29. The semantic load of the piano as an icon of civilization is apparent, even overburdened, in Jane Campion's *The Piano* (1993).

30. Bailey, Review of *The Phosphateers*, 146.

31. Ellis, *Ocean Island and Nauru*, 127.

32. Deleuze and Guattari, *A Thousand Plateaus*, 6–7.

33. According to the ethnographic filmmaker Gary Kildea (pers. comm.), "hair in the [camera] gate" was a real problem for early filmmakers and was constantly checked by shining a torch onto the lens to make sure no dust or hair was caught on film.

34. Macdonald, *Cinderellas*, 120.

35. This image for me resonated greatly with Enere's story about the two Ellice Island sisters, discussed in the next chapter.

36. See, for example, Hereniko's discussion of ritual Rotuman clowning in *Woven Gods: Female Clowns and Power in Rotuma*.

37. BPC Archives CA244: MP1174/1093.

38. Sontag, *On Photography*, 64.

39. Ibid., 65.

4. Remembering Ocean Island

1. See Morton, "The Subaltern," 96–97; and Zinn, *A People's History of the United States*.

2. Manterys et al., *New Zealand's First Refugees*.

3. Hunt, "My Life on Ocean Island," 220–2225.

4. Hunt, "Excerpt from the Memoirs of Mary Hunt," 1.

5. Hunt, *My Life*, 13.

6. Hunt, "Excerpt from the Memoirs of Mary Hunt," 1.

7. Ibid., 2.

8. Ibid.

9. Hunt, "Excerpt from the Memoirs of Mary Hunt," 3.

10. Hunt, *My Life*, 14.

11. Ibid., 16.

12. Ibid., 15. The work hours are different from those described in a 1903 pamphlet: 6–8 AM, 9–1 PM, and 2–5 PM (BPC Archives, CA244, R138/1, box 1, items 1–25).

13. Frigate bird taming was an important cultural practice for Banaban men.

14. Hunt, *My Life*, 16. There is a Gilbertese word for butterfly, *bwebwe*, and according to the Kiribati dictionary a black one often seen at sea is called *bwebwe ni marawa*. I have a Banaban cousin named Atanibwebwe, which means either "understanding butterflies" or "chief [for lack of a better word] of butterflies." Mary's memoirs, however, were the first account I had ever heard of using butterflies as hair decorations.

15. Ibid., 17.

16. Ibid., 18.

17. Ibid.

18. Dobson, "On Banaba," 1.

19. Williams and Macdonald, *The Phosphateers*, 65.

20. Dobson, "On Banaba," 1–2.

21. Ibid., 3.

22. Ibid., 6.

23. Ibid.

24. Ibid., 7.

25. "Aussie Rules Football" is a national sport that to me looks like a mix of rugby, basketball, and soccer. Australians in certain states, especially Victoria, are mad about the sport while rugby dominates New South Wales and Queensland.

26. Dobson, "On Banaba," 8.

27. Dobson, "On Banaba," 9.

28. Ibid., 11.

29. The pillowcases are often embroidered with people's names, a blessing like "Sweet Dreams," and colorfully stitched flowers.

30. Zausmer, "Ocean Island, Paradise of the Pacific," in "The Chronicles of Mary Beatrice Roche Critch." Mary wrote her memoirs over a five-year period with the final version edited when she was seventy-seven years old.

31. Zausmer, "The Chronicles of Mary," 95.

32. Ibid., 96.

33. Ibid., 97.

34. Ibid., 98.

35. Ibid.

36. Ibid., 99.

37. Ibid.

38. Piccanini, which is usually spelled "pickaninny," was a term used by British and Australians for indigenous children. It is still used for "child" in the Melanesian pidgins of Papua New Guinea, the Solomon Islands, and Vanuatu. It is usually seen as derogatory and offensive in the United States, Australia, and Britain today.

39. Zausmer, "The Chronicles of Mary," 101.

40. While Gilbertese and Banabans do not regularly name themselves after material things, colonialism did introduce some quirky naming practices among Pacific Islanders. I was once told by a Samoan woman that she knew a girl named "Veteran's Association." She was called "Va" for short.

41. This is likely the song "Po Atarau," or "Now Is the Hour," a well-known Māori farewell song.

42. Margaret O'Brien was born in 1937 and became one of the most famous American child actors in cinema history, appearing in films such as *Babes on Broadway* (1941), *Journey for Margaret* (1942), *Jane Eyre* (1943), and *Meet Me in St. Louis* (1944).

43. Zausmer, "The Chronicles of Mary," 106–107.

44. Ibid., 104.

45. "Like an Oyster: Lonely Phosphate Islands/Deepest Mooring in the World," *Auckland Star* (1929; no further date information), in BPC Archives, CA244, MP1174/1093.

46. Shlomowitz and Munro, *The Ocean Island (Banaba) and Nauru Labour Trade,* 4.

47. Ibid., 5.

48. Zausmer, "The Chronicles of Mary," 101.

49. Macdonald, *Cinderellas,* 118.

50. Ibid., 120.

51. Shlomowitz and Munro, *The Ocean Island (Banaba) and Nauru Labour* Trade, 7–8.

52. Ibid., 10.

53. Williams and Macdonald, *The Phosphateers,* 453–454.

54. Interview with Booti, Enere, and Temokou in Tanaeang village, Tabiteuea, Kiribati, March 2000.

55. Ibid.

56. *Aomata* directly translates as "people" but is usually used to refer specifically to people of one's own ethnic group. So when Banabans say "te aomata," they usually mean other Banabans, and the same pertains to Gilbertese.

57. Interview with Booti, Enere, and Temokou in Tanaeang village, Tabiteuea, Kiribati, March 2000.

58. Shlomowitz and Munro, *The Ocean Island (Banaba) and Nauru Labour Trade.*

59. Folk song lyrics and translation by John Teaiwa.

60. A marae is a public space where people gather for sports or other important events.

61. From his time on the island, Temokou recalled a woman named Nei Baorita, who lived on Banaba in the 1970s. She married a man named Kurae, who has now passed away. They once lived in Lautoka in Fiji, where my own family lived from 1976 to 1980. My father remembers meeting this woman and her husband there. Nei Baorita had a gift for locating missing items as well as those used in sorcery to harm people. She did this by communicating with her deceased father in her dreams; he was always able to direct her to the missing or destructive items.

62. He also remembered that for the most part relations between the workers were good, despite some problems with alcohol. They went fishing together and had sports events together, including soccer and wrestling competitions.

63. Neither Hockings, *Traditional Architecture in the Gilbert Islands,* nor Koch, *The Material Culture of Kiribati,* mention any houses with these types of walls, and they are probably innovations along with two-story houses. According to Hockings, however, bata (small dwellings) were traditionally on the ground, not raised. See Hockings, *Traditional Architecture in the Gilbert Islands,* 145–187.

64. Gerd Koch has more on different fishing styles. He lists taumata as the method used for catching *awai* fish. See Koch, *The Material Culture of Kiribati,* 49.

65. Williams and Macdonald, *The Phosphateers,* 284.

66. I go into more detail on this part of fieldwork in Teaiwa, "Multi-Sited Methodologies."

67. See Teaiwa, "Body-Shop Banabans and Skin-Deep Samaritans"; and Sigrah and King, "Abara Banaba."

68. See Sigrah and King, "Abara Banaba."

69. Nauruans, unlike Banabans, remained on their island and were paid much higher royalties for their lands. Their money was invested all over the world, but long-term financial problems resulted in a struggling economy, the kind of economy that now participates in the "Pacific solution" and its more recent manifestation: housing refugee camps on behalf of Australia for cash. See Fry, "The Pacific Solution?"

70. Malkki, "News and Culture," 92.

71. See Nei Teienemakin in the bottom right corner of the photo of the "Kings village" in chapter 1.

72. From Arundel, "Six Months on a South Sea Island," 200.

5. Land from the Sky

1. See, for example, Edvard Hviding's exploration of this issue in "Between Knowledges."

2. Albert Ellis, "The Discovery of Phosphate," *New Zealand Farmer Stock and Station Journal* (August 1916), in BPC Archives, CA244, R138/1.

3. Populations with roots in England, Ireland, Scotland, and Wales arrived much earlier: as convicts and penal colony administrators in Australia in the 1780s and as settlers in New Zealand from the 1830s. Australia was administered as separate colonies until the commonwealth was formed on 1 January 1901. Indigenous peoples in both lands strongly resisted, but some cooperated with the new settlers resulting in the loss of many indigenous lives and customs.

4. Also see Frances Steel's discussion in *Oceania under Steam.*

5. This is the literal translation of Aotearoa, the *Māori* postcolonial name for New Zealand, and especially the North Island. Recently, however, the New Zealand government has accepted the names Te Ika-a-Maui (Fish of Maui) for the North Island, and Te Waipounamu (Waters of Greenstone) for the South Island. A shorter version of the New Zealand portion of this chap-

ter was published as Teaiwa, "Our Sea of Phosphate: The Diaspora of Ocean Island," in Harvey and Thompson, *Indigenous Diasporas and Dislocations,* 169–192.

6. See Geelen, *The Topdressers.*

7. See "Aerial Fertilizer."

8. Charles, "The Phosphate Flyers," is one of the tracks on *New Zealand Ballads,* a 45 rpm, extended-play recording issued by Tanza, Wellington, in 1959. The words are by Joe Charles, a farmer and ballad writer of Otago and Canterbury. The musical arrangements and vocals are by Les Cleveland.

9. Cleveland wrote to me on July 17, 2001 from Wellington, New Zealand. Until his retirement in 1987, he was a Reader in politics at Victoria University in Wellington with a long background as a folklorist and ballad singer. The author of *Dark Laughter: War in Song and Popular Culture,* as well as numerous articles on military occupational folk song, he collected, broadcast, and made sound recordings of rural ballads from the South Island of New Zealand during the 1950s.

10. Charles, "The Phosphate Flyers," 17–18.

11. Brooking, Hodge, and Wood, "The Grasslands Revolution Revisited," 176.

12. Holland, O'Connor, and Wearing, "Remaking the Grasslands of the Open Country," 69.

13. Ibid., 75, 78.

14. Ibid.

15. See Macdonald, *Massey's Imperialism,* which gives an important account of the significance of phosphate to New Zealand.

16. Brian Talboys, "Tribute to the Pacific Phosphate Mining Industry" (1962), cited in Tyrer, *Nauru and Ocean Islands Story,* 3.

17. See, for example, "Treaty Debated—The Treaty in Practice."

18. See, for example, Ruru, "A Politically Fuelled Tsunami," 57; and Bargh, "Changing the Game Plan."

19. Ellis, "New Zealand Farms and the Phosphate Islands," 56–57.

20. *Te Ara: The Encyclopedia of New Zealand* can be found at http://www.teara.govt.nz/en (accessed August 20, 2012). The Banaba permanent exhibition is featured in the *Tangata o le Moana: People of Moana* portion of the Museum of New Zealand Te Papa Tongarewa: http://www.tepapa.govt.nz/whatson/exhibitions/pages/tangataolemoana.aspx (accessed September 4, 2013).

21. Phillips, "Rural Mythologies."

22. Ibid., citing Parkinson, *A Journal of a Voyage to the South Seas.*

23. Duncan, "Superphosphate—Superphosphate History."

24. Qtd. in Tyrer, *Nauru and Ocean Islands Story,* 4.

25. See "Aerial Fertilizer," which recommends Janic Geelen's *The Topdressers* for further reading.

26. Borerei, "Dancing and Massage," 116.

27. "The Better Farming Train," originally published in the *Argus,* Melbourne, October 9, 1924. The Better Farming Train was also the subject of a book by Elvery, *Rural Education—By Steam.*

28. "The Better Farming Train."

29. "History of Rail in Australia."

30. Eliot discusses this inconvenient rail system in *Broken Atoms,* 188–189.

31. "The Better Farming Train."

32. Ibid.; this site attributes the quotes to the *Journal of Agriculture* (March 1925).

33. Ibid.

34. Ibid.

35. Tiffany, *Everyman's Rules for Scientific Living*, 7.

36. Centre for Resource and Environmental Studies, *Monograph on Phosphate*, cited in Costin and Williams, *Phosphorous in Australia*, xiii.

37. See "Dictionary of Unsung Architects: Rae Featherstone, 1907–1987."

38. See, for example, "Sheep Sales."

39. Interview with farmers, at the home of Andrew Vile, Burrumbuttock, New South Wales, April 2011.

40. Personal communication with Richard Simpson, Canberra, July 2011.

41. Papatuanuku is the earth, which is gendered in *Māori* cosmology as the wife of Ranginui, the sky. The Dreaming is the Aboriginal world view that links people, movement, the environment, and the spiritual. It includes place and space but is not necessarily fixed in time. See Walker, *Ka Whaiwhai Tonu Matou: Struggle without End*; Hokari, *Gurindji Journey*; and Salmond, *Two Worlds*.

42. Teaiwa, "Visualizing te Kainga, Dancing te Kainga."

43. Brett, *Kainga Tahi, Kainga Rua*.

44. Wilson Harris's work is discussed in Petersen and Rutherford, "Fossil and Psyche," 185–189.

45. For example, see Morrison's widely discussed novel *Beloved*.

46. See Harvey and Thompson, "Introduction."

47. Also see Sigrah and King, "Abara Banaba."

48. Clifford, *Routes*, 252.

49. Clifford, "Indigenous Articulations," 472, 482. Also compare with the chapters in Harvey and Thompson, *Indigenous Diasporas and Dislocations*.

50. This is my critique of most studies of the global where scholars focus more on presenting an architecture or metaphor for what they are observing, rather than considering the real impact of multiscalar connectivity and what this means for people who inhabit other ontological realities than those of the still-presumed and dominant urban, (post)modern, capitalist, and Christian West or the urbanized, hypermodern East.

7. *E Kawa Te Aba*

1. Hermann, "Emotions, Agency and the Dis/Placed Self of the Banabans in Fiji," 200.

2. See a similar translation ibid., 204–205; and the transcription of the song from live performances in Teaiwa, "Visualizing te Kainga, Dancing te Kainga." Binder, *Treasure Islands*, 10, gives a more triumphalist translation.

3. Mahaffy, *Report by Mr. Arthur Mahaffy on a Visit to the Gilbert and Ellice Islands*, cited in Kituai, "An Example of Pacific Micro-Nationalism," 10.

4. Williams and Macdonald, *The Phosphateers*, 53.

5. Eliot, *Broken Atoms*, 142. For a critical appraisal of the government's handling of the Banaban situation, see Eliot, "Ocean Island Affairs."

6. Qtd. in Williams and Macdonald, *The Phosphateers*, 64.

7. Ibid.

8. Ibid., 67.

9. Ibid., 79.

10. Ibid., 87.

11. Phosphate and Trees Purchases for July 1904, in BPC Archives, CA244, MP1174/1, 1052.

12. Williams and Macdonald, *The Phosphateers*, 90.

13. Ibid., 92.

14. Ibid., 97.

15. Ibid., and the *London Times* cited on 99.

16. Ibid., 100–101.

17. As a point of comparison, Williams and Macdonald highlight that the United States paid Spain £4.5 million for the whole of the Philippines. They also mention that the first UK commissioner, Alwyn Dickinson, initially wanted the company to be named the Imperial Fertilizer Board. See Williams and Macdonald, *The Phosphateers*, 144.

18. Ibid., 127.

19. Matters pertaining to Ocean Island in papers from the Department of Defense and the prime minister's office in the National Archives of Australia between 1920 and 1947 are filled with these tensions. The traces of the rivalry are still seen today on the field of rugby.

20. Williams and Macdonald, *The Phosphateers*, 193.

21. "Knights and Knaves of the Pacific," 45.

22. Williams and Macdonald, *The Phosphateers*, 226.

23. Macdonald, *Cinderellas*, 107.

24. Ibid., 107–108.

25. This was related to me by Councilor Ioane of Tabiang on Rabi in 2000.

26. Maude and Maude, "Social Organization," 266. *Nei* is a respectful term signaling a female.

27. Maude, *The Book of Banaba*.

28. Ibid.

29. Incorporated Council of Law Reporting for England and Wales, "The Ocean Island Cases," 24–25.

30. Achebe, *Things Fall Apart*, 176.

31. Incorporated Council of Law Reporting for England and Wales, "The Ocean Island Cases," 20–21.

32. Notes Taken at Meeting with Banabans, January 24, 1931, in Maude and Maude Papers, MS 0003, 1904–1999.

33. Ibid.

34. Notes Taken at Meeting with Banabans, January 31, 1931, ibid.

35. Letter from the Banabans to the Secretary of State for the Colonies in London, August 1932, ibid.

36. See a passionately written version of their plight in Pearl Binder's *Treasure Islands*.

37. See Grimble, *We Chose the Islands* and *Tungaru Traditions*.

38. See Grimble, *A Pattern of Islands*.

39. See Williams and Macdonald, *The Phosphateers*, 306–307.

40. Ibid., 324–336.

41. Shennan and Tekenimatang, *One and a Half Pacific Islands*.

42. H. E. Maude to the Western Pacific High Commission, "A Memorandum on the Future of the Banaban Population with Special Attention to Their Lands and Funds" (1946), in BPC Archives, CA244.

43. Shennan and Tekenimatang, *One and a Half Pacific Islands;* and King and Sigrah, *Te Rii ni Banaba*. Both highlight the atrocities during World War II, and King and Sigrah give a comprehensive list of all those killed, 329–340.

44. The transcript of Jenny Barraclough's *Go Tell It to the Judge* is in the Maude and Maude Papers, MS 0003. The spelling of Rambey is per the transcript.

45. Ibid.

46. Ibid. Pilchards are sardines, herring, and other small oily fish.

47. *Foreign Correspondent*.

48. Ibid.

49. Weeramantry, *Nauru*, 203–204.

50. Ibid., 221.

51. See Teaiwa, "Choreographing Difference," for a discussion of the politics of difference and the politics of dance with respect to Banaban and Gilbertese relations. The Gilbert Islands government produced a pamphlet, *Ocean Island: Some Facts the Banabans Ignore*, which can be found in the Maude and Maude Papers, MS 0003.

52. Silverman, *Disconcerting Issue*, 183.

53. Ibid.

54. Ibid.

55. Posnett, *Ocean Island and the Banabans*.

56. Aidney, Ratuvuki, and Teai, *Report of the Committee of Inquiry into the Rabi Council Affairs*, 12.

57. Shennan and Tekenimatang, *One and a Half Pacific Islands*, 126.

8. Remix

1. Ellis, "Reminiscences," 5.

2. Ellis, *Ocean Island and Nauru*, 55.

3. Notes Taken at Meeting with Banabans, January 24, 1931, in Maude and Maude Papers, MS 0003, 1904–1999.

4. Carrie Tiffany, *Everyman's Rules for Scientific Living*, 7.

5. Ellis, "Speech," Rabi Island, September 21, 1948, in Maude and Maude Papers.

6. *Coming Home to Banaba*.

7. Huxley, *Brave New World*, 66.

8. Teaiwa, "Yaqona/Yagoqu," 100. The essay is entirely in lowercase.

9. Incorporated Council of Law Reporting for England and Wales, "The Ocean Island Cases," 24.

10. See full text of this song in chapter 7.

9. Interlude: Coming Home to Fiji?

1. On Fijian politics, Indo-Fijian and indigenous Fijian (I-Taukei) relations, constitutional reform, the four Fiji coups, and the issue of democracy and ethnic politics, see Lal, *Fiji before the Storm*; Lal and Pretes, *Coup: Reflections on the Political Crisis in Fiji*; Scarr, *Fiji: The Politics of Illusion*; Ratuva, "The Fiji Military Coups"; and the documentary film *Where the Rivers Meet*.

2. While other Banaban property has been lost through bad investments, Banaba House is in an ideal location on Pratt Street in Suva and is one of the few purchases that the Rabi Council made with interest from the trust funds that they still retain. The slightly run-down building houses the Suva offices of the council as well as the Hare Krishna Restaurant and the Lantern Palace (a Chinese restaurant).

3. The first coup, led by Major Sitiveni Rabuka, took place on May 14, 1987, when I was in the eighth grade at Yat-Sen Primary School. Rabuka overthrew the elected government of Timoci Bavadra of the Labour Party. This marked a major change in a government primarily led by the Fijian high chief Ratu Sir Kamisese Mara, who was installed at the time of independence in 1970. The second coup happened in September 1987, when Rabuka, by then head of the military, deposed the governor-general, Ratu Penaia Ganilau. Rabuka eventually was elected prime minister in 1992 after the establishment in 1990 of a constitution that guaranteed Fijian domi-

nation of the political system. The third coup, described in my reflection here, occurred on May 19, 2000, led by the relatively unknown George Speight, the son of a former backbencher in the Rabuka government. There was a fourth coup in Fiji on December 6, 2006, led by the head of the military, Commodore Frank Bainimarama. This coup was claimed to be in the name of multiculturalism and anticorruption but has largely been criticized in the international community for its impact on human rights and freedom of speech.

4. See Lal and Pretes, *Coup: Reflections on the Political Crisis in Fiji*; and Emde, "Between Equality and Hierarchy."

5. After the first day of the coup, the military formed a barricade around Parliament. At first they let people in to join the Speight-led rebels, but later they decided to stop the flow of incoming food and bodies. This resulted in a riot at the barricade, which killed or injured several soldiers and civilians and at least one journalist. See the *Fiji Times* and *Daily Post*, May 19–July 2000.

6. What was also worrying was that traditional leaders, like Ratu Kamisese Mara and the hero of the first coups Sitiveni Rabuka, were clearly out of favor in 2000. It was a new breed of dissent, and no one was really sure who was at the helm. George Speight, for the most part, appeared to be a front man for other forces at work. Those forces eventually led to the coup in December 2006. This most recent coup, of a very different tenor from the previous ones, was entirely military in planning and execution and installed the head of the army, Frank Bainimarama, as the interim prime minister. With his closest advisor, Attorney General Aiyaz Sayed-Khaiyum, Bainimarama's goal is to suppress Fijian nationalism and foster regulated multiculturalism by diminishing the authority of indigenous chiefly institutions and changing the language of race and ethnicity so that all Fiji Islanders, of any ethnic background, can claim to be "Fijian." In reality the construction of this new Fiji by force has resulted in the suppression of freedom of expression and critique on the ground and has alienated Fiji from regional institutions, the Commonwealth, and the country's regular aid, development, and trading partners—Australia and New Zealand. However, a host of other international partners, including China, have happily filled this gap.

10. Between Rabi and Banaba

1. See *Laws of Fiji*, ch. 123, "Banaban Settlement," and ch. 124, "Banaban Lands."

2. In 2010 the Fiji government approved a decree to amend the law so that the term "Fijian" now refers to all citizens of Fiji and the term "I-Taukei" refers specifically to indigenous Fijians. Rotuma is a Polynesian island to the north of the main islands of Fiji that has politically been part of the Fiji jurisdiction since 1881. Rotuman language and culture is distinct from that of I-Taukei, but both I-Taukei and Rotumans are seen as indigenous to Fiji.

3. See Teaiwa, "Peripheral Visions?"

4. Silverman, *Disconcerting Issue*, 195.

5. See Maude and Maude, "The Social Organization of Banaba."

6. Compare with Silverman, *Disconcerting Issue*, 154.

7. Thomas Teai, Letter to the Editor, *Fiji Times* (September 9, 1976), n.p., in Maude and Maude Papers.

8. Smith, *An Island in the Autumn*.

9. See van Trease, "From Colony to Independence," 5–6; Toatu, "The Revenue Equalisation Fund," 183–189.

10. This knowledge I gained from talking to people in Tarawa and Tabiteuea about the tensions in the 1970s.

11. Gilbert Islands Government, *Ocean Island: Some Facts the Banabans Ignore,* in Maude and Maude Papers, file 6.5.

12. Ibid.

13. See Maude and Maude Papers, file 3.

14. According to Betarim Rimon, te bo is not adoption as traditionally understood in the Gilberts, where adoption is always between blood relatives, but instead refers to the joining of families unrelated by blood. See Rimon, "A Comparative Study."

15. Silverman, *Disconcerting Issue,* 163.

16. Letter to the Editor, *Fiji Times* (March 15, 1979).

17. This Letter to the Editor of the *Fiji Times* was found in the Maude and Maude Papers but was cut so that the month and day were missing; the year 1976 remained.

18. Letter to the Editor, *Fiji Times* (March 13, 1979), in Maude and Maude Papers. The Banaban and Gilbertese tensions are also elaborated in Teaiwa, "Choreographing Difference."

19. *Fiji Times* (March 12, 1979), in Maude and Maude Papers.

20. Kituai, "An Example of Pacific Micro-Nationalism," 39.

21. Personal communication with Tomasi Puapua, January 2012. Also see Johnston's interview with the former Tuvalu prime minister Bikenibeu Paeniu.

22. Aidney, Ratuvuki, and Teai, *Report of the Committee of Inquiry into the Rabi Council Affairs.*

23. See Silverman, *Disconcerting Issue,* 180–209.

24. Ibid., 323–324.

25. Personal communication with John Teaiwa, 1999. During my fieldwork on Rabi many people would visit our house to discuss the political problems playing out in Tabiang village in particular. Some people didn't want non-Banabans to participate in village committees and many non-Banabans felt like they were being excluded from decision-making activities. This caused much bitterness, cutting across family and church lines.

26. For example, see Kempf, "Songs Cannot Die."

27. This presentation was based on a video I initially created for the 1999 Pacific Studies Conference at the University of Hawai'i. See Teaiwa, "Out of Phosphate: The Diaspora of Ocean Island/ers."

28. Sigrah and King, *Te Rii ni Banaba.*

29. The Rabi Council of Leaders under the leadership of Paula Vanualailai (of Banaban and Fijian heritage) was once again dissolved in June 2013 due to corruption and a lack of activity in their administration of island services.

30. See Teaiwa, "Peripheral Visions?"

31. Benaia, "The History of the Protestant Church in Banaba and Rabi," 57.

32. See "Rabi Proves Too Strong," *Daily Post* (August 23, 2001).

33. Cakaudrove covers the eastern part of Vanua Levu and includes Buca and Natewa Bays, Savusavu, Taveuni, Rabi, and Kioa.

34. Meeting of three Banaban elders and the Rabi Island Council, November 11, 2000, recorded on video by Katerina Teaiwa. The dialogue of the meeting was translated with assistance from John Teaiwa.

35. The fourth Fiji coup was led by the commander of the Fiji military, Frank Bainimarama, in the name of "good governance" and "anticorruption." While his regime has decidedly been for multiculturalism and against Fijian nationalism, it also adjusted the law in order to protect the military from action in the courts, and it removed freedom of speech in the media and civil society.

36. Meeting of three Banaban elders and the Rabi Island Council, November 11, 2000.

37. Ibid.

38. Silverman, *Disconcerting Issue,* 14.

39. See Hermann, "Emotions, Agency and the Dis/Placed Self of the Banabans in Fiji"; Kempf, "Reconfigurations of Place and Ethnicity," "Songs Cannot Die," and "The Drama of Death as Narrative of Survival."

40. Kempf, "Reconfigurations of Place and Ethnicity"; Foucault, "Of Other Spaces"; Soja, *Postmodern Geographies* and "Heterotopologies."

41. See Stevenson, "Festivals and Cultural Identity," 55–57, and "The Festival of Pacific Arts."

42. Flores, "Art and Identity in the Mariana Islands."

43. See Grimble, *Tungaru Traditions,* especially Maude, "A Discourse on Gilbertese Dancing: Editor's Note," 314, where the editor (H. E. Maude) notes Grimble's defense of dance.

44. See Shennan and Tekenimatang, *One and a Half Pacific Islands.*

45. See Kempf, "Reconfigurations of Place and Ethnicity," 165; Dean, *Three Dances of Oceania* and *South Pacific Dance.*

46. Hermann, "Emotions and Relevance of Past," 282.

47. In Teaiwa, "Choreographing Difference," I explore the nontheatrical dances on Rabi and argue that the movement is explicitly Pacific, global, and inclusive in contrast to the political imperative of difference.

48. Shennan, "Approaches to the Study of Dance in Oceania," 193; also see Teaiwa, "Choreographing Difference."

49. See Teaiwa, "Choreographing Difference."

50. Silverman, *Disconcerting Issue,* 15.

51. Ibid., 171.

52. See Sigrah and King, *Te Rii ni Banaba.*

53. Members of the Te Aka clan are descended from what they claim to be the original inhabitants of Banaba, who were there even before Auriaria. They believe their ancestors are Melanesian. Evidence for their claims is manifested by the existence of the skull of an ancestor, Teimanaia, who was a "giant" who lived on Banaba many generations ago. This skull was removed from Banaba by Dr. Gould. An archeological excavation of the Te Aka site by an Australian National University and Bishop Museum team did not uncover any major pieces of evidence, but people are still searching for Teimanaia's skull. The Auriaria myth is based on the migrations between the Gilberts and Samoa, so all the gods of his time, especially the "red-skinned" ones, are probably more Polynesian in origin. See Lampert and Sigrah, "Documents Relating to Dr. Lampert's Archaeological Investigation."

54. Silverman, *Disconcerting Issue,* 171.

55. Ibid., 103.

56. Ibid.

57. Maude and Maude's handwritten catalogs of some of the Banabans indicate place of birth, and these include Tahiti and Hawai'i. See the Maude and Maude Papers.

58. See Teaiwa, "Ti Rawata Irouia"; Maude, *The Book of Banaba;* and Silverman, *Disconcerting Issue.*

59. Silverman also describes how in larger societies the everyday person has very little ability to impact the whole group—only people in power can do this—while on Rabi, the distance between the person and effecting island-wide action is much shorter. Silverman, *Disconcerting Issue.*

60. Clifford, *Routes,* 246.

61. *Foreign Correspondent;* Binder, *Treasure Islands.*

62. See Diaz and Kauanui, "Native Pacific Cultural Studies on the Edge," for a useful theoretical discussion; see also Hereniko and Wilson, *Inside Out;* and Harvey and Thompson, *Indigenous Diasporas and Dislocations.*

63. Teaiwa, "Militarism, Tourism and the Native," 50.

64. Benaia, "The History of the Protestant Church in Banaba and Rabi," ix.

65. Clifford, *Routes,* 251.

66. Kempf, "Songs Cannot Die."

67. Silverman, *Disconcerting Issue,* 157–210.

68. Ibid., 15.

69. Before the 1990s and the corruption in the Rabi Council, annuities were paid to all Banabans, including children, at US$175–US$200 per family member per year. For a family of ten, this was a significant amount of money to receive all at once.

70. Teaiwa, "Peripheral Visions?" 93.

71. Ibid., 195.

72. Teaiwa, "yaqona/yagoqu," 92.

73. Shennan and Tekenimatang, *One and a Half Pacific Islands.*

74. Kaake, "Women's Interest Group," 103.

75. See Hockings, *Traditional Architecture in the Gilbert* Islands, 107–130; and Sigrah and King, *Te Rii ni Banaba,* 128.

76. de Certeau, *The Practice of Everyday Life,* cited in Clifford, *Routes,* 53–54.

77. Those who have passed away are marked by (d.).

78. Many of these partnerships are not marriages in the legal sense.

79. The smaller squares are toilets, which are separate from the houses.

80. *Kaka* designates "grandparent" for Banabans. Female is Nei Kaka and male is Ten Kaka. It also designates all siblings in the same generation as grandparents so that grand-aunts and -uncles are also "Kaka."

81. Teaiwa, "Visualizing te Kainga, Dancing te Kainga."

82. Another popular action hero is Bruce Lee. My uncle Tekarika is often referred to as "Bruce Lee," and I once saw him perform a dance that was based on "karate."

83. Cynthia Rothrock played the character "China O'Brien" (pronounced China "Brain" in the song) in a number of popular films about a white woman who always saves the downtrodden through her martial arts skills.

84. Arundel, "Six Months on a South Sea Island," 187.

85. Tabucanon, "The Banaban Resettlement."

86. Sigrah and King, "Abara Banaba."

Coda

1. L. J. Thwaites and V. Conrad, "Banaba Excavation Report," Pacific Manuscripts Bureau, http://asiapacific.anu.edu.au/pambu/reels/manuscripts/PMB1136.PDF. Ronald Lampert Papers. A version of this story was also published in Sigrah and King, *Te Rii ni Banaba.*

2. Sigrah and King, *Te Rii ni Banaba,* 68–69.

3. Ibid.

4. Field, "Refugee Status Denied to Fiji Islander."

5. Field, "British Documents Hint at South Pacific 'Secrets.'"

6. Wilson Harris qtd. in Petersen and Rutherford, "Fossil and Psyche," 185.

Bibliography

Archives and Reports

British Phosphate Commissioners Archives, CA 244, 1900–1970: MP1174, R10, R32, R138, R140

Arthur Grimble Papers, Pacific Collection, Barr-Smith Library, University of Adelaide, South Australia

Lampert, Ronald, and Ken Sigrah. "Documents Relating to Dr. Lampert's Archaeological Investigation at Te Aka, Banaba Island 1965," PMB 1136, Pacific Manuscripts Bureau, Canberra

Henry Evans Maude and Honor Courtney Maude Papers, MS 0003, 1904–1999, parts I and II, Pacific Collection, Barr-Smith Library, University of Adelaide, South Australia

John Miller Photo Collection: 1908–1939, Ocean Island Photographs, courtesy of Frank Miller, Queensland

National Archives of Australia, Melbourne and Canberra

National Library of Australia, Canberra

New Zealand agriculture journals, 1950–1970

Pacific Collection, Barr-Smith Library, University of Adelaide, South Australia

Pacific Manuscripts Bureau, Canberra

Thwaites, L. J., and V. Conrad, "Banaba Excavation Report," Pacific Manuscripts Bureau

Alexander Turnbull Library, National Library of New Zealand, Wellington

Papers of Maslyn Williams, MS 3936, 1850–1995, National Library of Australia

Memoirs

Dobson, [William] Ray. "On Banaba (Ocean Island) in the Central Pacific 1950/51," 1998–2001, unpublished manuscript in author's possession.

Hunt, Mary. "Excerpt from the Memoirs of Mary Hunt (nee Robertson)," 1945–1950, unpublished manuscript in author's possession.

Zausmer, Mary Critch. "The Chronicles of Mary Beatrice Roche Critch, 1922–1955: A Family Entertainment," 1997–2002, unpublished manuscript in author's possession.

Films

All Islands—Phosphate Seq No. 2. N.d. BPC Archives, CA 244, R125, box [33], National Archives of Australia.

Coming Home to Banaba. 1998. Written and produced by Jeremy Cooper, transcript by

Michael Kaukas, Open University and BBC, 30 mins. Online transcript: http://www.olioweb.me.uk/banaba/coming_home/html/banabascript.html (accessed August 23, 2012).

Exiles in Paradise. 1993. Sixty Minutes, Channel 9 (Australia), 20 mins.

Foreign Correspondent. 1995. "The Banabans," ABC (Australia), 20 mins.

Go Tell It to the Judge. 1975. Produced by Jenny Barraclough, BBC (UK), 60 mins.

Land from the Sky. 1959. National Film Unit (New Zealand, 35mm b&w, National Archives of New Zealand, Te Whare Tohu Tuhituhinga O Aotearoa, Wellington, 24 mins. http://www.youtube.com/watch?v=_TTlnGq5WwM (accessed October 25, 2013).

Missing Paradise in the South Pacific. 1997. Japanese National TV and Banaban Heritage Society Inc.

The Spirit of Kiribati. 2000. Nei Tabera ni Kai (Kiribati), 90 mins.

Te Eitei: The Banaban Story. 2007. Directed by Paul Wolffram, Handmade Films, New Zealand, 32 mins.

A Visit to Ocean Island and Nauru. 1951. BPC Archives, CA 244, R125, box [34], National Archives of Australia, 18 mins.

Visualizing te Kainga, Dancing te Kainga: History and Culture between Rabi, Banaba and Beyond. 2002. Katerina Teaiwa, visual portion of PhD diss., Australian National University, Canberra, 90 mins.

Where the Rivers Meet: A Divided Community and Its Struggle for Peace. N.d. Directed by Atu Emberson Bain, In Focus Production for the World Council of Churches, 36 mins.

Books, Articles, and Journals

Achebe, Chinua. *Things Fall Apart.* London: Heinemann, 1958.

"Aerial Fertilizer." *An History of Technological Innovation in New Zealand.* http://www.techhistory.co.nz/OntheLand/aerial_top-dressing.htm (accessed October 25, 2013).

Aidney, Cyril, Luke Ratuvuki, and Taomati Teai. *Report of the Committee of Inquiry into the Rabi Council Affairs.* Suva: April 8, 1994.

Appadurai, Arjun. "Disjuncture and Difference in the Global Cultural Economy." *Public Culture* 2, no. 2 (1990): 1–24.

Arundel, Lillian. "Six Months on a South Sea Island." In *One and a Half Pacific Islands: Stories the Banabans Tell of Themselves,* ed. Jennifer Shennan and Makin Corrie Tekenimatang, 177–200. Wellington: Victoria University Press, 2005.

Asimov, Isaac. *Asimov on Chemistry.* 1959. Rpt., London: Doubleday, 1974.

Bailey, Eric. Review of *The Phosphateers. Journal of the Polynesian Society* 96, no. 1 (1987): 146.

Ballard, Chris. "It's the Land, Stupid! The Moral Economy of Resource Ownership in Papua New Guinea." In *The Governance of Common Property in the Pacific,* ed. Peter Larmour, 47–65. Canberra: National Centre for Development Studies, 1997.

Barak, Phillip. "Essential Elements for Plant Growth." Department of Soil Science, University of Wisconsin, Madison (ca. 1997), http://www.soils.wisc.edu/~barak/soilscience326/lawofmin.htm (accessed October 25, 2013).

Bargh, Maria. "Changing the Game Plan: The Foreshore and Seabed Act and Constitutional Change." *Kotuitui: New Zealand Journal of Social Sciences Online* 1,

no. 1 (2006): 13–24, http://www.tandfonline.com/doi/abs/10.1080/1177083X.2006
.9522408#.UuygRHeSxhw (accessed October 10, 2014).

Barley, Shanta. "Might as Well Face It You're Addicted to Phosphorus." *Climate Change: The Blog of Bloom* (June 23, 2009), http://www.bbc.co.uk/blogs/climatechange /2009/06/forget_oil_were_running_out_of.html (accessed October 11, 2013).

Bayer CropScience. "Food Security: A Race against Time" (September 12, 2012), http:// www.bayercropscience.com/bcsweb/cropprotection.nsf/id/EN_Topic_The _Second_Green_Revolution (accessed October 8, 2013).

Benaia, Temaka. "The History of the Protestant Church in Banaba and Rabi." B.D. thesis, Faculty of Pacific Theological College, 1991.

"The Better Farming Train." Department of the Environment and Primary Industries, State Government, Victoria (ca. 2010), http://new.dpi.vic.gov.au/about-us/publications /library/virtual-exhibition/better-farming-train (accessed July 20, 2011).

Binder, Pearl. *Treasure Islands: The Trials of the Banabans.* Cremorne, NSW: Angus and Robertson, 1978.

Boiling Ocean II. Produced at the Oceania Centre for Arts and Culture, Suva; performed at the Center for Pacific Islands Studies Conference, Honolulu, 2000.

Borerei, Kaiao. "Dancing and Massage." In *One and a Half Pacific Islands: Stories the Banabans Tell of Themselves,* ed. Jennifer Shennan and Makin Corrie Tekenima- tang, 116–117. Wellington: Victoria University Press, 2005.

Brooking, Tom, Robin Hodge, and Vaughan Wood. "The Grasslands Revolution Re- visited." In *Environmental Histories of New Zealand,* ed. Eric Pawson and Tom Brooking, 169–182. Melbourne: Oxford University Press, 2002.

Charles, Joe. "The Phosphate Flyers." In his *Black Billy Tea: New Zealand Ballads.* Christchurch: Whitcoulls, 1981.

Cleveland, Les. *Dark Laughter: War in Song and Popular Culture.* Westport, Conn.: Praeger, 1992.

Clifford, James. *Routes: Travel and Translation in the Late Twentieth Century.* Cam- bridge, Mass.: Harvard University Press, 1997.

———. "Indigenous Articulations." *Contemporary Pacific* 13, no. 2 (2001): 468–490.

Collings, Gilbeart H. *Commercial Fertilizers: Their Sources and Use.* London: McGraw- Hill, 1955.

Conniff, Richard. "Fast-Tracking Could Breed a Second Green Revolution." *Christian Science Monitor* (March 14, 2012), http://www.csmonitor.com/World/Making-a -difference/Change-Agent/2012/0314/Fast-track-breeding-could-bring-a-second -Green-Revolution (accessed October 8, 2013).

Cordell, Dana. "The Story of Phosphorus: Sustainability Implications of Global Phos- phorus Scarcity for Food Security." PhD thesis, Institute for Sustainable Futures, University of Technology of Sydney; and Department of Water and Environmen- tal Studies, Linköping University, 2010.

Cordell, D. J., and S. White. "Peak Phosphorus: Clarifying the Issues of a Vigorous De- bate about Long-Term Phosphorus Security." *Sustainability* 3 (2011): 2027–2049.

Costin, A. B., and C. H. Williams. "Introduction." In *Phosphorus in Australia,* ed. A. B. Costine and C. H. Williams, xi–xxi. Canberra: Centre for Resource and Environ- mental Studies, Australian National University, 1982.

Costin, A. B., and C. H. Williams, eds. *Phosphorus in Australia.* Canberra: Centre for Resource and Environmental Studies, Australian National University, 1982.

Cushman, Greg. *Guano and the Opening of the Pacific World: A Global Ecological History*. Cambridge: Cambridge University Press, 2013.

Dean, Beth. *Three Dances of Oceania*. Sydney: Sydney Opera House Trust, 1975.

———. *South Pacific Dance*. Sydney: Pacific Publications, 1978.

de Castell, Suzanne. "One Code to Rule them All" (n.d.), http://web.mit.edu/comm -forum/mit5/papers/decastell_plenary_notes.pdf (accessed October 26, 2013).

de Certeau, Michel. *The Practice of Everyday Life*, trans. Steven Rendall. Berkeley: University of California Press, 1984.

Deleuze, Gilles, and Felix Guattari. *A Thousand Plateaus: Capitalism and Schizophrenia*. London: Athlone, 1988.

Diaz, Vicente, and J. Kehaulani Kauanui. "Native Pacific Cultural Studies on the Edge." *Contemporary Pacific* 13, no. 2 (2001): 315–342.

"Dictionary of Unsung Architects: Rae Featherstone, 1907–1987." *Built Heritage* (n.d.), http://www.builtheritage.com.au/dua_featherstone.html (accessed October 14, 2013).

Duncan, Arthur. "Superphosphate—Superphosphate History." *Te Ara: The Encyclopedia of New Zealand* (updated March 1, 2009), http://www.TeAra.govt.nz/en /superphosphate/1 (accessed October 14, 2013).

Eisenstein, Sergei. *The Film Sense*, trans. and ed. Jay Leyda. New York: Harcourt, Brace, 1942.

Eliot, Edward Carlyon. *Broken Atoms*. London: G. Bles, 1938.

———. "Ocean Island Affairs: Gilbert and Ellice Islands Protectorate (Later Colony), 1913–20." In his *Broken Atoms*, 138–185. London: G. Bles, 1938.

Ellis, Albert. *Ocean Island and Nauru: Their Story*. Sydney: Angus and Robertson, 1935.

———. "New Zealand Farms and the Phosphate Islands." *New Zealand Geographer* 4, no. 1 (1948): 55–68.

———. "Reminiscences." Auckland: Institute Printing and Publishing Society, 1951.

Elvery, David H. *Rural Education—By Steam*. Victoria: Victoria Department of Agriculture, Victorian Railways, 1996.

Emde, Sina. "Between Equality and Hierarchy: Articulating the Multicultural Nation in Postcolonial Fiji." PhD thesis, Australian National University, 2007.

Emsley, John. *The Shocking History of Phosphorus: A Biography of the Devil's Element*. London: Pan Macmillan, 2000.

Escobar, Arturo. *The Making and Unmaking of the Third World*. Princeton, N.J.: Princeton University Press, 1995.

Fernandez, Ramona. *Imagining Literacy: Rhizomes of Knowledge in American Culture and Literacy*. Austin: University of Texas Press, 2001.

Fertilizer Industry Federation of Australia. "Soil Fertility," http://www.fifa.asn.au/public /soil_fertility/fifa_13.html (accessed June 2001, no longer available).

Field, Michael. "Refugee Status Denied to Fiji Islander." *Fairfax NZ News* (February 8, 2012), http://www.stuff.co.nz/national/6380998/Refugee-status-refused-to-Fiji -islander (accessed October 12, 2013).

———. "British Documents Hint at South Pacific 'Secrets.'" *Stuff.co.nz*, http://www.stuff .co.nz/world/south-pacific/9632699/British-documents-hint-at-South-Pacific -secrets (accessed January 21, 2014).

Flores, Judy. "Art and Identity in the Mariana Islands: The Reconstruction of 'Ancient' Chamorro Dance." In *Pacific Art: Persistence, Change and Meaning*, ed. A. Herle,

N. Stanley, K. Stevenson, and R. L. Welsch, 106–113. Adelaide: Crawford House, 2002.

Fortune, Kate. "Lever Brothers." In *The Pacific Islands: An Encyclopedia,* ed. Brij V. Lal and Kate Fortune, 217–218. Honolulu: University of Hawai'i Press, 2000.

Foster, Susan Leigh, ed. *Choreographing History.* Bloomington: Indiana University Press, 1995.

Foucault, Michel. "Of Other Spaces." *Diacritics* 16 (1986): 22–27.

Fry, Greg. "The Pacific Solution?" In *Refugees and the Myth of the Borderless World,* ed. William Maley, Alan Dupont, Jean-Pierre Fonteyne, Greg Fry, James Jupp, and Thuy Do, 23–31. Canberra: Department of International Relations, Australian National University, 2002.

Geelen, Janic. *The Topdressers.* Te Awamutu: NZ Aviation Press, 1983.

Ghai, Yash, Robin Luckham, and Francis Snyder, eds. *The Political Economy of Law: A Third World Reader.* New York: Oxford University Press, 1987.

Gilbert Islands Government. *Ocean Island: Some Facts the Banabans Ignore* (pamphlet, n.d.).

Graham, Brett. *Kainga Tahi, Kainga Rua: New Work on Banaba by Brett Graham.* Exhibition in Te Pataka Toi/Adam Art Gallery, July 4–August 15, 2003, http://www.adamartgallery.org.nz/past-exhibitions/brett-graham (accessed October 15, 2013).

Grimble, Arthur Francis. *We Chose the Islands: A Six-Year Adventure in the Gilberts.* New York: Morrow, 1952.

———. *A Pattern of Islands.* BBC Records (1969), http://www.discogs.com/Sir-Arthur-Grimble-A-Pattern-Of-Islands/release/1495247 (accessed October 15, 2013).

———. *Tungaru Traditions: Writings on the Atoll Culture of the Gilbert Islands.* Honolulu: University of Hawai'i Press, 1989.

Hanlon, David. "'The Sea of Little Lands': Examining Micronesia's Place in Pacific Studies." *Contemporary Pacific* 21, no. 1 (2009): 91–110.

Haraway, Donna. "Situated Knowledges: The Science Question in Feminism and the Privilege of Partial Perspective." *Feminist Studies* 14, no. 3 (Fall 1988): 575–599.

———. *Primate Visions: Gender, Race, and Nature in the World of Modern Science.* 1989. Rpt., London: Verso, 1992.

———. *How Like a Leaf: An Interview with Thyrza Nichols Goodeve.* London: Routledge, 2000.

Harvey, Graham, and Charles D. Thompson Jr. "Introduction." In *Indigenous Diasporas and Dislocations,* ed. Graham Harvey and Charles D. Thompson Jr., 1–12. Aldershot, England: Ashgate, 2005.

Harvey, Graham, and Charles D. Thompson Jr., eds. *Indigenous Diasporas and Dislocations: Unsettling Western Fixations.* Aldershot, England: Ashgate, 2005.

Hau'ofa, Epeli. "Our Sea of Islands." *Contemporary Pacific* 1 (1993): 148–160.

———. "Pasts to Remember." In *Remembrance of Pacific Pasts: An Invitation to Remake History,* ed. Robert Borofsky, 453–472. Honolulu: University of Hawai'i Press, 2000.

Haynes, T.W. *Our Daily Bread; or, A Story of the Phosphate Islands.* London: Houghton, 1933.

Hereniko, Vilsoni. "Representations of Cultural Identities." In *Tides of History,* ed. K. R. Howe, 406–434. Honolulu: University of Hawai'i Press, 1994.

———. *Woven Gods: Female Clowns and Power in Rotuma.* Honolulu: University of Hawai'i Press; and Suva: Institute of Pacific Studies, 1995.

Hereniko, Vilsoni, and Terence Wesley-Smith, eds. *Back to the Future: Decolonizing Pacific Studies*. Special issue of *Contemporary Pacific* 15, no. 1 (Spring 2003).

Hereniko, Vilsoni, and Rob Wilson, eds. *Inside Out: Literature, Cultural Politics, and Identity in the New Pacific*. Lanham, Md.: Rowman and Littlefield, 1999.

Hermann, Elfriede. "Emotions, Agency and the Dis/Placed Self of the Banabans in Fiji." In *Shifting Images of Identity in the Pacific*, ed. Toon van Meijl and Jelle Miedema, 191–217. Leiden: KITVL, 2004.

———. "Emotions and Relevance of Past: Historicity and Ethnicity among the Banabans of Fiji." *History and Anthropology* 16, no. 3 (September 2005): 275–291.

"History of Rail in Australia." *Australian Government: Department of Infrastructure and Regional Development* (May 15, 2013), http://www.infrastructure.gov.au/rail/trains/history.aspx (accessed October 15, 2013).

Hockings, John. *Traditional Architecture in the Gilbert Islands: A Cultural Perspective*. Queensland: University of Queensland Press, 1989.

Hokari, Minoru, *Gurindji Journey: A Japanese Historian in the Outback*. Honolulu: University of Hawai'i Press, 2011.

Holland, P., K. O'Connor, and A. Wearing. "Remaking the Grasslands of the Open Country." In *Environmental Histories of New Zealand*, ed. E. Pawson and T. Brooking, 69–83. Melbourne: Oxford University Press, 2002.

Hunt, Mary. *My Life*, ed. Dina Dunavan, Judith Richards, and Llewelyn Richards. Wellington: Te Taa Haeretahi/Hand in Hand Press, 1999.

———. "My Life on Ocean Island." In *One and a Half Pacific Islands: Stories the Banabans Tell of Themselves*, ed. Jennifer Shennan and Makin Corrie Tekenimatang, 220–225. Wellington: Victoria University Press, 2005.

Hutchinson, G. E. "Phosphatic Guano on the Atolls of the Pacific Ocean," in *The Biogeochemistry of Vertebrate Excretion. Bulletin of the American Museum of Natural History* 96 (1950): 160–259.

Huxley, Aldous. *Brave New World*. 1932. Rpt., Middlesex, England: Penguin, 1972.

Hviding, Edvard. "Between Knowledges: Pacific Studies and Academic Disciplines." *Contemporary Pacific* 15, no. 1 (Spring 2003): 43–73.

Incorporated Council of Law Reporting for England and Wales. "The Ocean Island Cases." In *The Political Economy of Law: A Third World Reader*, ed. Yash Ghai, Robin Luckham, and Francis Snyder, 11–34. New York: Oxford University Press, 1987.

Iremonger, Lucille. *It's a Bigger Life*. London: Hutchinson, 1948.

Johnston, Ian. Interview with former Tuvalu prime minister Bikenibeu Paeniu. *Radio New Zealand International* (2011), http://www.rnzi.com/newflagsflying/tuval-in t.php (accessed October 20, 2013).

Kaake, Arariki. "Women's Interest Group." In *One and a Half Pacific Islands: Stories the Banabans Tell of Themselves*, ed. Jennifer Shennan and Makin Corrie Tekenimatang 102–104. Wellington: Victoria University Press, 2005.

Kaplan, Elisabeth. "Many Paths to Partial Truths: Archives, Anthropology, and the Power of Representation." *Archival Science* 2 (2002): 209–220.

Kaplan, Martha. "Fijian Water in Fiji and New York." *Cultural Anthropology* 22, no. 4 (2007): 685–706.

Kempf, Wolfgang. "'Songs Cannot Die': Ritual Composing and the Politics of Emplacement among the Banabans Resettled on Rabi Island in Fiji." *Journal of the Polynesian Society* 112, no. 1 (2003): 33–64.

———. "The Drama of Death as Narrative of Survival: Dance Theatre, Travelling and Thirdspace among the Banabans of Fiji." In *Shifting Images of Identity in the Pacific*, ed. Toon van Meijl and Jelle Miedema, 159–189. Leiden: KITLV, 2004.

———. "Reconfigurations of Place and Ethnicity: Positionings, Performances and Politics of Relocated Banabans in Fiji." *Oceania* 75 (2005): 368–386.

Kirsch, Stuart. "Environmental Disaster, Culture Loss and the Law." *Current Anthropology* 42, no. 2 (2001): 167–178.

Kituai, August. "An Example of Pacific Micro-Nationalism: The Banaban Case." *Bikmaus* 3, no. 4 (1982): 3–48.

"Knights and Knaves of the Pacific." *Pacific Magazine* (1997): 45.

Koch, Gerd. *The Material Culture of Kiribati: Nonouti, Tabiteuea, Onotoa*. Suva: Institute of Pacific Studies, University of the South Pacific, 1986.

Lal, Brij V. *Fiji before the Storm: Elections and the Politics of Development*. Canberra: Asia Pacific Press, 2000.

Lal, Brij V., and Kate Fortune, eds. *The Pacific Islands: An Encyclopedia*. Honolulu: University of Hawai'i Press, 2000.

Lal, Brij V., and Michael Pretes, eds. *Coup: Reflections on the Political Crisis in Fiji*. Canberra: Pandanus, 2001.

Lefale, Penehuro Fatu. "*Ua'afa le Aso* Stormy Weather Today: Traditional Ecological Knowledge of Weather and Climate: The Samoa Experience." *Climatic Change* 100 (2010): 317–335.

Lougheed, Tim. "Phosphorus Paradox: Scarcity and Overabundance of a Key Nutrient." *Environmental Health Perspectives* 119, no. 5 (May 2011): A208–A213, http://www .ncbi.nlm.nih.gov/pmc/articles/PMC3094441 (accessed October 11, 2013).

Macdonald, Barrie. *Massey's Imperialism and the Politics of Phosphate*. Palmerston North, NZ: Massey University Press, 1982.

———. *Cinderellas of the Empire: Towards a History of Kiribati and Tuvalu*. Canberra: Australian National University Press, 2001.

MacDougall, David. *Transcultural Cinema*. Princeton, N.J.: Princeton University Press, 1998.

Mahaffy, Arthur. *Report by Mr. Arthur Mahaffy on a Visit to the Gilbert and Ellice Islands, 1909*. London: Darling, 1910, http://www.wdl.org/en/item/2367 (accessed October 15, 2013).

Malkki, Liisa. "News and Culture: Transitory Phenomena and the Fieldwork Tradition." In *Anthropological Locations: Boundaries and Grounds of a Field of Science*, ed. Akhil Gupta and James Ferguson, 86–101. Berkeley: University of California Press, 1997.

Manterys, Adam, Stefania Zawada, Stanislaw Manterys, and Jozef Zawad, eds. *New Zealand's First Refugees: Pahiatua's Polish Children*. Wellington: Polish Children's Reunion Committee, 2004.

Mar, Tracey Banivanua, and Penelope Edmonds, eds. Making Space: Settler-Colonial Perspectives on Land, Place and Identity. London: Palgrave, 2010.

Marcus, George E. "The Modernist Sensibility in Recent Ethnographic Writing and the Cinematic Metaphor of Montage." In *Visualising Theory: Selected Essays from V. A. R.*, ed. Lucien Taylor, 37–53. London: Routledge, 1994.

———. "Ethnography in/of the World System: The Emergence of Multi-Sited Ethnography." *Annual Review of Anthropology* 24 (2005): 95–117.

Maude, H. C., and H. E. Maude. "The Social Organization of Banaba or Ocean Island, Central Pacific." *Journal of the Polynesian Society* 41, no. 4 (1932): 262–301.

Maude, H. C., and H. E. Maude, eds. *The Book of Banaba*. Suva: Institute of Pacific Studies, University of the South Pacific, 1994.

Maude, H. E. *Slavers in Paradise: The Peruvian Slave Trade in Polynesia, 1862–1864*. Stanford, Calif.: Stanford University Press, 1981.

———. "A Discourse on Gilbertese Dancing: Editor's Note." In Arthur Francis Grimble, *Tungaru Traditions: Writings on the Atoll Culture of the Gilbert Islands*, ed. H. E. Maude, 217. Honolulu: University of Hawai'i Press, 1989.

McFarlane, Colin. "Translocal Assemblages: Space, Power and Social Movements." *Geoforum* 40, no. 4 (2009): 561–567.

McLeish, Kathy. "Nauru: The World's Smallest Republic" (October 23, 2013), http://www.abc.net.au/news/2013-10-23/nauru-worlds-smallest-republic/4983548 (accessed October 25, 2013).

Merlan, Francesca. "On Indigeneity." *Current Anthropology* 50, no. 3 (2009): 303–333.

Mintz, Sidney. *Sweetness and Power: The Place of Sugar in Modern History*. New York: Viking Penguin, 1985.

Morrison, Toni. *Beloved*. New York: Plume, 1987.

Morton, Stephen. *Gayatri Spivak: Ethics, Subalternity and the Critique of Postcolonial Reason*. Malden, Mass.: Polity, 2007.

Myers, Richard L. *The One Hundred Most Important Chemical Compounds: A Reference Guide*. Westport, Conn.: Greenwood, 2007.

Narayan, Kirin. "How Native Is a Native Anthropologist?" *American Anthropologist* 95, no. 3 (1993): 671–686.

"Nauru Country Brief." Australian Government, Department of Foreign Affairs and Trade, http://www.dfat.gov.au/geo/nauru/nauru_brief.html (accessed October 28, 2013).

Oliver, Douglas. *The Pacific Islands*. Cambridge, Mass.: Harvard University Press, 1989.

Owen, Launcelot. "Notes on the Phosphate Deposit of Ocean Island: With Remarks on the Phosphates of the Equatorial Belt of the Pacific Ocean." *Quarterly Journal of the Geological Society of London* 79, no. 313 (1923): 1–15.

———. "The Phosphate Deposit on Ocean Island: Discussion." *Economic Geology* 22 (1927): 632–634.

Parkinson, Sydney. *A Journal of a Voyage to the South Seas, in His Majesty's Ship, the Endeavour. Faithfully Transcribed from the Papers of the Late Sydney Parkinson, Draughtsman to Joseph Banks, Esq. on His Late Expedition. With Dr. Solander, Round the World. Embellished with Views and Designs, Delineated by the Author, and Engraved by Capital Artists*. London: Stanfield Parkinson, 1773. Online version published by South Seas (2004), http://southseas.nla.gov.au/journals/parkinson/title.html (accessed October 15, 2013).

Pearce, Fred. "Phosphorus: A Critical Resource Misused and Now Running Low." *Yale Environment* 360 (July 7, 2011), http://e360.yale.edu/feature/phosphate_a_critical_resource_misused_and_now_running_out/2423 (accessed August 13, 2012).

Perry, Richard. "Sad History of Tiny Island Is Evoked in Many Forms." *New York Times* (January 20, 2013), http://www.nytimes.com/2013/01/21/arts/music/d-j-spookys-nauru-elegies-at-metropolitan-museum.html?_r=0 (accessed October 8, 2013).

Petaia, Ruperake. *Patches of the Rainbow*. Apia: Samoa Observer, 1992.

Petersen, Kirsten Holst, and Anna Rutherford. "Fossil and Psyche." In *The Post-Colonial Studies Reader,* ed. Bill Ashcroft, Gareth Griffiths, and Helen Tiffin, 185–189. London: Routledge, 1995.

Phillips, Jock. "Rural Mythologies: First Traditions." *Te Ara: The Encyclopedia of New Zealand* (updated July 13, 2012), http://www.teara.govt.nz/en/rural-mythologies /page-1 (accessed October 14, 2013).

"Phosphorus: Micronutrient Information Center." *Linus Pauling Institute: Micronutrient Center for Optimum Health,* http://lpi.oregonstate.edu/infocenter/minerals /phosphorus (accessed August 23, 2012).

Pincock, Stephen. "Peak Phosphorus Fuels Food Fears." *ABC Science* (August 5, 2010), http://www.abc.net.au/science/articles/2010/08/05/2973513.htm (accessed October 11, 2013).

Ponting, Clive. *A Green History of the World: The Environment and the Collapse of Great Civilizations.* London: Penguin, 1991.

Posnett, Richard. *Ocean Island and the Banabans: A Report to the Minister for Foreign and Commonwealth Affairs.* London: Foreign and Commonwealth Office, 1979.

Power, F. Danvers. "The Phosphate Deposits of Ocean and Pleasant Islands." *Proceedings of the Australasian Institute of Mining Engineers* 1, no. 1 (May 1904), http://trove .nla.gov.au/work/34660313?q&versionId=42923311 (accessed February 1, 2014).

Rainbird, Paul. "Taking the Tapu: Defining Micronesia by Absence." *Journal of Pacific History* 38, no. 2 (2003): 237–250.

Ratuva, Steven. "The Fiji Military Coups: Reactive and Transformative Tendencies." *Journal of Asian Political Science* 19, no. 1 (May 2011): 96–120.

Report on Banaban Affairs. Suva: Rabi Council of Leaders, 1980–1995. In possession of author.

Resture, Jane. *Banaba: Aspects of History* (June 22, 2012), http://www.janesoceania.com /kiribati_banaba_history/index.htm (accessed October 15, 2013).

Rimon, Betarim Robuti. "A Comparative Study of Family Structures in the Kiribati and Banaban Societies" (n.d.). Unpublished manuscript in possession of author.

Rockefeller, Stuart Alexander. "Flow." *Current Anthropology* 52, no. 4 (August 2011): 557–578.

Rockström, Johan, et al. "A Safe Operating Space for Humanity." *Nature* 461 (September 2009): 472–475.

Roosevelt, Franklin D. "Message to Congress on Phosphates for Soil Fertility." *American Presidency Project* (May 28, 1938), http://www.presidency.ucsb.edu/ws/index.php ?pid=15643 (accessed October 11, 2013).

Rosemarin, Arno, Gert de Bruijne, and Ian Caldwell. "Peak Phosphorus: The Next Inconvenient Truth." *Broker Online* (August 4, 2009), http://www.thebrokeronline .eu/Articles/Peak-phosphorus (accessed October 11, 2013).

Rubinstein, Helen J., and Paul Zimmet. *Phosphate, Wealth and Health in Nauru: A Study of Lifestyle Change.* Gundaroo, NSW: Brolga, 1993.

Ruru, Jacinta. "A Politically Fuelled Tsunami: The Foreshore/Seabed Controversy in Aotearoa Me Te Wai Pounamu/New Zealand." *Journal of the Polynesian Society* 113, no. 1 (March 2004): 57–72.

Sabatier, Ernest. *Gilbertese-English Dictionary.* Sydney: South Pacific Commission Publications Bureau, 1971.

Sahlins, Marshall. "Poor Man, Rich Man, Big Man, Chief: Political Types in Melanesia and Polynesia." *Comparative Studies in Society and History* 5, no. 3 (1969): 285–303.

Salmond, Ann. *Two Worlds: First Meetings between Maori and Europeans: 1642–1772.* Auckland: Viking, 1991.

Scarr, Deryck. *Fiji: The Politics of Illusion.* Kensington: New South Wales University Press, 1988.

"Sheep Sales." *Kilmore Free Press* (September 26, 1940): 8.

Shennan, Jennifer. "Approaches to the Study of Dance in Oceania." *Journal of the Polynesian Society* 90, no. 2 (1981): 193–208.

Shennan, Jennifer, and Makin Corrie Tekenimatang, eds. *One and a Half Pacific Islands: Stories the Banabans Tell of Themselves/Teuana ao teiterana n aba n te Betebeke: I-Banaba aika a karakin oin rongorongoia.* Wellington: Victoria University Press, 2005.

Shlomowitz, Ralph, and Doug Munro. *The Ocean Island (Banaba) and Nauru Labour Trade: 1900–1940.* Bedford Park: Flinders University of Australia, Discipline of Economic History, 1990.

Sigrah, Raobeia Ken, and Stacey M. King. "Abara Banaba (Our Land of Banaba)." *Nature Pacific* (ca. 2001), http://www.banaban.com (accessed October 15, 2013).

———. *Te Rii ni Banaba.* Suva: Institute of Pacific Studies, University of the South Pacific, 2001.

Silverman, Martin G. *Disconcerting Issue: Meaning and Struggle in a Resettled Pacific Community.* Chicago: University of Chicago Press, 1971.

Skaggs, Jimmy. *The Great Guano Rush.* New York: St. Martin's, 1995.

Smith, John. *An Island in the Autumn.* Kinloss, Scotland: Librario, 2011.

Soil and Water Conservation Research Division. *Superphosphate: Its History, Chemistry and Manufacture.* Washington, D.C.: Agricultural Research Service, U.S. Department of Agriculture, 1964.

Soja, Edward W. *Postmodern Geographies: The Reassertion of Space in Critical Social Theory.* London: Verso, 1989.

———. "Heterotopologies: A Remembrance of Other Spaces in the Citadel-LA." In *Postmodern Cities and Spaces,* ed. Sophie Watson and Katherine Gibson, 13–34. Oxford: Blackwell, 1995.

Sontag, Susan. *On Photography.* London: Penguin, 1979.

SOPAC. *Water Resources Assessment, Banaba (Ocean Island), Republic of Kiribati.* Technical report 334, Overmars and Butcher (2000), http://ict.sopac.org/VirLib/TR0334.pdf (accessed October 18, 2013).

Steel, Frances. *Oceania under Steam: Sea Transport and the Cultures of Colonialism c. 1870–1914.* Manchester, England: Manchester University Press, 2011.

Stevenson, Karen. "Festivals and Cultural Identity." In *Garland Encyclopaedia of World Music, vol. 9:* Australia and the Pacific Islands, ed. Adrienne Kaeppler and Jacob Love, 55–57. New York: Garland, 1998.

———. "The Festival of Pacific Arts: Its Past, Its Future." *Pacific Arts* 25 (2002): 31–40.

Stoler, Ann Laura. "Imperial Debris: Reflections on Ruins and Ruination." *Cultural Anthropology* 23, no. 2 (2008): 191–219.

———. *Along the Archival Grain: Epistemic Anxieties and Colonial Common Sense.* Princeton, N.J.: Princeton University Press, 2010.

Tabucanon, Gil Marvel P. "The Banaban Resettlement: Implications for Pacific Environmental Migration." *Pacific Studies* 35, no. 3 (2012): 343–370.

Talu, Sister Alaima, et al. *Kiribati: Aspects of History.* Suva: Institute of Pacific Studies, University of the South Pacific, 1984.

Teaiwa, Katerina Martina. "Body-Shop Banabans and Skin-Deep Samaritans." *Pacific Science Information Bulletin* 49, nos. 3–4 (1997): 13–18.

———. "Ti Rawata Irouia: Re-presenting Banaban Histories." M.A. thesis, University of Hawai'i, 1998.

———. "Out of Phosphate: The Diaspora of Ocean Island/ers." Paper presented at the Center for Pacific Islands Studies Conference, Honolulu, October 1999.

———. "Visualizing te Kainga, Dancing te Kainga: History and Culture between Rabi, Banaba and Beyond." PhD thesis, Australian National University, 2002.

———. "Multi-Sited Methodologies: Homework between Fiji, Australia and Kiribati." In *Anthropologists in the Field,* ed. Jane Mulcock and Lynne Hume, 216–233. New York: Columbia University Press, 2004.

———. "Our Sea of Phosphate: The Diaspora of Ocean Island." In *Indigenous Diasporas and Dislocations: Unsettling Western Fixations,* ed. Graham Harvey and Charles D. Thompson Jr., 169–192. Aldershot, England: Ashgate, 2005.

———. "Choreographing Difference: The (Body) Politics of Banaban Dance." *Contemporary Pacific* 24, no. 1 (2012): 65–94.

Teaiwa, Teresia. "Mine Land: An Anthem." In her *Searching for Nei Nimanoa.* Suva: Mana, 1995.

———. "Yaqona/Yagoqu: Roots and Routes of a Displaced Native." *UTS Review: Cultural Studies and New Writing* 4, no. 1 (May 1998): 92–106.

———. "Peripheral Visions? Rabi Island in Fiji's General Election." In *Fiji before the Storm: Elections and the Politics of Development,* ed. Brij V. Lal, 93–110. Canberra: Asia Pacific Press, Australian National University, 2000.

———. "Militarism, Tourism and the Native: Articulations in Oceania." PhD diss., University of California, Santa Cruz, 2001.

Te Ara: The Encyclopedia of New Zealand. http://www.teara.govt.nz/en (accessed October 23, 2013).

Tekenimatang, Karoro. "Catching a Frigate Bird." In *One and a Half Pacific Islands: Stories the Banaban People Tell of Themselves,* ed. Jennifer Shennan and Makin Corrie Tekenimatang, 49–52. Wellington: Victoria University Press, 2005.

Thaman, Konai Helu. "Decolonizing Pacific Studies: Indigenous Perspectives, Knowledge, and Wisdom in Higher Education." *Contemporary Pacific* 15, no. 1 (2003): 1–17.

Thomas, Nicholas. *In Oceania: Visions, Artifacts, Histories.* Durham, N.C.: Duke University Press, 1997.

Thoughts on Screen by Dave Sag (1997), http://dave.va.com.au/the_future/networked_forces1.html (accessed August 23, 2012).

Tiffany, Carrie. *Everyman's Rules for Scientific Living.* New York: Scribner, 2006.

Toatu, Teuea. "The Revenue Equalisation Fund." In *Atoll Politics: The Republic of Kiribati,* ed. Howard van Trease, 183–189. Christchurch: Macmillan Brown Centre, University of Canterbury; and Suva: Institute of Pacific Studies, University of the South Pacific, 1993.

"Treaty Debated—The Treaty in Practice." *New Zealand History* (updated December 20, 2012), http://www.nzhistory.net.nz/politics/treaty/the-treaty-in-practice/the-treaty-debated (accessed October 22, 2013).

Tyrer, Thomas Grace. *Nauru and Ocean Islands Story.* Wellington: Hutcheson, Bowman and Stewart, 1962.

Van Kauwenbergh, Steven. *World Phosphate Rock Reserves and Resources.* Muscle Shoals, Ala.: *International Fertilizer Development Center,* 2010, http://pdf.usaid.gov/pdf_docs/PNADW835.pdf (accessed September 15, 2013).

van Trease, Howard. "From Colony to Independence." In *Atoll Politics: The Republic of Kiribati,* ed. Howard van Trease, 3–22. Christchurch: Macmillan Brown Centre, University of Canterbury; and Suva: Institute of Pacific Studies, University of the South Pacific, 1993.

van Trease, Howard, ed. *Atoll Politics: The Republic of Kiribati.* Christchurch: Macmillan Brown Centre, University of Canterbury; and Suva: Institute of Pacific Studies, University of the South Pacific, 1993.

Viviani, Nancy. *Nauru—Phosphate and Political Progress.* Canberra: Australian National University Press, 1970.

Walker, Ranginui. *Ka Whaiwhai Tonu Matou: Struggle without End.* Auckland: Penguin, 1990.

Warakai, Vincent. "Dancing Yet to the Dim Dim's Beat." In *Nuanua: Pacific Writing in English since 1980,* ed. Albert Wendt, 246. Auckland: Auckland University Press, 1995.

Ward, Gerrard, and Elizabeth Kingdom. *Land, Custom and Practice in the South Pacific.* Cambridge: Cambridge University Press, 1995.

Watson, Sophie, and Katherine Gibson, eds. *Postmodern Cities and Spaces.* Oxford: Blackwell, 1995.

Weeramantry, Christopher G. *Nauru: Environmental Damage under International Trusteeship.* Melbourne: Oxford University Press, 1992.

Whitten, David O., and Bessie E. Whitten, eds. *Manufacturing: A Historiographical and Bibliographical Guide.* New York: Greenwood, 1990.

Wild, Matthew. "Peak Soil: It's Like Peak Oil Only Worse." *Peak Generation* (May 12, 2010), http://peakgeneration.blogspot.com.au/2010/05/peak-soil-its-like-peak-oil-only-worse.html (accessed October 25, 2013).

Williams, Maslyn, and Barrie Macdonald. *The Phosphateers: A History of the British Phosphate Commissioners and the Christmas Island Phosphate Commission.* Melbourne: Melbourne University Press, 1985.

Zinn, Howard. *A People's History of the United States.* New York: HarperCollins, 2003.

Index

Page numbers in italics refer to illustrations

KATERINA MARTINA TEAIWA is Convener of Pacific Studies and Head of Department of Gender, Media, and Cultural Studies in the College of Asia and the Pacific at the Australian National University. Born and raised in the Fiji Islands, she is of Banaban, I-Kiribati, and African American heritage.

CPSIA information can be obtained
at www.ICGtesting.com
Printed in the USA
BVOW11s1727200917

495433BV00018B/541/P